The flight from work

by
Göran Palm

Translated by Patrick Smith

Introduction by Dorothy Wedderburn
*Director of the Industrial Sociology Unit
of the Imperial College of Science
and Technology, London*

with a foreword by Peter Docherty, PhD
*The Economic Research Institute of
the Stockholm School of Economics, Sweden*

CAMBRIDGE UNIVERSITY PRESS

CAMBRIDGE
LONDON · NEW YORK · MELBOURNE

Published by the Syndics of the Cambridge University Press
The Pitt Building, Trumpington Street, Cambridge CB2 1RP
Bentley House, 200 Euston Road, London NW1 2DB
32 East 57th Street, New York, NY 10022, USA
296 Beaconsfield Parade, Middle Park, Melbourne 3206, Australia

Published by agreement with Lennart Sane Agency, Malmö 25, Sweden

Printed in Great Britain by
Western Printing Services Ltd, Bristol

ISBN 0 521 2/6680 hard covers

Contents

Introduction

The attraction of Sweden, even for some people in the United States but for many in Britain, lies in its apparent ability to create an acceptable face for capitalism. It is a country which combines economic success, as measured by traditional criteria of economic growth and profitability, with social policies marked by compassion and concern for misfortunes such as unemployment, disability and old age, which in Britain and the USA still result in poverty and deprivation. It has also shown a willingness to engage in social experiments in education, and with policies to expand opportunities for women. Private enterprise dominates in a society where Social Democratic governments had, until 1976, been almost continuously in power for over 40 years, and where their policies had had significant effects upon the distribution of income, and via the educational system, upon the openness of the society in class terms. This background of a pluralist society is important to the understanding of Göran Palm's book.

Sweden is a small country, only 8 million people, and compared with the United States, for example, has a homogeneous population. The last 20 years have seen an influx of immigrants – Turks, Yugoslavs and Finns – but they are still very much the minority. Industrialization occurred late, towards the end of the last century, with the result that Sweden's manufacturing industry is based upon advanced technology. The engineering industry predominates. Approximately one fifth of total production, and almost one half of industrial production, is exported. Many Swedish companies are household names abroad, and their products carry a reputation for quality and good design. But these companies are, for the most part, privately owned. Some activities are nationalized but the public sector is smaller than that of Britain. Moreover there is a degree of industrial concentration in

private industry in Sweden that is higher than that to be found in
the rest of Western Europe or in the USA. There are, of course,
many small firms. Indeed 70% of all firms have less than 4 employees but they provide only 9% of total employment. At the
other extreme the fifty largest companies, among which LM
Ericsson is one, provide a fifth of employment. Within the private
sector too, the ownership of capital is highly concentrated.
Swedish industry and the banks are still predominantly owned
by a few families. So, while Swedish companies are not large
by international standards, within the country economic policy
and the employment condition of the majority of the labour
force are dictated by a few enterprises governed by a management characterized by an aggressive, competitive and innovative
approach to their role. In this the private sector has been encouraged and supported both by government policy and by the
attitudes of the trade unions. The tri-partite labour market policy
developed within this framework has been the envy of many
other West European governments. Among other things it provides one of the most extensive training programmes in the world
which helps to produce an adaptable and mobile labour force.
Economic growth has been steady, and today the standard of
living in Sweden is probably the highest in the world. This is not
to suggest that the country has been free of economic problems.
'Wage drift' and its consequent impact upon prices was first
diagnosed in Sweden. Unemployment has also been considered a
problem at times. But it must be seen in perspective. In 1976 when
unemployment in Britain was creeping up to 5% and in the
United States was 8%, it was only 2% in Sweden. This economic
prosperity and the improvement in material standards is reflected
in the lives of Palm's workers.

Even though Swedish industry is predominantly capitalist, many
people consider Sweden a socialist country, not only because of
the long rule of the Social Democrats, but also because of the
influence of its trade union movement. Union membership is
probably the highest in Europe. Of the workforce 87% are members of trade unions as compared with 50% in Britain and only
28% in the United States. Trade union structure is simple. There
is a well established and highly centralized system of bargaining
between the main trade union confederations, LO for the manual
workers and TCO for the white collar workers on the one hand,

and SAF, the employers' federation, on the other. This system has extended bargaining far beyond wages to include many other issues such as safety, training and the status of shop stewards. An agreement between SAF and LO made in 1946 provides that all enterprises employing more than 50 workers will have works councils to provide a forum for consultation between management and trade unions. We find the Ericsson works council figuring in Palm's account of his life on the shop floor. In 1973 Sweden legislated for trade union representation on the unitary boards of all companies employing more than 100 workers. Initially this was experimental, but in 1976 the legislation was extended and now also applies to smaller enterprises. The power of the trade unions, which at national level is considerable, is exercised within a system of shared values. They have accepted the need for technical change and rationalization, and they have cooperated with companies to increase productivity and efficiency. In their turn, managements have accepted trade unions and have sought their cooperation. Until very recently, at least, the normative framework surrounding the industrial relations systems has been such that the use of sanctions, traditional and much used in Britain and North America, such as over-time bans, work to rule and strikes, have been rarely used or even contemplated. Nationally trade union employer relationships have been shaped by the so-called 'peace formula'.

The close relationship between the trade unions and the Social Democratic government has produced a welfare state as extensive as any in the world. A generous pension policy providing some 60% of earnings on retirement was introduced in 1962. Standards of health care are high and there are imaginative schemes of support for the disabled and single parent families. Such provision has its price. To effect extensive transfers, Swedish taxation is one of the highest in Europe. But there is no complacency. There has been public debate, including a Royal Commission, about the continuing extent of inequality. There have been conscious attempts by the trade unions to narrow employment differentials, particularly between manual and non-manual workers in a policy known as 'wage solidarity'. Another important social development of the last twenty years has been the adoption of the first completely unstreamed educational system in Western Europe. Already this has affected the proportions of working class children transferring to the gymnasium and gaining access to university education. It might therefore be said that the dedication of the Social Democratic Party to a policy of 'welfare' and 'social reform' within the framework of a capitalist system had been successful.

Finally, Sweden made its own contribution to an issue which, in the late sixties and early seventies, emerged as of great interest in many advanced industrial countries. It has become known world-wide as the 'quality of working life' debate. In the United States an official study 'Work in America' was commissioned. In Britain the government set up a Work Research Unit. In 1972 SAF and LO in Sweden signed an 'Agreement on Rationalization'. Its goals were 'to attain increased productivity, greater job satisfaction, a better working environment and security of employment'. From 1969 to 1974 many experiments in the reorganization of work were embarked upon in several hundred Swedish factories. Those at the Saab engine assembly plant at Södertalje and the newly built Volvo car assembly plant at Kalmar acquired international fame. The object was to increase the interest of work, as well as its efficiency, by organizing around semi-autonomous work groups. The Kalmar plant incorporated a new approach to automobile assembly by breaking up the flow line into small work stations, or shops, within which each work group is free to organize its work as it wishes. Some of these developments have influenced Palm's own thinking about the problems of work organization, although his suggestions go beyond them in important ways.

But here we are faced with a puzzle. How can we relate the general picture of this concern with well-being at work with Göran Palm's picture of life on the shop floor written after a year spent in one of Ericsson's factories (LM), assembling telephone equipment? Even the title of his book *The Flight from Work* begins to raise questions. The first, perhaps startling, feature of his account is that any British or American worker will recognize and identify with the concerns, the complaints and the frustrations of the workers whose portraits Palm so skilfully paints. Even if some allowance should be made for possible shock which the reality of industrial life may produce in poets and academic sociologists, industrial readers will find in these pages a life which they themselves know.

Roland at sixty has difficulty in coping with the increased piece-
work and complains of the 'bloody awful work environment'.
Jaakko, the immigrant Finnish worker with his strange Swedish
accent, is afraid of losing his job and is also ground down by the
'carrot bastard' of piece-work. The complaints about the canteen
food, the noise, the fumes, the bad organization of the work flow,
the poor rates of pay, the boredom of the work could be heard in
Detroit or in Birmingham. But there are also some work features
which appear more unfavourable than those to which many
British and American workers will be accustomed. The complaints
about piece-work and about the way in which the speed of working has increased are overwhelming. The shop floor rules are very
tight. Speaking during working hours is prohibited; entering
closets more than one at a time is prohibited; leaving places of
work is prohibited; washing before the buzzer goes is prohibited.
Another example of the tight control is that payment for the
holiday is lost if the worker is late by even one hour the following
day. Many workers in Britain know such rules exist, but they can
often be bent or ignored up to a point. The fear of the supervisor,
at least among the middle-age group at Ericsson's (Palm comments on the more open attitude of the young) is striking. In
Britain and America some workers might also find the apparent
distance of the shop steward, or local trade union representative
familiar. Yet others, however, would find the extent of managerial
prerogative in the organization of work surprising. Palm was
writing when the 1906 agreement between the trade unions and
employers was still in force. He refers to it as 'Paragraph 32'.
This stated that the employer was entitled to 'direct, assign work
and dismiss workers at will and to employ workers whether they
are organized or not'. But shop stewards in Britain would not
hesitate to challenge managements' right to re-allocate labour or
to change working practices where these were inimical to the
workers' interests if they felt that they could command the support of their members. The overwhelming impression left by
Palm is of the weakness of local shop floor control and of the
failure of trade union representatives to be concerned with the
individual workers' problems.

Palm's book has been widely debated in Sweden. This suggests that although there may be disagreement about some of his
findings they have not been dismissed out of hand. But there

is also other evidence to suggest that management control in Swedish factories has been much tighter than in either Britain or America. In 1974 six American car workers from Detroit spent four weeks working in the engine assembly plant at Saab. Their reactions were interesting. They valued highly the superior physical working conditions at the Saab plant. But they, too, objected to the pace of work, to the tightness of rules and the social distance of the foreman. These American workers felt that the Swedish trade unions were not as effective at plant level and not so concerned with the needs of individual workers as were their own American union. How then can the general picture of Swedish progressiveness be reconciled with this picture of industrial life with less freedom and autonomy for the worker? Has this been the price for a higher standard of living?

There are three things to be borne in mind. First, national negotiations and agreements in Sweden, and elsewhere, take time to have their effect at lower levels in the system. The rationalization agreement of 1972 seems better known outside Sweden than it was to Palm's workers at Ericsson's, and even within Sweden it has been acknowledged that the Volvo and Saab experiments had received publicity of a kind which over-rates their importance. Second, and more important, there are ongoing conflicts and pressures within Sweden which have begun to produce some significant changes in industrial life and which are rooted in the discontents expressed by Palm's workers. As we see from Palm's account, the late sixties were a time when, to maintain profitability in the face of increasing international competition, employers were tightening piece-rates, dismissing workers, re-allocating labour within the plants. At that time there was little official opposition at national or plant level from the trade union. They had the desired effect of increasing profitability. But they also produced spontaneous grass roots response. The early seventies saw one or two unofficial strikes, all the more startling because they had previously been so rare. In the last two or three years the issue of piece-rate payments has been tackled more directly with a vigorous campaign conducted officially by the unions. Already there have been some modifications to the individual piece-work system. In 1977 the 'Democracy at Work' Act was passed which ended the period of managerial prerogative. It gives to the trade unions extensive new rights covering such things as priority of interpretation in disputes concerning members' rights and duties; it places upon employers the duty to negotiate about important changes in company activities; and it gives the union the right to examine the company books, and to receive information about production trends and plans. Potentially such legislation could have a considerable impact upon the balance of power at plant level.

Changes are also apparent at a wider social level. Goran Palm's account of life on the Swedish factory floor makes it clear that there is still a class system in Sweden. 'They really do spoil us chars', says Deidre with her gold watch and four company shares after forty years of service with Ericsson's. We are aware of a gulf between the shop floor and the office workers, while the top managers and directors of the company do not figure in the world of Ericsson's workers. Other evidence, however, tells us that Swedish workers compare themselves and their conditions with a much wider range of social groups than British workers. They do not take for granted that their pay, working conditions, career prospects should be less favourable than those of white collar workers. Palm's young workers are less ready to accept authority, and have more open attitudes. Thus we can perceive tensions in a society where the impact of educational changes and the widespread acceptance of certain social values are producing aspirations in direct conflict with the constraints of the work situation and the play of market forces, which still limit access to top jobs.

The third issue is a much wider one which concerns the nature of autonomy at work. It may well be the case that Swedish workers have paid a price for their high standard of living and welfare. They work harder under tighter control than their British or American counterparts. But the autonomy exercised by the British shop steward or American automobile worker is certainly not the 'freedom, status, coherence and meaning in work' that Palm is seeking. As a first step he would like to see what he calls the 'worst obstacles removed' – the labour legislation rewritten (as we have seen that it has to some extent been since he made his study), payment by results systems ended, the workshop rules relaxed and more power to the grass roots of the trade unions. He is even in favour of quite traditional methods of job enlargement based upon teamwork.

But in the last analysis Palm is concerned with a problem

which is unlikely to be fundamentally touched by such measures and yet which is also common to Swedish and British and American industrial life. He sees the pressure of the trade unions and the Social Democrats as having been concerned with 'increasing the yields which workers get from work, not the yields that they get *in* work'. This is also the concern of British and American trade unions. But this is not enough, says Palm. Contemplating his Finnish friend Jaakko's concern to do an honest job and useful work of good quality, he speculates upon the 'funds of human productive power. . .' which 'lie bound and concealed and are only occasionally released during leisure time.' 'The consequences of industrial work as at present organized are twofold. First a split within the individual. . .one-half at work with no expectation of freedom or self-fulfilment, the other which "is born when the sun goes down" which seeks in leisure all those qualities denied in work.' Hence 'the flight from work'. But in addition to the personal split, these conditions prevent the development of cooperation between workers. Nationally the Swedish unions may pursue their policies of 'wage solidarity' but this is at the expense of solidarity in pursuit of shared objectives and fulfilment in work itself. Palm's preoccupation is with alienation.

His prescription is a gradualist one. He believes that autonomous production teams can be built up which will increasingly absorb all supervisory functions. He sees the work's engineer placing orders for products with these teams as though they were independent sub-contractors. He believes such a development to be possible even within a company still retaining some hierarchy of authority and within a private enterprise economy. He speaks of 'the employees' and when he does so he means all of them – blue collar, white collar, technicians, salesmen as well as managers – taking over the running of the factories.

This is one man's – a poet's – vision of a system of employee participation. It is of widespread interest because in most of Western Europe this question is on the agenda. Various experiments, particularly with formal board-level worker participation, are to be found in countries including Germany, Denmark and Holland. Britain has recently received the report of the Bullock Committee of Inquiry into Industrial Democracy. Such proposals are different in kind from those of Palm. Indeed he is quite scathing about the Swedish legislation for board level trade union representation. But the connection between formal institutional worker participation and workers' control over their immediate work situation is not something which can be easily developed and yet is one which has to be explored. It is also the case that interest in such connections may be influenced by current economic conditions. At a time of rising unemployment or of falling standards of living such issues may seem less central. But the longer term developments in industrial society are such that the questions will re-emerge. It is not, therefore, the prescriptions of Göran Palm which are the most important thing in this book. It is his ability to increase our understanding of the so often hidden aspirations and emotions of routine manual workers which is the book's strength and which is essential for the future successful solution of industrial problems.

March 1977   Dorothy Wedderburn
London   *Professor of Industrial Sociology*
                     Imperial College

Foreword

In this book the poet-author presents his understanding of the workers' situation based on his personal experiences in a factory of one of Sweden's largest export manufacturing companies. That a well-known author should choose to work in a factory in a country where he would be eligible for a cultural stipend is possibly more unusual than would be the case in the UK or the USA. The author had several reasons for this move. One of them is a social curiosity to acquire a deeper understanding of the workers' situation, partly to test his own personal frame of reference and partly to fill a gap in his personal experiences and generate a personal basis for future writings dealing with workers' conditions. He experienced a certain confusion, the disillusionment, frustration not uncommon among intellectual socialists who have lived all their life in a social democracy when faced with the ideas and experiences of the new left reaching Sweden in the mid-sixties.

A key issue for the author is the relationship between the worker as an individual and the workers as a social class. Study visits to a large industry give rise to a flood of impressions which leave one with a general picture of the workers' situation. One knows, of course, that each worker is a unique individual but what one sees is a joint labour collective, the working class. A restricted and extended visit to a single work group would give quite different results. The impression of the collective would be replaced by a keen appreciation of the individuality of each worker. The author aims in this book to present both these views in a balanced perspective.

An increasing number of authors and journalists have made serious efforts to portray the lot and experiences of workers in different industrial and service settings. These inputs in the current social and political debate may be termed social reporting. The most common form for such reports is extended interviews with individual workers, sometimes complemented with photographs from the relevant environments. The quality of the descriptions presented depends naturally on the social skills of the interviewer and on the readiness and ability of those interviewed to present an open and nuanced picture. Göran Palm felt that the interview method runs too high a risk of yielding superficial, stereotype results. To gain a real understanding of the workers' situation he felt he must share or participate in their day-to-day activities as a 'guest worker'. He had no real illusions about completely identifying himself with them or being identified by them as 'one of us'. His membership in the group, however, would allow the gradual development of social relationships with his work colleagues which would lead to the insights he sought.

This participant study differs however from the reports of such authors as Günther Walraff in that the author was motivated strongly by a desire to test his values and preconceived ideas about the workers' world in industry rather than seeking out clear-cut exemplifications of his thesis. Two basic ideas behind this report are that preconceived ideas can only be really tested by direct personal experience, as distinct for example from reading books or watching television programmes, and that many of the socialist and marxist analyses of the situation of the working class pay insufficient attention to the rich variety existing within the members of that class. He wished to penetrate more deeply, to understand what lay behind the 'flight from work' – the workers' tendency to regard work as a more or less depressing overture to the leisure time constantly in their thoughts – to the passivity in union affairs, to the variety in their experiences of their situation.

Palm worked for a year as an hourly-paid worker in different assembly departments at L. M. Ericsson's main factory in Stockholm. On the basis of his experiences he wrote *A Year at LM* which described his first contact with the firm, a number of personal surprises (preconceived ideas which were not substantiated), and an analysis of the validity of a number of his prejudices, as well as portraits of different typical figures he met among the work-force. In his foreword to the book he made an open appeal to his former colleagues at LM, management, the unions and any other interested reader to contact him with reactions to and comments on the book. These were incorporated in a new analysis of the material which resulted in a second volume entitled *The Final Account from LM*. This volume included separate analyses of the reactions to the book from workers, management and unions, further portraits of individual workers, a popular review of the findings of psychological and social-psychological studies of industrial workers as well as the author's suggestions for improving working conditions.

The translation presented here is an abridgement of the two Swedish volumes. The abridgement has been accomplished by selecting chapters from the two books as distinct from précising the total contents. In making our selection we have in a first instance retained the majority of the individual portraits which we feel provide the most important material for understanding the workers' situation. The abridgement decisions were made jointly by the author, the translator and myself. In addition, we selected the discussion of a number of preconceived ideas and prejudices which we feel may well be shared by people in most Western industrial countries. We conclude this volume with the author's recommendations for action.

The form of publication of the two Swedish books indicates a distinct aim on the part of the author which evolved during his employment at LM, namely to influence the current political and social debate. The first volume was published in 1972, the second in 1974. How have they been received as an input into the educational, scientific and political areas?

There is a growing debate in the Scandinavian countries, among others, regarding the values behind and the methods used in social science research. Some of the consequences of this debate are increasing awareness of the role of values in research and of the limited roles played by scientists in the past. There is a gradual shift in emphasis towards the need to understand and not just explain the phenomena and situations studied, the need to play an active role and not just to be a bystander, a desire to share experience and not just observe or record, and a desire to do research with and not research on different groups in society. This has meant that social scientists at the universities and other research institutions are beginning to show a greater interest in and receptiveness to impulses from each other and from outsiders. The formation of cross-disciplinary research groups orientated to specific problem areas is becoming more widespread. The methods used in social anthropology, political science and journalism are finding their way into the curricula and research projects in the field of psychology, sociology and business administration.

These developments are not of course solely the result of an internal process – they are also the result of new pressures on the research community. New demands have been made on researchers from quarters of society previously disinterested in their activities. An important group here is the trade unions. Previously very sceptical to research, voices can now be clearly heard within their ranks calling for research efforts on problems of direct interest to their members, carried out within frames of reference understandable to the unions and compatible with or incorporating their values. Government legislation in May 1976 ratified the plans for setting up a special research centre to study issues concerned with working life. This confirmed the need to conduct research from the workers' perspective and provided a number of research posts at the centre for non-professional researchers, i.e. industrial workers, union officials or journalists can suitably be employed as research assistants in specific projects.

Against this background the two Swedish volumes have been positively received by the universities and have been and are utilized as textbooks in several social science and engineering faculties at major universities. The books are used primarily in courses in business administration and industrial engineering from which future Swedish managers will emerge.

It was natural that the author's reactions were both positive and negative and that his straightforward presentation of his negative experiences has trodden on sensitive toes and this has guaranteed sharp reactions from both the management and trade union quarters. Management's stance has been that the author's methods of collecting, structuring and analysing his data do not conform with any scientific standards for objectivity and thus the data and conclusions presented do not warrant comment. They represent the charming but highly subjective notes of a poet. It may however be relevant to compare this work with the brochures, information articles and press releases produced by public relations departments in companies whose managements would hasten to assure potential readers of their objectivity.

A common reaction from trade union officials has been that

the criticisms raised of private industry are old hat and that the author's demands have been pushed by the unions behind the scenes for many years. An answer to this criticism is that the only reasonable starting point for social criticism is to regard every problem as new as long as it still exists. The difficult and important thing is not constantly to hit upon new problems to expose; the difficult and important thing is to find new ways of describing those problems which are already known – so that they may be rediscovered and thereby new efforts may be made to deal with them.

If it is not possible to create an opinion by fiery protest articles, one can attempt to use statistics, and if statistics fail one can attempt to use concrete examples, and if concrete examples fail one can utilize satire etc. The author has utilized all these methods and thus regards this work formally as a cross between a documentary and fiction.

The strongest criticism in Sweden from both management and unions was addressed to the first book. The second *Final account from LM* received a more positive reception. It was the subject of a series of debate articles in the magazine of the Metal Workers' Union, Sweden's largest industrial union. A major correspondence course institute has produced a study handbook to be used together with the book, many company managements and local trade unions have invited the author to lead debates and discussions on the book and perhaps most important, the trade union congress and the confederation of salaried workers' trade unions have both presented reports to their 1976 congresses – reports which strongly reflect the author's ideas regarding the meaning and content of work. The debate which has taken place in Sweden during the last two or three years regarding the abolition of Paragraph 32 in the statutes of the Swedish Employers' Confederation has also provided a climate more receptive to the experiences and observations in the second book. (Paragraph 32 refers to the employers' right to direct and allot work, to hire and dismiss workers at will, and to employ workers whether they are union members or not. Legislation passed in May 1976 makes these issues the subject of joint negotiation between unions and management.)

The book has been an important bestseller in Sweden but what relevance has it for the USA and the UK? The problems and some of the developments would seem to be the same, but they occur in different contexts. What aspects of the Swedish context would it be useful to bear in mind when reading this book? Sweden is a country with a small population which underwent late industrialization and in which the same party (the Social Democratic Labour Party) was in power from 1932 until 1976. During the 30 year period from roughly 1940 to 1970 the Government observed a policy of non-intervention in the labour market which was controlled through joint agreements between the main parties, the Employers' Confederation and the Trade Union Confederations for labour and staff (LO och TCO). These organizations are very strong and exert a tight influence over their members; 95% of the workers are members of 29 industrial unions and 70–80% of the staff personnel are members of 22 professional unions. The unions have succeeded in cultivating a strong sense of solidarity, evolving a correspondingly strong authority among their members. There is a marked agreement between the values and opinions of the rank and file members and their representatives.

There are definite signs of a change in the relationship between the main parties on the labour market: the focusing on harmony, joint interests and collaboration is giving way to a focus on differences, conflicts and even possibly confrontation. This shift is also noted in the change in Government strategy during the 1970s. The Social Democratic Party, closely aligned with the Confederation of Trade Unions (LO), has introduced ten new laws regarding conditions of the labour market during the last six years. This change in strategy reflects partly a response to the radical ideas emerging in most Western industrial countries, new aspirations and militancy amongst the workers and the change of generations in the Social Democratic Party and central union organizations.

Swedish management and unions are also characterized by a marked innovativeness and openness in thinking in which there is a strong rivalry between the parties to maintain the initiative. This condition reflects the late industrialization of Sweden, its exposure to a highly competitive export market and to certain ingredients from its educational system. For example non-streamed schools have existed in Sweden for some time. Already it has been found that this has a significant effect on the proportion of working-class children transferring to the gymnasium and gaining access to the universities. Moreover, Sweden is one of the capitalist countries with the longest average number of years of education.

These factors may be summarized by characterizing Sweden as in a state of permanent reform.

Stockholm School of Economics   PETER DOCHERTY
August 1976

First contact with LM

The procedure followed when applying for an industrial job has a healthy simplicity. No written applications, no documents to be submitted, no uncertain waiting for a reply by post; all you do is ring up or walk in on spec with your testimonials in your hand and you will usually get an answer on the spot. As a rule, firms don't even bother to advertise unqualified jobs, hence the poor supply of vacancies at the labour exchange. The snag in my case was that I did not have any testimonials to show.

'Don't you have an employment book?' the staff officer said hesitantly and regarded me from the other side of his desk as though I had spent the last fifteen years behind bars.

'Actually I'm a teacher', I explained eagerly as though reciting a lesson, which was in fact what I was doing. 'There's a shortage of teaching posts in Stockholm just now, and I'd like to make a change and do industrial work while I'm waiting. One gets rusty just sitting reading.'

I intended to smile when I said this last part but my face felt stiff as tarpaulin.

'So it'll only be for a short time', the staff officer said.

'No, I reckon on staying six months at least. If I can manage the job, that is. I saw that LM needs truck drivers. Here. . .here are my references.'

By now my mouth was dry, and my hand shook noticeably when I handed over a paper with a teacher's name at the top. And yet I had not actually told any lies. I *do* have a basic university degree, and I *have* been a teacher. It was just that I had omitted to say what my real occupation is, and I thought that the staff officer could read the word BLUFFER in letters of fire across my forehead.

'I see', was all he said, apparently reassured, and he let his gaze glide from the references to me. 'Yes, graduates are beginning to come into industry now. Unfortunately the truck job went straight away, but we'll have to find something else. Göran. . .Palm was the name.'

Anyone who might happen to think that those who work in the staff departments of a large company should recognize the name or face of a 'well-known' author has no realistic concept of the limits of cultural fame or of the reading habits prevalent in Swedish industry. When Honken Holmqvist, the Swedish ice-hockey star, turned up at LM during a break between matches and training camps a buzz passed through the dining room, even amongst the Finns, but an author can move around unnoticed. Unless he has 'been on telly' or something like that. Perhaps no more than a dozen of the workshop employees who heard my name or saw my mug at LM associated me with politics or literature. About half of those could place me at once. The others, including supervisors, probably thought of intellectuals in general when they saw my face and of Prime Minister Palme when they heard my name.

How can I be so sure of this? I am not completely sure, of course. But the surreptitious glances that come one's way say more than the giver realizes. Above all it is easy to see through the glances which try to pretend that they do not recognize one.

Like most of the others, my own foreman did not know who I was until I had been working in his department for six months. He has said so himself in *Dagens Nyheter*. It was not until after six months had passed that I became active in union matters. 'Seen at LM' rather than 'seen on TV', so to speak. Right enough, he never pushed me around after that. But he did before.

I almost certainly could not have anticipated all this if my year at LM had been my first turn-out as an industrial worker. But I had jumped the gun as far back as 1968 at the Holmens paper-mill in Hallstavik. In those days I walked around the community waiting for my first shift, excited thoughts running through my head in the egocentric manner of those who believe themselves well known: Now I am going to be recognized! Now I am going to be recognized! But everyone seemed to be minding his own business in Hallstavik. Nobody cast any particular glances in my direction. There was only one fitter in the entire paper-mill who knew who I was, and he happened to live in the same barracks as I did. Otherwise we would probably never have met.

But the point is that I had already taken all the measures I *could* take then. During the years 1968–70 I turned down all offers to appear on TV and asked the major newspapers not to publish photos of me when I wrote new books. Publishing people's photographs in the daily press is usually regarded as publicity or free advertising but in sensitive situations the correct name for it is facial theft. If my face had been well-known when I started at the Hallsta papermill or at LM, my chances of getting to know what working conditions were like would have been limited straightaway. I would have been received and treated in a special way and not simply as one of the employees.

Another point: those who are often seen soon find it difficult to see.

As a result of all this, I wasn't particularly worried about being 'discovered' when I sat there in the LM staff office. The only thing I could not know – and this was what made me tense – was how this particular staff officer might react. After all, he might have a deep and personal interest in modern literature or else he might have a blacklist, drawn up by the Wallenberg Group or by the Employers' Federation, of left-wingers interested in industrial firms. There was no way of knowing.

'I don't mind taking an ordinary piece-rate job', I said when the danger seemed to have passed...

'Yes, you look fairly robust', the staff officer said doubtfully, 'but the presses...that might be a bit too tough. I think the assembly department would be better. Most of the work is piece-rate there too. I'll speak to one of the foremen in 36', he added decisively, 'and we can book time at the medical centre in the meantime.'

Perhaps he didn't say the presses. Perhaps my memory of other minor details is also incorrect. But what I am certain of is that the employment interview went very smoothly indeed, that it never touched on politics and that the whole thing was over in two or three minutes. But then of course, I was in possession of all the negative merits which are so highly valued when industry needs labour. I was not handicapped, I was not over 40, I was not a woman, and I was not a foreigner.

'He's Swedish!' is by no means an uncommon remark when new employees are introduced in the various departments at LM, particularly in departments where immigrants are in the majority. The import of foreign labour to industry tends to make the word 'Swedish' a positive characteristic.

But of course the major companies have concentrated on bringing in undemanding foreigners *instead of* improving working conditions to an extent which would attract Swedish workers to industry.

The company doctor

The medical examination I went through the following day took all of 25 seconds. This is not including the x-ray screening which a nurse carried out. Twenty-five seconds for testing whether or not a body might withstand factory work seems remarkably short, but I actually timed it. '20–25 seconds', is entered in my LM diary. Perhaps the last five seconds were used to write out the certificate of health. At any rate, the doctor devoted the remainder of the time to listening to my heart, looking at my tongue, shining a light in my eye, tapping my knee, listening to my cough and stating that I was healthy – all in rapid sequence.

No blood sample, no urine sample, no hearing test. Readers in the know will already have realized that it was Dr Sjöberg who examined me. Anyone who has had anything to do with this tough old army doctor, known as one of the most skilful sawbones at the Södersjukhuset hospital and a legendary figure at LM, will also know that 25 seconds is by no means a record for him. I once went to him with a swollen elbow which I had struck against a wall and Dr Sjöberg devoted five seconds to squeezing it, ten seconds to making a diagnosis – bursitis – and then went his way with an encouraging shout. Fortunately the nurse took more time to apply the bandage.

Dr Sjöberg has finished at LM now, missed by every employee who prefers brusque treatment at lightning speed to any form of gentle and time-consuming care. And this is no small group in a piece-rate industry. The fact that the workers do not have salaries means that they lose part of their income when they sit waiting in the medical centre, and there were seldom queues at Dr Sjöberg's. The lack of queues was not, however, solely a result of the doctor's acknowledged speed. One day I came in with a distressing lump under my foot and before I had time to protest Dr Sjöberg took a large scalpel and hummed as he began to open the lump with rapid cuts. When I bellowed he asked quietly if I thought he was 'unkind', though he didn't rest the scalpel for a moment. Total time on this occasion: less than a minute. My foot did actually become better, but it is not only elderly workers who pale when they hear stories like this and who prefer to keep their pains to themselves or spend expensive hours in the waiting rooms of gentler surgeons.

For my own part, I rather liked Dr Sjöberg. He always seemed to go directly to the source of the trouble no matter who whimpered when he cut. He was almost certainly scrupulous in following the old butcher's motto 'no pampering' no matter who paid for his knife. Nor can I imagine him ever taking people who were sick at LM off the sick list simply because top management said they were short of staff or anything like that. But perhaps it is best not to be too certain. Even Dr Sjöberg had been known to let company arguments fall from his lips in moments of impatience. A piece-rate worker, who has now left LM and is, consequently, safe, told me that he had a backache for a number of years from working in a standing, forward-leaning position and that he asked Dr Sjöberg to certify that it would be better for his back if he could work sitting down so that his suspicious supervisor could be persuaded to arrange seated work. But instead of a certificate, this worker was given the following reply: 'If the work doesn't suit you, you can always leave.'

I am *not* mentioning this example simply to be able to dismiss Dr Sjöberg as a 'company man'. I mention it to provide concrete support for a demand which has been put forward from many quarters in recent years and which has not yet led to any results: industrial medical officers should be released from their morally stressing intermediate position and should be paid by the county councils instead of being paid by management.

Why has this elementary demand not yet been met? Is it because it is not just the employers but also the doctors themselves who are against it? If so, I cannot quite grasp what arguments the doctors may have. After all, the economic ties with the employer must first be severed before a company doctor can be relieved of double loyalties and devote himself to exercising his profession without being disturbed or insulted by justified and unjustified charges of corruption from dissatisfied patients. Or is it just that the doctors are afraid they may be paid less by the county councils?

A few facts

The LM Ericsson telephone company was founded in 1876. It employs more staff and labour than any other Swedish company – 67 000 people all over the world. Slightly more than 57% of these are employed abroad.

Gross sales amounted to SKr 3700 million in 1971, and profits before tax came to SKr 477 million.

Europe excluding Sweden (42%), Sweden (23%) and South America (20%) comprise the major markets for the Ericsson Group.

Investments abroad, above all in the EEC countries and in South America, are increasing at a considerably faster rate than are investments in Sweden.

LM (as the company is known in Sweden) has subsidiaries or offices in 45 countries and representatives in such far-flung places as Bolivia, the Dominican Republic, Formosa, Greece, Guatemala, Hong Kong, Jordan, Liberia, Macao, Mozambique, Namibia, Paraguay, the Republic of Vietnam and South Africa.

In 1970 the 12 891 workers (40% immigrants) who were employed at the Group's Swedish factories shared a total wage sum of SKr 275 million. The 7414 salaried employees shared a total sum of SKr 273 million that year. In other words, the mean annual wage for a worker was less than SKr 22 000, while the mean annual salary for salaried employees (including directors) exceeded SK 36 000.

Movements are measured in units of TMU in time-and-motion studies carried out in accordance with the MTM system. According to the data cards used at LM, it takes 2 TMU for an average worker to open his or her hand, 3.5 TMU to grasp a thin object lying on a flat surface, 7.3 TMU to focus his or her eyes, 8.5 TMU to move his or her foot 10 cm without pressure, 18.6 TMU to turn his or her body 45–90° with the aid of two legs and 29 TMU to bend to knee level. One second corresponds to approximately 28 TMU.

Piece-work wages are opposed by 91% of the members of the Swedish Metalworkers' Union.

Two-thirds of Sweden's industrial workers regard their work as nothing more than a means to create resources to satisfy leisure time needs through various forms of consumption.

More than 80% of the members of the Swedish Confederation of Trade Unions say that they are exposed to health hazards in their work.

A large minority of the active members and a clear majority of the passive members of the Metalworkers' Union consider that wildcat strikes may, on occasion, be justifiable.

Five surprises

I found the work fairly easy

My first job was soldering. Then I stood and cut out power rails. Finally, I screwed anchoring brackets in position, assembled connectors and tapped guide bars into long telephone racks. Did I have to work like a dog? I'm sorry, but I never saw as much as a trace of the inferno of stress, noise, dirt and supervision which is portrayed in so many presentations of industrial work in recent years.

The pace was not particularly forced. I could smoke, drink coffee, if I had brought any with me, go to the toilet whenever I wanted to. Nothing prevented me from going to make a telephone call or visiting other departments whenever I had got a little ahead with my work, despite the fact that the shop rules at LM expressly forbid any such movements. Sometimes my foreman came with pompous rebukes like, 'Put away that newspaper!' (Paragraph 25 in the shop rules), but for the most part those of us who worked together were permitted to determine breaks and working periods to suit ourselves. Although the foreman often saw us sitting talking when he passed, he never made any direct admonitions. Never. We knew what he wanted anyway.

Nor was the work itself particularly heavy. I mainly sat like most others in the telecommunications sector and pottered with small components. Sometimes it was interesting, sometimes it was deadly dull. Standing bent over a rack for hours at a time is scarcely very healthy, but as a rule one could switch over to lighter work when one felt tired. All in all, the monotony was less than I had feared. None of my three jobs forced me to repeat the same thing all the time. The unit assembly work comprised roughly ten different operations and the rack assembly work comprised about 70 – though, of course, each operation was repeated ad nauseam as time went by.

All of the cupboards were covered with a thick layer of dust and the floors were worn out, but otherwise my surroundings were fairly clean. The floor was swept every afternoon. The constant clatter of the machinery in the department was, of course, tiresome, sometimes extremely tiresome. But as a rule the noise was not so high as to prevent the music from the loudspeakers getting through. The cold neon lighting was not pleasant to work in but one could not fault the intensity or direction of the light itself. The bad air was the worst problem. It is rather fantastic that enormously rich large-scale industries like LM Ericsson still satisfy themselves with opening a window to provide the main ventilation in smoky workshops when even easily aired, small offices install air conditioning. The air in the workshops was unfailingly putrid after no more than a few hours work; the pungent soldering smoke made many noses run and when the windows were opened two or three times a day during the winter months, warm smoky air at 25°C was mixed with freezing outdoor air. The result: a steady stream of colds.

Apart from this, *my* work environment was quite decent.

It must be borne in mind, of course, that I worked in the light telecommunications sector and not in the mechanical sector. In the Low Block, as the two-storey mechanical building is called, there is more than one department which produces high levels of noise and dirt. In some places one cannot even make oneself heard. In some places the machines and work benches were so closely spaced that the air around each worker was limited to a smoky and noisy minimum. And the stress is worse, too, in the Low Block, particularly in the departments dominated by immigrants.

Above all, it must be remembered that my jobs were not based on piecework. Those of us who assembled units and racks did, admittedly, have job cards to punch, but during a trial period while the piece-rate was being set we got the same wage whether we worked hard or took things easy. Consequently, we took things easy. But round about us in Department 36, and throughout the entire factory, there were performance maniacs who seemed to have a diabolical little foreman of their own built into their brains, a slave driver with eyes shining with gold fever, for their arms moved like the wings of a lark day after day, and they seldom as so much as stretched their legs.

The most distressing of all to regard were those who were forced through economic circumstances, or through their dreams of a luxury car, to abandon their human and natural working rhythm and bit by bit coerce their arms and hands into a mechanical movement pattern. Single mothers. Immigrant bachelors. Breadwinners encumbered with debts. Formerly phlegmatic craftsmen who had allowed themselves to be reschooled to robots. But there were just as many pieceworkers who *refused* to toil as though they were to be pensioned off at 45. They preferred to let their income drop a few kronor rather than wreck their nervous systems in advance or compromise with their customary working rhythm. Some took long breaks between concentrated working periods. Some worked at full speed for five hours and then slackened off. Some kept at it all the time, calmly and methodically. Some talked quite a lot between the work benches.

And quite a lot of the workers at LM had jobs and working conditions which were roughly as easy-going as my own. This applied to a large number in the High Block, quite a few in the Low Block and, probably, most of those in the stores and transport departments.

In saying this I do not want to claim that the considerably more depressing picture of Swedish industrial work which has been presented in recent plays about Volvo and the state-owned North-Bothnian Steelworks or in Sara Lidman's book on the mining industry (*Gruva*) or Marit Paulsen's book on low-income workers (*Du, Människa?*) are in any way false.

Far from it.

All I want to say is that it is dangerous to generalize using these fearful portrayals of industrial work as a basis – something which I found myself doing when I started at LM. I expected something similar there. But the assembly line at Volvo is not representative of the Swedish engineering industry, and the oppressive conditions in the mines and the steel mills, with their shift work and serious accident risks, tell us little about the work situation in large-scale industries like LM which are, technically and environmentally, more refined and where most of the employees work during the daytime and where there are no counterparts to the silicosis hazards of the mining industry or the falls of the building industry.

In fact, looking back on it now, I find it easier to identify myself with work-place descriptions where the emphasis is on facts rather than on indignation.

What is particularly striking at LM are the considerable differences between the various departments and sections. The dirt and stench are insufferable in one place; in the next everything is neat and tidy. The clamour is deafening in one section; not a sound is to be heard in a store nearby. The pace is forced to an inhuman degree in one spot; people sit playing games in the next.

That is what it is like at LM. That is how much things are dissimilar at LM. And this type of engineering industry employs, fortunately, considerably more Swedish workers than do the mines, steelworks and car assembly lines combined. Those who devote themselves to fundamentally changing Sweden's industrial society may find this a troublesome fact, as though the wind of change had suddenly lost its source. But if one ignores this fact it is impossible to work for a fundamental change. A revolutionary programme which is based on selected parts of reality only is bound to be shattered by those parts of reality which it has elected to ignore.

I think it is equally dangerous to generalize using the willingness to strike which started in Svappavaara in 1969 (and which was later to be so clearly manifested in the mines and on the docks as well as at numerous building sites and automotive factories) as a basis. The workers are in a state of ferment! people said. Since I started at LM when the wave of strikes reached its climax in the spring of 1970, I immediately set about seeing whether people were in a state of ferment there too. But there was no ferment to be seen at LM, possibly a gentle simmering but no more. Very few had the faintest notion of striking. Dissatisfaction existed, and it found expression daily. But for several reasons some of which I have intimated already, this dissatisfaction was individual rather than collective. The *common* dissatisfaction was weak and appears to be so still. When the Confederation of Trade Unions gave notice in June 1972 of spot strikes which would have embraced practically all of the labour force at LM the labour force had already arranged its holiday plans and would have nothing to do with any strikes – whether they be tame or wildcat.

Anyone who wants to get far away from talk of revolution should take a job at LM Ericsson in Midsommarkransen, Stockholm.

Do not misunderstand me. Something *could* happen at LM tomorrow. And there are certainly engineering industries with a fighting spirit which is a good deal more developed than it is at LM. There are industries of this type even within the LM Group, e.g. the factories at Karlskrona. I just want to warn against making too much out of the wave of strikes which has taken place. It has meant a clear step forwards for the entire working class of Sweden, but it was limited. It did not spread like a prairie fire. Once again unrest and strikes occurred at the work places where unrest and strikes *usually* occur in Sweden – at places where there was a fighting tradition which could be used as a basis, principally in the mining industry but also amongst the automotive workers, the dock workers and the building workers. But what sort of fighting tradition exists at SKF, Asea and LM, to name only three of Sweden's largest industrial firms?

Ever since 1969 young revolutionaries have been drawn to the ore mines like moths to a flame. But there are plenty of people already working up there who are fit for fight. There is far more to do at LM quite simply because so little has been done there.

The manner in which one *experiences* a job in industry depends to a considerable extent on where one comes from and where one is going. For my own part, I came from a study in which I found, for several reasons, that I could neither write nor read. I could get nothing done. In a situation like that it felt marvellous to enter the manufacturing sector and do something useful. To manufacture products which were needed – and not non-returnable bottles or plastic casing for splinter bombs. Assembling telephone exchanges made a big change from sitting at a typewriter and using the letter 'x' more than any other.

Before that I had come from one of the most physically trying jobs to be found in the paper industry (at least in 1968). I stood with a boat hook at the Holmen paper-mill and fed timber logs which were to be converted to pulp into an inexorably sinking moist – a sort of individual production line. During the first five shifts I had only one exhausted thought in my head: I must not give up! Every finger was blistered and the muscles of my back were ruptured. After brutal drudgery of this type, the jobs which LM had to offer were bound to be a pleasant surprise. Compared with the paper-mill, the entire telecommunications sector looked like a vast therapeutic institution for basket weaving.

All of this meant that I ran the risk of regarding the work done at LM in too favourable a light right from the beginning.

But what is particularly important is where one is going, and I was on my way *out* the whole time. I was no more than a guest at LM, an ex-National Serviceman on a refresher course. I could return to my ordinary writing work – or at least to a job at the Central Bureau of Statistics – at any time. Anyone who has a brighter future up his sleeve the whole time can *afford* to experience his work in a more favourable manner than those whose whole future consists of LM. Even if I had had a tough piece-rate job, which was what I applied for, I should never have needed to know the true harshness of piecework stress since this harshness consists partly of being forced to hurry in order to earn one's living and partly of the fact that there is no end in sight, the job fills whatever future may lie ahead.

But I was by no means the only one who experienced LM as a stop on the road to somewhere else. Many of the workers there finished after a shorter time than I did, and many of the others could not imagine remaining much longer.

Why? *None* of those I spoke to gave the stress, the noise, the dirt or the supervision as a decisive reason. They all gave other reasons: wage reductions, piecework conflicts, compulsory moving around – in short, labour policy, the feeling of being a small replaceable cog in a giant machine which one cannot survey: 'Almost like a number.'

If criticism of the vast engineering sector is to be precise and effective it must aim at exactly these conditions.

There are plenty of smiles at LM

Working conditions being what they are and wages being set in the apparently haphazard manner in which they are set, what is there to be happy about at LM? Are not faces necessarily dogged and smiles rare in an arduous piece-work industry? Do not the few smiles which do appear seem a little tired or bitter?

One might expect them to be so. It seems only natural that they should. But one does not need to spend long at a factory to realize that gloomy expectations of this type ignore the fact that workers are human beings.

Having spent a year seeing workers, southern Europeans as well as Scandinavians, make the most of their opportunities for joking, laughing, chatting and relaxing, even of singing at times, I am almost inclined to claim that the opposite is true. It is precisely when the pressure really is on that smiling contact becomes a vital necessity.

So does black humour. No one can describe the worst jobs at LM as drastically and funnily as those who have carried them out for ten years.

Obviously most piece-rate workers do not exactly laugh themselves to death when they are in the middle of a difficult work operation. But even then it happens that they shout or flirt or whistle a little to themselves without a thought for the fact that the LM shop rules forbid 'whistling and other noise' (Paragraph 28). Two women who cannot make their voices heard in the noise from the machines, despite the fact that they work no more than a few metres apart, help make daily life supportable for each other by exchanging a smile now and then. And as soon as a demanding operation is finished or a machine breaks down most workers take the chance to smooth out their features, cast an eye around for mates who feel like a chat, give their neighbour a dig in the ribs, clap a fellow countryman on the back or steal off for a natter at the coffee dispenser. And many of those employed in the workshops regard these furtive breaks and the furtive interchanges with their mates as the only (or at any rate as particularly) attractive elements in the working day.

Management at LM sometimes tries to regard the existence of smiles and jokes in the factory as a sign that the work environment is not, despite all, as inhuman as left-wingers try to make out – or even as a sign of job satisfaction and pleasure. Those who set the headlines and write the captions at *Dagens Nyheter* were equally dishonest when they picked out and twisted everything I said about smiles at the factory when interviewing me about my LM experience last year and made it look as though the LM management should take the credit for these expressions of joy. This form of interpretation is just as erroneous as when a company commander regards the existence of laughter and joking in the barracks as a sign that the recruits enjoy doing their national service.

It is precisely when work is felt to be joyless and inhuman that the need for joy and human contact becomes so palpable that it suddenly breaks out where one least expects it. In the midst of drudgery. As a powerful counteracting force; as a means of protest and of enduring; as unexpected dandelions on an asphalted road.

The ability to smile against all odds and to find cause for rejoicing where there seems to be cause only for sorrow is an ability which outside visitors to the factory often find as perplexing as tourists in Africa do when they see slave workers laugh or dance during their breaks. This is a talent which can only be acquired during the daily struggle for survival at the bottom level of the class society. This is the capital held by the working class, acquired during decades and centuries of chronically getting the worst of things, a treasure of popular culture which can never be stolen or commercialized, only temporarily buried.

Rock bottom joy. The hidden spring which only the oppressed can find.

This does not mean that joy is greatest in the worst departments at LM. There is a limit to what human beings can stand, and every smile will freeze below a certain level of oppression. But the impression I have received both from LM's workshops and from the rice paddies of Guinea-Bissau is that this limit is extraordinarily elastic.

When time-and-study engineers came to LM during the 1940s and prohibited spontaneous coffee breaks, unnecessary conversations and running about in the departments, many of the workers felt as though the smiles had disappeared from the workshop according to Elsa Appelquist in *Krig med räknesticka* (*Slide-rule war*), the only novel written about LM. But she goes on to say that nicknames, jokes and stories soon grew up around the new conditions and that necessity, the mother of invention, found numerous ways of getting around the new prohibitions. The smiles returned through the back door, so to speak.

Shortly before I started at LM, I visited some of the poorest villages in West Africa, villages where daily work still constitutes a struggle for existence. Yet a smile was by far the most common means of communication amongst those who worked, both in the fields and outside the huts where the women crushed rice with huge cudgels. Smiles were the most common means of communication, next came chatting, then laughter and song.

The spring to which only the oppressed can find the way does not easily run dry.

Party dictatorship prevails in the union

Union matters at LM give plenty of cause for surprise.

Most of the workers called the union 'they' as though themselves were not members. 'All they do is fleece you for contributions.' Only a few seemed to know what their own union representatives were called. It seemed to be extraordinarily difficult to find willing *and* competent candidates for all sorts of union positions, even at the departmental level. The piece-work system was not so much as mentioned at any of the four quarterly meetings arranged by the union during my time at LM. Many of the members could not imagine attending a union meeting under any circumstances whatsoever. 'I was at a meeting once four years ago, that was enough.' When the chairman of the local union branch (i.e. the shop union) visited a department or came into the toilet, the normal conversations between the workers often died down. Apart from this, it was as though the shop union did not exist. Despite the fact that one-third of the union members at LM were immigrants, no foreign words ever occurred at the shop union meetings or on the posters announcing the meetings. Not once!

I was less surprised by the noticeable contrast between the enthusiastically industrious contact men, safety officers and study circle organizers who were often to be seen in the workshops, and the polished leader types who ran things in the shop union and the Social Democratic Club – ran things and dealt with the contacts upwards to the Metalworkers' Union and the Labour Party (i.e. The Swedish Social Democratic Labour Party – SAP).

But one must be careful not to make too much of this contrast. Some of the self-sacrificing contact men were far too uninformed and easy-going to stand up to the bosses when they began to get tough. And some of the leader types were sufficiently knowledgeable and stubborn to deal with difficult negotiations with the company, e.g. temporary lay-offs, local pay rises for low-income groups and piece-work disputes. It would be wrong to believe that the top ranks in the union spend their time scheming or gorging themselves when they meet the LM directors. Completely wrong. Nor is it only careerists who are voted onto the shop union committee. People who are deeply devoted to union matters, who would have nothing to do with scheming for personal advantages are also to be found there – although seldom in key positions. I am not introducing these qualifying aspects to smooth over the contrast between the top level and the rank and file within the union but merely to reach the heart of the contrast easily. As I see it, the boundary line can be drawn between those active in the union who are in daily touch with the members and who primarily devote themselves to what is best for the members on the one hand and, on the other, those active in the union who seldom ask their members anything and who primarily devote themselves to what is best for themselves or for the party.

In other words, there are plenty of competent people in the union at LM – and that is precisely why the party dictatorship which has been developed at the top level of the union is so objectionable.

Of course I knew beforehand that LM has been one of the strongest bastions of the social democrats in the engineering industry since the metalworkers' strike in 1945 and that the communists in particular have suffered many defeats there. But it surprised me that the one-party rule could be exercised as openly as it was, almost as though it were an unquestionable axiom that democracy and trade union work do not belong together.

In addition to the shop union, in which almost all the shop workers are still members (though young people and immigrants are grumbling to an increasing extent), two voluntary local labour clubs have been in existence for many years – one social democratic and one communist. The level of activity is not exactly overwhelming in either of these clubs. In fact, the Art Society at LM is probably a great deal more active, to say nothing of the Athletics Association. There may be a handful of truly active members in the communist club and perhaps fifteen in the social democratic, a total of twenty active members out of 2200 conceivable members.

But unfortunately what is decisive is not the degree of activity and labour support but rather the degree of influence, and the social democratic club has a tremendous, an even decisive, influence over the entire range of union activities at LM. It is there, for instance, that the candidates for all elective posts in the shop union are nominated and elected in practice.

How is this possible? The answer is very simple. The social democratic club is the only strong party organization at LM and those who are in control of it fill all of the important posts in the shop union committee as well as acting as representatives for the Metalworkers' Union. Party comrades elect each other. Communists, members of other parties, non-party members, or headstrong or left-wing social democrats do not hold as much as a single post, even as deputies. Nothing but faithful party members all the way. Competent or colourless toe-the-line social democrats. And the shop union connections upwards, with the Labour Party (SAP) leadership, are close, durable and extensive. The party whips often visit the meetings since the Labour Party attaches considerable importance to its local union branches in industry.

If you work at LM and you want to know what is going on in the trade union sphere you quite simply *have to* be a member of this local social democratic club.

For my own part, I first began to smell a rat when the chairman of the shop union meeting held in November 1970 asked for suggestions for contact men in the departments and an elderly member immediately requested the floor, drew out a paper and read up 29 names in rapid sequence. Only the names, without any presentation of any sort. How many of those present could place those names straight off? LM is a large factory and most of those working there know only the people in their own departments. The chairman seemed satisfied anyway and confined himself to asking quickly if there were any other suggestions before he let his mallet fall to indicate that the 29 had been elected as contact men for the union for 1971.

By acclamation.

Formally, there was nothing to remark on. The statutes say that the contact men may be elected as a group and that they shall be elected at a shop union meeting, i.e. by a central assembly that cannot possibly know which of the proposed representatives have the confidence of the workers – and not at the meetings held in the various departments. In other words, the procedure was correct. But the entire election not only *seemed* to have been decided in advance, it *must* quite simply have been decided in advance. Where could the old boy have got the paper from otherwise?

The picture became even more clear at the combined nomination and annual meeting in 1971. This time the board and the representative assembly were to be elected as well as the members of the joint works council and the canteen council. In many factories the shop union arranges a special nomination meeting before the annual meeting, but this is not 'necessary' at LM since the social democratic club arranges the only meeting which is acceptable. It was no great surprise to see that the council election came fairly far down the agenda for the annual meeting so that many of those who were interested had already gone home when the new front man stood up and struggled through the list of names he had been given at the nomination meeting. The club chairman had not even bothered to appoint different front men for each particular nomination; the same old boy stood up seven or eight times and read out names from the same sheaf of papers. Despite this, a few of us tried to break through the list by proposing a different chairman than 'A' and a different member than 'B' but, disappointingly, our candidates declined to stand. And the list of names was soon pushed through unchanged.

Were the union opposition to be better prepared than we were it *could*, of course, get several rival candidates nominated; at least the elections are democratic enough for that. But what happens when two names are set, one against the other, in this way? The *entire* committee usually gives in and the election is postponed until a later occasion. Consequently, what most of those who are dissatisfied would like to do – replace a few individual and detested members with others – is particularly difficult and frequently impossible. Instead, what is known as a 'list election' takes place. In this election two complete lists are put forward – on the one hand the social democratic proposal and on the other an opposing proposal which the social democrats usually brand as communist during the election campaign. In the building and mining industries, where the communists are traditionally strong, list elections of this type can develop into tough and, in many ways, clean party fights. But at LM, and at most other large-scale industries, the union opposition is so mixed that branding opposition proposals as communist and fighting party battles between the Labour Party (SAP) and the Left Party Communists (as the largest communist party in Sweden, VPK, is called) seem more like ghosts from the past, conjured up to conceal the one-party rule.

Many of the opposition workers at LM are not members of any party today; a growing number are members of the Centre Party, a growing number are social democrats opposed to dictatorship, a number are convinced communists and most seem to be more or less enthusiastic advocates of a united trade union front *without* any party ties. The snag is that this opposition is unorganized, and it is easy to see what will happen as long as it remains unorganized. The Centre Party will continue to fish for votes on the quiet while the social democratic club continues its secret nominations, package elections, list elections and smear campaigns against the left and thus maintains union dictatorship.

Until the bubble bursts one day and the stink of underhand scheming makes everyone hold their noses.

'Democracy is the life breath of the trade union movement', Ragnar Casparsson writes at the end of his history of *LO – bakgrund utveckling verksamhet* (*The Swedish Confederation of Trade Unions – background, development, activities*), published by Prisma 1966. And he adds: 'A free trade union movement can neither endure nor assert itself without democracy.' I agree with this unreservedly. But, unfortunately Casparsson's fine words must be changed to suit the central union activities at LM:

> One-party rule is the life breath of the trade union movement. A social democratic trade union movement can neither endure nor assert itself without party dictatorship.

LM does not appear to be a particularly well-run firm

For a number of years the employee turnover at the main factory has exceeded 50%. Fortunately, this does not mean that half the labour force finishes every year; many finish after a far shorter time. But the matter is serious, nevertheless. A halt in recruitment for two months was required to get the figure down to about 40% in 1971.

For a long time I was surprised that a large-scale, profit-making concern like LM, known to the outside world as a well-run, smoothly and skilfully organized company, one of the best shares on the Exchange, with an international competitive ability which can match up to giants like ITT, with secure monopolies in many countries and a research department which is said to be quite remarkable, should find it so difficult to retain its labour force. It seems to be quite as difficult for LM to reduce its employee turnover as it is to reduce absence due to sickness. Many of the workshops show a steady increase in sick-leave figures which were high to begin with.

What does the expression 'well-run' mean when applied to a firm where employees come and go as though visiting a department store?

By the time I had made myself acquainted with the conditions described above, my surprise had diminished. The strange wage-setting system, the daily price conflicts, the sudden wage reductions, the equally sudden transfers to Gotland or Finland, the constant movement of people within the company, the extremely brief introduction one was given, the disregard for the trade union and the incipient linking of the medical centre to the personnel department were all shortcomings which seemed to me to more than suffice to explain why LM Ericsson's reputation is as thoroughly bad at the Stockholm labour exchange as it is thoroughly good on the Stockholm stock exchange.

Good business and poor personnel policy can, evidently, be easily combined.

And to all this must be added the inhuman stigmatizing attitude which is fairly commonly adopted among LM supervisors, towards employees who are partially disabled ('social welfare cases', 'second grade', 'parasites', 'lazy-bones') and the constant lag in the industrial safety sector. I shall return to these two conditions, but I should like to give a concrete example of what a lag in industrial safety means. Quite simply, it means that accidents and near-accidents generally precede the safety measures.

Someone falls down steep stairs first, and then the stairs are made less steep. Someone crushes a finger when he lifts something, and then a lifting machine is purchased. Week after week and year after year the industrial safety officers present their demands for safety devices, enclosures of machinery and rebuilding operations of various types but at least one good near-accident is required before anything is done and not merely promised. It is as though management first needed tragic and palpable proof that the safety measure is justified.

Am I exaggerating? If only I were! Management is as careful in seeing to it that the *workers* follow the stipulations of the Workers' Protection Act and cooperate in 'preventing ill-health and accidents' (Paragraph 37 in the LM workshop rules) as it is careless with its own obligations. Hence the number of accidents increases from year to year despite the fact that many heavy jobs have been removed through rationalization; 123 accidents at work were recorded in 1969, 137 in 1970 and 139 in 1971 according to the annual accounts presented by the trade union.

An intensive public debate on work environment and industrial safety issues has been carried on in recent years, but it is difficult to see any trace of this debate at LM. The company *did* arrange a course on work environment, full of learned, expert lectures on lighting technology and the like, but unfortunately industrial safety is not improved by *talking* more about it. And as long as we still have a Workers' Protection Act which gives management considerable opportunities for avoiding measures or for obtaining a dispensation ('where it is deemed necessary', 'as far as possible' and 'reasonably can be required' are painfully common formulations in this Act), the old order of things will almost certainly remain: as a rule, an accident must occur for something to be done.

This may be a somewhat heightened description of a procedure which is now, fortunately, to be reformed. But if so, the description has been heightened by people who should know – the principal trade union industrial safety officer and the company industrial safety engineer. I have heard them express themselves in roughly the same manner: 'First someone must get injured. . .'

Does this mean that the employees must be ignored if one is to be able to call LM Ericsson a well-run company?

I find it more difficult to assess the administration and decision-making process as a whole since I was confined to regarding activities from the worm's view of the shop workers. But it is depressingly obvious that many decisions at LM are reached numerous floors and salary grades above the points where they are to be implemented and that those who are to execute them are frequently not consulted until the decisions have actually been made. This procedure sometimes has bizarre consequences which can best be observed at shop floor level.

One of many possible examples: the story of the *anchoring bracket*.

An anchoring bracket is a grey plastic sheet, large as a large gauntlet and provided with a number of holes and with a cock's crest instead of fingers. About 40 anchoring brackets are screwed in position on each telephone rack so as to provide a support for the units when they are soldered together. During my time there were three types of anchoring brackets, and the third type was provided with three extra holes which were so difficult to make that the production costs for this anchoring bracket alone amounted to SKr 18 per bracket whereas the other two cost no more than SKr 2 per bracket. We learnt this from one of the few engineers who ever visited our department. The economic section could not tolerate a difference in price of this magnitude. Consequently, the design section was given the task of finding a new standard anchoring bracket. After a number of sketches and conferences all of the technical and economic requirements had, it was thought, been met and a prototype was created. The only snag was that they had forgotten to ask anyone in the assembly department if the assembly work could be carried out with the aid of the new anchoring bracket. It was not until several thousand brackets had been produced and no changes of any importance could be made that one of the designers came down to us to show us the brilliant new product. He showed us a comb, the spikes of which had been bent and reinforced so that it was impossible to fit any outer tubes over them; he showed us a plastic rivet with edges which were too broad to permit manual clamping in tight corners; he showed us an upper section from which the very base on which the units were to rest had been removed. When we pointed out these weaknesses, the designer first pretended that he was well aware of them but when the time came to show us how the bracket functioned he was soon forced to admit that he had not thought of them. He was quite simply unable to solve the problems they entailed.

What had happened was not a complete catastrophe. The anchoring bracket could be used. All we had to do was alter the assembly technique, acquire a pair of shears for the outer tubes and a hammer for the plastic rivets – and there was, of course, a drop in the number of racks we could produce during the first month following the changes. It did not matter to *us* that the production rate dropped. But the ridiculous part of the whole thing was that the problems which had occurred were, for the most part, unnecessary. They could easily have been avoided if we had been allowed to borrow the prototype for ten minutes six months earlier.

It is not likely that something of this type could happen in a small workshop where the engineers and the workers are in closer physical contact. But it is *bound* to happen in a large workshop – and how often should it be *allowed* to happen in a workshop which claims to be well-run? There is no shortage of stories at LM about decisions which drop down from above and all of which seem to have been reached in a vacuum. One sometimes has the impression on the shop floor that high-ranking staff members feel that their position and their salary obliges them to know best even when they do not.

Those who deal with long-term planning, research and international marketing in our leading export firms are, without doubt, highly skilled people. Otherwise the firms would obviously have been devoured long ago by the multi-national giants. LM, Aga, SAAB, the whole lot would have vanished. But if one confines one's view to how things are run at LM's main factory one quickly becomes less impressed. I find it very difficult to imagine that, were the employees to take over the running of the factory, they would make a worse job of, for example, the work distribution, wage setting, personnel welfare and decision making than top management does at present.

LM might even become a well-run firm into the bargain.

Alienation can be seen at a glance

Workers numbering 2200 and salaried employees numbering approximately 4000 make quite a large number of people in one work place. The equivalent of six regiments. The equivalent of a small town from which all the parks, waterways and cemeteries have been removed and in which the inhabitants have been crowded together in a cluster of high-rise blocks. Yet I never saw any thousand-headed multitudes at LM.

I had not exactly expected to see 6000 people lined up in the yard, but I had expected that the employees would flood into the factory in the morning and that there would be an enormous crowd when the bell went in the afternoon. I had expected vast workshop departments swarming with workers and a giant factory complex in which most of the employees were housed.

Reality was quite different.

Instead of one enormous building for everyone, there were at least ten different units, most of them offices, spread over 100 000 square metres. A couple of the workshop departments were noticeably large – workshop landscapes existed in Sweden long before the first office landscape was built – but if these departments swarmed with anything they swarmed with machines and not with workers. Even if I stood on my toes at one end of the major machine shop I could not see more than about 70 workers. Most of them were screened off by machinery, partitions and cupboards. Few departments contained more than a hundred workers. Many of the departments contained less than 50 workers. And numerous work places had no more than ten workers. The employees *trickled* in to work in the morning, one by one or in small groups, at different times and through different entrances. Not even those of us who came rushing across Telefonplan at the last moment numbered more than ten or twenty. There was more crowding when work finished for the day – but never as much as in the underground at rush hour. This was because work finished at different times for different groups of employees. When those of us who worked in the High Block clocked out at half past four the workers in the Low Block had already left the factory and the office workers still sat in the high-rise office block. But not even those of us who clocked out at half past four went home in a single group. Several hundred took the rear exit to the cars parked in the yard at the back.

In fact it was only in the large workers' canteen, 'Scandinavia's largest self-service restaurant' (no longer in use) which could seat 2000 persons at one time, that one got the impression of a massive quantity of people. Otherwise the total number of employees might have amounted to 600 instead of 6000.

All of this is obvious to those who work in a large-scale industry but outsiders like myself are easily surprised. If I were to say that I had lived for a year in Gubbängen, a suburb which contains

almost as many inhabitants as LM, none of my non-factory-
working friends would have asked questions like: 'What did they
think of you?', 'How did they treat you?' – which are the questions
I received when I said I had worked a year at LM. Everyone
knows that I could not possibly have met more than a few of the
inhabitants in Gubbängen, that the suburb is extensive and that
most people stay indoors even if I should happen to pass by.
Things are no different at LM. Most people one sees there are
just as much strangers after a year as most of those one might see
in Gubbängen would be. Just as many have recently moved in
and take the wrong turning or the wrong stairs just as easily.
And most people at LM seem to have been just as randomly
pushed together in impersonal high-rise blocks and hesitate to
greet each other.

I knew that a remote acquaintance of mine, who was an
engineer, worked at LM so I kept an eye out for him sometimes
in the yard. It was first after a few months that I realized that this
was as pointless as walking around in a suburb looking for
someone whose address one has forgotten. Hundreds of people
can work for decades at LM without being in the least aware of
each other's existence.

But there is also a lack of contact between different groups of
employees at LM and this lack can only partly be explained by
the size of the company.

During my year there I never saw a single one of the fairly
numerous directors of the Group. Which goes to show how non-
existent personnel contact is downwards. Sometimes delegations
passed through. Foreign guests were piloted around. But if there
were any directors with them, they never stopped long enough to
be recognized as directors. When the Managing Director celebrated his 50th birthday, the shop workers read about it in the
same way everyone else in Sweden did – in their daily newspaper;
we never saw the Managing Director himself. Consequently,
even industrial workers can cultivate strange misconceptions of
what directors are like. They can see them as being fat or smoking
cigars, for example. After all, the workers only see their company cars and chauffeurs. They only see the large windows in
the directors' suites. They only see the written orders which the
managers send down to the production floors. By messenger.

Can power be exercised in a more impersonal manner?

But surprisingly watertight bulkheads also separate the lower grades of salaried employees from the workers at LM. After decades of separate eating, joint dining rooms were built for office workers and shopworkers in 1971. Neat pleasant dining rooms. Three of them. But just the same, the lowest of the new dining rooms is used almost exclusively by workers; it is the only one where they can fill their thermos flasks with coffee. And those workers who do not have thermos flasks, who eat on the floor above, seldom if ever eat at the same table as the office workers. This is because shop workers and office workers are seldom acquainted. The *only* things they have in common are the dining rooms. Work places, working hours, wage conditions and social benefits all differ. And several of the differences deserve a more outspoken name: injustices.

> The salaried employees have a fixed monthly salary.
> The salaried employees do not have to punch their cards during lunch.
> The salaried employees always have windows to look out through.
> The salaried employees are not subjected to deductions when they go to the doctor.
> The salaried employees are allowed to whistle during working hours.
> The salaried employees are not constantly supervised in their work.

When the workers at LM Ericsson see that even the lower grade salaried employees are more trusted by management, they are by no means giving expression to prejudice but rather to bitter reality. The workers can reach considerably higher incomes, by means of piece-work and over-time, than can most clerical workers – at least during the best years – *but the workers are treated unfairly in everything connected with trust.* After all, there is no need to adopt military regulations, clocking in during lunch and other checks for a group of employees one trusts.

But the possibilities for contact were noticeably limited amongst the workers themselves.

'Workers may not leave their work place unnecessarily during their work', states Paragraph 3 in LM's workshop rules. The term 'work place' as it is used here does not mean the factory or even

the department but the individual work station. As soon as a
worker takes a few steps from his own work bench, he immediately becomes an *unauthorized person*. The toilet and the foreman's desk are the only destinations available to him. Otherwise
he is expected to stick to his machine.

Naturally many workers break this unusually stupid rule which
in practice acts as a prohibition for every shop employee to
acquaint himself with the production of which he forms a part.
But there are few who do so without suffering from a bad con-
science. Everyone moves freely within their specific preserves,
which comprise the nearest work benches, and most feel there is
nothing to prevent them stopping on their way to the toilet at
one of the work benches within the area covered by their foreman
– usually one third of the department. But visiting a work mate
who works under another foreman in the same department or
going to the dining room or making a telephone call or visiting a
totally different department all constitute illegal actions which
every worker is expected to carry out with a beating heart and
trembling legs, i.e. extremely seldom. All of that vast part of the
industrial regiment which falls outside one's own group and
one's own platoon is and remains the preserve of *others*.

In any case, most workers cannot afford the time to make any
furtive excursions. Maintenance burdens, reduced piece-work
rates and fear of being transferred generally keep them tethered
in their own pens. I could afford the time better since I was paid
by the hour and I could also afford the risk of being fired, but
even my excursion possibilities were markedly limited. After a
year's work most of those employed at LM were still as unknown
personally to me as they had been when I started – even in my
own department.

The observations in this book have, in other words, a limited
applicability. 'One year in Department 36' might have been a
better title. (And yet I do not think it is presumptuous to generalize from these experiences. Many of those I got to know had
worked for long periods in other departments.)

But even the permissible contact with those who sat in one's
immediate vicinity was made difficult in various ways. The noise
was not particularly troublesome in my department, one could
make oneself heard. The distance between the eight work benches
in the group where I sat and soldered was not too great for

conversational contacts. But how does one talk with a Finn or a
Turk who does not understand a word of Swedish? And how does
one talk with a Swede who has instruction headphones on his ears?
One simply does not. In practice there were only three of us who
could exchange phrases during the course of our work and even
we were hampered by a third obstacle: the foreman sat within
hearing distance. In addition to this we had the workshop rules
prohibiting 'unnecessary talking' and 'agitation' (Paragraph 42).
Noise difficulties, distance difficulties, language difficulties, supervision difficulties – there was always something to prevent those
workers who were close to each other at LM from becoming real
work mates.

No one who has followed the political debate held in recent
years can be surprised on encountering alienation amongst
the workers in a large-scale industry. But what surprised me was
that the alienation could be seen at a glance and could be heard
without effort. Wads of cotton wool, headphones, protective
goggles, partitions, glazed walls, prohibition signs, spaces, supervisors' desks, TV screens, closed doors and thundering machinery
all comprise palpable signs of the distance, subdivision and isolation, in brief of the alienation amongst LM's workers.

As I mentioned before, those who assemble plastic components
are cut off from the entire decision-making process which leads
up to how and where these plastic components are to be manufactured and assembled. But there is more to it than that. They
are also forbidden to so much as visit the department from which
the plastic components are sent to their work benches. It goes
without saying that conditions like this provide little to tempt an
employee to find out which factory in Sweden delivers the plastic
components to LM. And he or she is even less tempted to finding
out where the plastic components factory gets its plastic. And still
less to find out which countries supply the oil for the plastic –
or what conditions apply to workers in these countries. If the local
production at their place of work is experienced as chaotic and
inaccessible by most workers, it is scarcely surprising that the
international production context appears even more inaccessible.

Like a strange world to which workers alone cannot get a visa.

These were a number of the conditions which surprised me for
various reasons during my year at LM. However, one gets used

to almost anything. And I soon forgot my surprise in connection with my introduction to the factory, the manual work, the wage-setting policy, the smiles and a great many other things. But I never managed to grow accustomed to – and still less to under-stand – the alienation and subdivision of the workers, the relation-ship the workers had to each other and my own relationship to the workers. The questions which arose from this have occupied my brain and my pen ever since I finished at LM.

Seven of the two thousand

Say the word 'worker', close your eyes and see what sort of image appears while you get the feel of the word. 'Worker'. What is it in *your* language which gives the word worker its colour and feeling and part of its import?

Readers who come from a working class environment will probably give completely different answers than those who come from other environments, and the individual variations will in all probability be considerable in both cases. But I should imagine that most of the answers can be roughly broken down into one of the following four groups:

1. You see before you a rough male figure in overalls who drills holes in a street, stands at a production line or talks to a politician on television, wearing a safety helmet in a mine gallery. If so, you probably have a *marked tendency* to stereotyped thinking when it comes to workers.

2. You see a row of men queueing in front of a punch clock at a factory or drinking beer in a site cabin, all of them dressed in working clothes but with considerable differences with regard to age, appearance, behaviour and nationality. If so, you probably have a *fair tendency* to stereotyped thinking when it comes to workers.

3. You see before you a pretty girl making her face up and pulling on shining leather boots before she goes tripping off to her piece-rate job in a process industry or to shift work in a bus company. If so, you probably have *little tendency* to stereotyped thinking when it comes to workers. (The very fact that the word 'worker'

has masculine connotations has undoubtedly provided nourishment for innumerable prejudices.)

4. You see before you pair after pair of gainfully employed persons who are, for the most part, each other's opposites: an elegant young waiter from Naples beside a worn-out female steel-mill worker from Rovaniemi; a female announcer, who also happens to be a member of the Baptist Church and who works in a bingo hall, beside a process supervisor who divides his free time between a temperance lodge and a study circle in genealogy; an ex-smallholder, who also happens to be a member of a Christian political party and who has been forced to become a packager in a corset factory beside a home helper who is a member of an extreme left-wing propaganda team; or a precision mechanic who is strong as a bear and interested in nothing but professional boxing beside a weak and introspective rock blaster who devotes every free moment he has to reading poetry? If so, you have probably no tendency at all to stereotyped thinking when it comes to workers.

If so, you have, perhaps, realized that workers do not lose their individuality when they enter the working class but that the entire working class consists, just like other social classes, of distinctive individuals.

I say perhaps, because it is very difficult to say with certainty. A linguistic test like this does not go very deep. Prejudices do.

The piece-rate star

is a woman who is well in with the foreman, something which is otherwise confined to male workers in our department. But then she is also assured and frank in a way which few of her sister workers are and prefers to bandy words with the men around her. When she complains of something, she never sounds anxious or repressed and entreating, which is the maid-servant attitude otherwise often adopted and which daily tempts the foreman to use a domineering tone to the other girls. Instead she automatically receives the bantering boyish tone which the foreman uses to his male subordinates.

Perhaps this is the real reason why she gets the best jobs. The reason which is given is that she is unusually skilled in her work, which is also true. She is both fast and accurate at the same time.

She is at least 25 years of age, and as big-bodied as Birgit Nilsson. Born the daughter of a farmer from Österlen, she is now married to an engineer. Now and then she changes the colour of her hair or her nail varnish. Since her husband has a good income, they have tax problems. They also have large instalments to pay on their terrace house. If she cannot achieve an hourly rate of around 17 kronor on average she may as well give up, she says. Most of the others earn less (the average is about 12 kronor an hour or 480 kronor per week), but she is fully aware of her own value.

Things are so arranged in our department that it is the men who make the decisions, who assemble and carry the cases, since this is deemed suitable work for men, and it is the women who solder, connect wiring or fill cases with small components, since this is deemed suitable work for women. The girls have deft fingers I am told when I ask. 'There's no getting away from that.' No, there is no getting away from prejudice. In fact, according to the foreman the girls are dexterous 'by nature' – as though they had started knitting or doing crochet work in the womb.

The piece-rate star is one of those who connects wiring.

Things are also arranged in our department so that each individual job, whether it takes two hours or two weeks to carry out, is priced separately – on different dates and with different workers as guinea pigs, and frequently by different time-and-motion engineers. As a result of this, some jobs in the wiring sector give an average income of at least 17 kronor per hour while others give a maximum of 10.50 kronor. And yet the work contribution is roughly the same in both cases. According to the inscrutably wise laws of the piece-work system things are also so arranged that wiring whole racks in *all* series while standing pays several kronor more than wiring smaller units while sitting – and this is where the fact that the piece-rate star gets on well with her superior is so significant. She works only on the well-paid rack connections while the other women are happy if they are permitted to nibble at the golden egg a few days a month.

This means that she is amongst the best paid workers in the whole department despite her sex and despite her youth.

Her sister workers come from many different countries – Sweden is just one of them. But their shyness knows no national boundaries and for a long time they confine themselves to complaining about the situation amongst themselves. They complain about their situation, look askance at the piece-rate star and now and then new time-and-motion studies are carried out on the worst paid jobs. But one day they gather their courage and march up to the union contactman in a single body. They have a concrete proposal. No more time-and-motion studies; 13.50 kronor an hour for all unit wiring; rack wiring according to the piece-rate prices in force; and general rotation on all wiring jobs.

Four girls from four countries join forces to demand their rights – even this is a victory for solidarity which otherwise usually gives way to the golden rule of the piece-work industry: every man for himself. In addition, the girls' demand for a common unit wage contains a direct challenge to the piece-work mania of those in charge.

There is only one snag. If the proposal is to have any chance of being accepted the piece-rate star must back it up. And the piece-rate star will have nothing to do with it. When the time comes, she wants things to stay the way they are. She would, undoubtedly, make an excellent leader for the group of shy girls with her bold manner, and she undoubtedly has nothing against the others being better paid. She just cannot accept that this must take place at her expense.

'Am I supposed to accept several kronor an hour less voluntarily just so that you others get more? Am I the one who is supposed to pay out money here instead of the pay office? I'd rather leave!'

A tragically high number of conflicts at work are actually solved in exactly that manner; one of those most victimized gives in his or her notice. But the piece-rate star does not give in her notice. Instead she appeals for understanding for her point of view while the girls continue to speak for theirs. One of the girls, who is Finnish, has to bear the full burden of maintenance since her husband became unemployed. She has no wish, she says, to work overtime one more evening a week just to help the piece-rate star meet the instalments on her terrace house. The Finnish girl lives with her family in a semi-modern 3-room flat an hour's journey from LM and already works overtime two evenings a week to support her family.

How dreadfully easy it is to understand the arguments on both sides!

Gradually, more and more of those in the department are drawn into the discussion, and the results are the same as they always are when piece-work conflicts go on and on without being settled. Tears and gnashing of teeth, tears and gnashing of teeth. Sick-leave absence increases noticeably amongst those immediately involved. Even the tough piece-rate star suffers a great deal from sleeplessness for a time.

Since discord is everyday stuff in Department 36, there are many who do not react at all. They just go on with their work without even looking up. But those who do react seem to take up positions on a personal level. Some of them think that the piece-rate star is disobliging and selfish, others think that the immigrant girls should be grateful and should not cause trouble. Some blame the dissension on the foreman's inability to get on with the female employees, others blame the dissension on the union big-wigs who do not interfere.

But the criticism is always directed towards *persons* – and not towards the wage system which aims at producing, on the one hand, piece-rate stars and, on the other, insoluble conflicts. The criticism is not even directed towards those persons, the time-and-motion engineers, who primarily represent this infernal wage system. It is as though most of those involved could only become angry with people they *see* frequently. Like the immigrant girls, like the foreman, like the piece-rate star.

And everything returns to the old order.

The apprentice

is called Kent-Åke and has spent two years at LM's apprentice school, which is for boys only. Now he is getting practical experience in our department by cutting out copper rails and assembling them in plastic sections. A purely routine job.

He is rather tall and long-haired, wears purple corduroy jeans and has puppyish movements. As soon as he sees anything lying on the floor, he is taken by an irresistible urge to kick it at once, but he misses quite often. He is far better at *happening* to knock over chairs or plastic coffee cups as he passes by. BOW-WOW is written on the front and BEWARE OF THE DOG is written in Swedish on the back of his turtle neck sweater. He makes 3.85 kronor an hour at the age of 18, a starvation wage which is both common and in accordance with the labour agreements for LM apprentices.

'Isn't it bloody awful?' is the first thing Kent-Åke says to us. Before we even know that he answers to this strange name. 'Isn't it bloody awful? They practically promised I'd get to work on an exchange straight off and here I bloody well stand in this sheet metal shed, and what the *hell* is this?'

He holds up a twisted plastic channel as though it were a rattlesnake.

'Take it easy, lad', Jörgen says.

'You've got the best job in the whole department', I tell him.

'Ahhh', Kent-Åke says.

The BEWARE OF THE DOG sign seems justified. He kicks a cardboard box on the floor and tumbles cursing down into a seat in the coffee-break area where he has already laid out the four objects which will make his period of practical experience bearable day by day: a packet of cigarettes, a large Coca Cola and two new girlie magazines. One thing is immediately certain. We need never fear missing any issue of the major girlie magazines during Kent-Åke's guest performance amongst us.

At the same time, he is interested in technology and can sit for hours pottering with an amplifier he has brought along with him or filing off the insulation on LM cables until a pile of grey plastic rises under his chair. Then he gets up and tries to kick the pile away before starting on something new. But the fact that he ended up in the technical-practical line at school and then went on to LM's apprentice school seems mainly to be due to his low marks. Those who achieve any sort of decent results in their final year seldom come to LM's apprentice school nowadays; they apply for admission to the vocational schools instead.

'A bloody detention centre, that's what school is if you want my opinion', Kent-Åke says. 'They were always on top of you; they never left you alone.'

'Did you go to school to be left alone?'

'Look, let's talk about something more pleasant.'

Nonetheless, he voluntarily took part in the confirmation course after hours during his second last year in school. Why? Is he pious despite all?

'Like hell I am. But all my mates were going to get confirmed. And the old lady pleaded and went on about it.'

This sounds familiar. Ten out of the twelve vocational orientation students – boys only there too – who have worked in our rack-assembly group during the school year have given us exactly the same answer. The eleventh one wanted to find out about the lofty world of the spirit, and the twelfth refused to be confirmed because he did not believe in God – two independent 14-year-old souls. But the remainder had taken lessons from the priest despite the fact that they did not believe in God, just as Kent-Åke had. According to what they say themselves, they would have got their confirmation suit and confirmation watch just the same. All of them were working-class children. If this selection is in any way representative, dechristianization amongst the working class does not seem to have got very far.

Is it easier to rid oneself of God than it is to rid oneself of baptism, confirmation and a church marriage – in the same way as it is easier to change one's political opinion than it is to change one's table manners?

Kent-Åke seems to consider everything connected with religion as 'drivel', so he has no viewpoints on this matter. 'Drivel people's mums carry on with.' Nor does he have anything to say when we discuss politics. When I ask him directly what he thinks of the Centre Party or of the USA, he just smiles evasively, almost a little in wonder as though it were the first time anyone had assumed that *he* might have a political opinion worth putting forward. But he takes part all the more eagerly when we begin to talk about prison problems.

'What are they going on about anyway? Vocational training and leave-of-absence. . .all this togetherness behind the walls, telly and rooms for fucking in and things like that. . .like some sort of resort where the prisoners can pretty well walk in and out. . .What? Aren't they supposed to atone for their crimes nowadays? Murderers should be beheaded and prison sentences should be longer, that's what I think.'

Kent-Åke is astonished when he notices that I become upset because the papers say that numerous countries still have the death penalty. A few days later he is just as astonished when he notices that I do *not* become upset because the papers say that pigs have been used and sometimes killed in conjunction with scientific experiments. How on earth can I be so sloppy about cold-blooded criminals and at the same time be so indifferent when dumb animals are tortured? Since he can make neither heads nor tails of this, no matter how he tries, he switches over to kicking things on the floor instead, including a dumb animal which seems to have been included in the latest dispatch from the stores, an earwig.

'Innocent pigs', he mutters between kicks. 'They should bloody well. . .have used murderers and sex criminals instead.'

It almost seems as though he was trying to kick all the educationalists and teachers who have told him down through the years to listen better, to study better, not to be so sluggish, not to throw his legs about, to sit still, to use his head, to make an effort. . .All these well-meaning oppressors who only asked that he should say: 'Yes, sir' when they made it clear to him that he was no good as he was.

'BOW-WOW!'

A contact man tries to interest Kent-Åke in becoming a member of the union, but without success. For one naive moment I think that Kent-Åke is about to criticize the party rule or the lack of democracy in the union but instead he answers as most apprentices I have met at LM do:

'The union? What bloody use is the union? All they want to do is take your money off you.'

He is supported by a couple of the young northern Swedes in the assembly section who have already been reminded several times to fill in their application forms. Saying that money is needed to form a dispute fund, that everyone must join in if the dispute is to have any effect, is the sort of argument which seems to have no effect on them.

'Membership should be voluntary', they say instead. 'It's undemocratic to try to force people to join the union.'

This new definition of democracy appeals to Kent-Åke. Democracy in the sense of the right not to have to do things. Democracy in the sense of the right not to have to use one's democratic rights.

'Undemocratic is exactly what it is!'

After a month of slaving with the power rails, he suddenly gives a shout one day, gathers up his girlie magazines, pulls on his leather jacket so forcefully that his arm strikes the wall, walks jauntily towards the exit, giving a friendly kick to our racks on the way, half turns and calls 'Cheerio!', bumps into a metal cabinet at the exit and finally makes off to his next point of practical experience. But he returns six months later to visit us together with an apprentice mate. He looks more grown-up now. The sweater with the lettering has been replaced by a check sports shirt and his hair is cut. But above all he looks more cheerful. He has finally managed to get out and do exchange work.

'Proper installation work. Tough but technical. We decide our own working hours in the group. Big difference to this sort of rubbish', he adds laughing and points at a twisted plastic channel which a silent student from Madagascar has been told to straighten out again.

'How can you have that good-for-nothing out on an exchange?' we ask his mate. 'Doesn't he kick everything to pieces out there?'

Kent-Åke too pretends to address himself to his increasingly embarrassed mate for support: 'I put up with these nuts for a whole month. Incredible the patience you can learn!'

As he says this he is already on his way towards the exit again, and we wait for him to bump into the sheet-metal cabinet as he usually did. But instead, he gives it a kick so that the boom fills the entire room. Then he calls 'Cheerio' and disappears out of our lives in the best of humours.

Jaroslav

considers that a woman should brush her husband's shoes, should iron his shirts, should make his bed, should cook his food and should take care of his children; otherwise marriage becomes unbearable. Even if both husband and wife have full-time jobs, it is the wife alone who should be responsible for all household duties, including child care.

'Why?' I ask him one day.

'Look, Palm. Should women be allowed to marry if they can't iron shirts and can't cook food, is that what you mean?'

'Of course.'

'You have to get below the surface of the problem, Palm. Do you or do you not mean that there's a difference between men and women?'

'Yes, there's a difference.'

'In that case women must do feminine things, do you get my point? Men do masculine things, so women must do feminine things. They have different hormones.'

Jaroslav is 34 years of age and is short and lightly built. Luckily for him his wife is even more lightly built. And as a rule his shirts are freshly ironed. Certain of his facial features remind one of Alexander Dubcek, above all the narrow protruding nose, but Jaroslav is a more cautious man. He seldom leaves his work station. Even when he feels like flirting with the girl sitting 15 metres away he generally confines himself to broad gestures and smiles from his bench. At close range this looks like deaf-and-dumb language. And he never goes into the foreman to ask for a rise or to get a better rate for badly paid piece-work.

And so he remains in the low-income group.

Jaroslav had gone through the technical *gymnasium* (upper secondary school) at home in Slovenia, and after that he had worked for eight years in an electrotechnical factory; but here at LM he is put doing the same unqualified semi-skilled work as I am. Nobody inquires about his vocational experience.

At home in Slovenia he and the other workers in the factory were invited at regular intervals to take part in the factory council votes and to participate in the various decision-making bodies during working hours. But here nobody asks for his opinion. No union meetings are arranged during working hours, nor any language training either for that matter (though beginners do get such training nowadays), and his only contact with the trade union is the 40 kronor deduction for the membership dues made on his wages each month.

Unemployment was considerable at home in Slovenia. Despite this, no one was ever dismissed or rationalized out of a job at the factory, Jaroslav says. But here in Stockholm he has seen so many people laid off during five years that he has determined never to do anything that might attract the displeasure of those in charge. He never complains about the work. He never goes to any political or union meetings. He avoids sensitive subjects in discussions. When I show him a newspaper article with the head-

line 'Yugoslavia threatened by Bulgaria and by internal disin-
tegration', he becomes interested at once but after half a minute
of intensive reading he returns the paper without comment and
goes back to his work. He knows that there are Ustasja supporters
amongst the Yugoslavs at LM. Nor does he permit himself to be
provoked by open criticism of Marshal Tito or of Yugoslavia's
dependency on the USA. All he does is frown heavily and ask me
to look deeper into the problem. Not until more than a hundred
other foreigners have signed a protest list against some obviously
unsatisfactory state of affairs at LM can he persuade himself to
put his own name to it.

There is no rebel concealed inside Jaroslav.

At home in Slovenia life was, above all, poor, and Jaroslav
frequently gets letters asking him to make a lot of money in
Sweden so that he can make life easier for his dependents when
he returns. And he does live *extremely* simply with his wife and
his children. Once a week he walks all the way down to the
Central Station to buy a Yugoslav magazine which he sits at home
reading in the evenings until the next issue is available. This
seems to be the only expenditure the family permits itself on
entertainment. They never go to a restaurant or a cinema and
never buy anything more than the necessities of life. Perhaps his
wife bakes a cake on Saturday. Perhaps they have a second-hand
TV set.

There are southern European bachelors who can save up to
30 000 kronor in a few years using methods like this, particularly
if they have managed to get into one of the dirtiest and most
lucrative piece-work departments in the Low Block. Sometimes
they buy a Mercedes with the money. But Jaroslav has not kept
himself to the fore in that way. Nor is he a bachelor. Besides, all
his savings have gone to a flat-renting agency. He was forced
to get hold of a 2-room flat on the black market ('masculine
matters') so as to be able to provide something better than a
furnished room when his second child arrived, and his wife was
forced to give up her gainful employment ('feminine matters').

'Fifteen thousand kronor under the table for two small rooms
– how can things get to be like that, Palm?' he asks indignantly
'How can they?'

'That's capitalism', I say.

'Isn't there anything that isn't politics for you?' Jaroslav laughs

Then he becomes serious again. 'Your problems are small, Palm. Mine are big. Big problems.'

He returns to this question of small and big problems so often that my head spins.

'It doesn't matter what I do', he sighs, for example, when I ask if he wants to sort out a new order or continue with the guide bars. 'Unpack this or unpack that, what difference does it make? I have big problems. You read the newspaper and books and you think sometimes, Palm. You have small problems.'

For a long time I wonder whether his views are merely narrow or whether they are, in fact, wise. Can he believe that the things Jörgen and I usually discuss, Vietnam, union passiveness at LM, industrial safety or the Common Market, are minor problems compared to his own housing troubles, debts and poor relatives? I do not think he is as self-centred as that. Or does he, perhaps, instead mean that Jörgen and especially I have solved our fundamental problems and are, precisely because of that, at liberty to interest ourselves in the affairs of the world?

To tell the truth, it was not until I had finished at LM that I began to think about this probable interpretation of his attitude. But that is probably exactly what he did mean. And he was probably right, too. Not that those of us who discuss things and take the initiative lack personal problems but that the fundamental material questions have, undeniably, been solved as far as we are concerned. Our livelihoods are secure. We can work in our own country. We need never be afraid of being discriminated against or thrown out, and we have no debts worth talking about – none of which applies to Jaroslav.

And he also seems to see the rest of us as basically free of problems. While he himself sits there worrying about his situation, he hears us discuss general social problems easily, almost lightly. While he feels himself forced to go on working, he sees us take a break or go out and make a telephone call – as though we never ran the risk of being sacked. While he himself treads water simply to keep his head above the surface, he sees us wandering around on the shore, dry-footed and apparently at liberty to add the problems of others to our own.

In his own way he agrees with Brecht: 'Erst kommt das Fressen, dann kommt die Moral.' (First comes food and then come morals.) Or, to put it more comprehensively: 'If only I could get my basic problems solved I'd join in your political discussions and union activities. I and all those like me who are still stuck in the muck. Don't get the idea that you'd be involved in the questions you are involved in if you sat in the muck with us. Your lives would be filled with your own problems then too. And then you'd begin to understand.'

This does not mean that only the food and the basic conditions can make Jaroslav sigh at his work bench – when he does not suddenly jump up and dance or flirt with the girls. Morals, too, make him sigh to a considerable extent, particularly questions of matrimonial morals. He often broods about what he should do to make his wife agree better with the picture he has been given of what a good wife should be like. He broods about what he should do to make his wife clean up the way a wife should clean up and polish shoes the way a wife should polish shoes.

So that the uppers shine.

I suggest that he solve the problem by taking his fossilized ideal picture of 'The Wife' and putting it away in an old sack and polishing his own shoes instead. But Jaroslav will not listen to a word of that. When Jörgen and I, talking about Rhodesia, discuss the part played by violence in the colonial struggle, Jaroslav takes up the part played by violence in the marital struggle instead.

'You have to beat your girl until she becomes good and obedient', he says eagerly as though he had finally found the solution to his problems. 'If she doesn't obey like a woman should obey there's only one way to teach her, by beating her.'

I feel somewhat nonplussed, since Jaroslav is probably the one immigrant amongst all those in the department who is most anxious to avoid every form of conflict at work. But he obviously makes up for it when he gets home.

Does this mean that one must get one's head above water to be able to get rid of the prejudices one grew up with, too?

Desirée

cleans up at LM. She has been doing that for forty years now.

In order to qualify for a gold medal from the Marcus Wallenberg medal fund, the number of years of an employee's life and the number of years of his or her employment must amount to at least 95 combined, otherwise he or she will have to be satisfied with a bronze plaque. Evidently Desirée is 60 years of age because she is included amongst the gold medallists one day. 'Desirée Jonsson Vt 24'. We congratulate her when she comes as usual and cleans up under our work benches in the afternoon.

'Just think how old I've become! I can hardly believe it. And now I'm going to be a shareholder too.'

'Shareholder?'

'Yes, they give four LM shares to everyone who gets the gold medal. They really do spoil us chars in this firm, don't they?'

Not until she says this last part does she interrupt her cleaning, straighten her back and look with a half smile from one face to the other as though to make sure that the people working here are the same ones as those who were here yesterday. She often complains that people are constantly being replaced where she works.

'The floors are much the same, but the faces are often new when I look around.'

Not many people in Sweden get a worm's-eye view of the workers in their daily job, but Desirée is one of them. If she is rushed, all she has time to see are the shoes and legs of the workers she cleans for. She has a light-blue overall over her uniformly heavy body, but she does not wear a char's turban. Wisps of hair hang freely over her ruddy-complexioned face. An incipient moustache catches some of the drops of sweat which are formed when she bends over her brush. All in all, she looks as though she had a solid, traditional name like Svea or Tekla. But instead she has the rather royal-sounding name of Desirée – just like the Swedish princess.

'So you're going to start playing the stock market now?' Jörgen asks.

'Not on your life! I was in the Stock Exchange once and heard how they go on. They were in the middle of a call. I didn't understand a word. But you can't put your trust in shares, I know that much. In 1930 – I expect you people weren't even born then? In 1930 LM's shares suddenly fell to 25 öre apiece. That was just about enough to buy a cheap magazine. Ordinary folks had best leave shares alone.'

As she says this she opens the cover of her shovel as though she had thought of sweeping up the shares on to it.

'I'm going to sell mine as soon as I get hold of them. The very same day!'

As a rule, Desirée confines herself to short, occasional messages or calls so that she can continue to clean without having her work rhythm upset by any formulation problems. During the election campaign, which the cleaning women at LM come in particularly close contact with since it is they who have to clean up all the leaflets which lie around the workshop, she has only one comment to make: 'They're like small boys fighting.'

On the other hand, she says this with such emphasis that the party leaders would pale if they heard her. She gives herself more time to talk during the breaks, except when a new issue of the women's magazine *Svensk Damtidning* appears. Sometimes she gets talking about 'Sweden's most beautiful landscape' Ånger-manland, where she grew up. She talks about Pelle Molin's cottage and about the poetry tradition of the area.

'He had a theatre there, Pelle Molin, a theatre constructed by nature. Ever been in Versailles?'

I nod, to her surprise.

'You have? Well then, you know, one of those outdoor theatres that slopes downwards. I said to my husband when we saw Pelle Molin's theatre in Ådalen, he's dead now, I said that's like the theatre in Versailles. Only smaller.'

Desirée did not like Bo Widerberg's film about Ådalen.

'It wasn't like that. There was no working lad had it off with any upper-class hussy, I can tell you. Not in those days. It was impossible. The film was really beautiful, but then it couldn't be anything else since it was made in Ångermanland! All you have to do is set up a camera there when the summer's come. But reality. . .*reality* was different than the film. Completely different.'

Desirée worked as a cleaning woman at LM during the Ådalen events in 1931. In those days the factory was located at Tulegatan in central Stockholm, and the day after the five workers were shot to death in Ådalen all of the employees at LM went to the Norra Bantorget square to march to Gärdet.

'There must have been a hundred thousand workers there. We had the day off. Norra Bantorget wasn't big enough. But there were no soldiers there. They had been forbidden to go out during the demonstration. I've never seen anything like it. The march was completely silent.'

According to Desirée, cleaning work has been easier since those days. Equipment is better and the factories cleaner. Oil no longer drips from pulleys in the roofs in the turning shop. And employees deal with their personal hygiene in a better way, particularly in the toilets. Nevertheless, she preferred cleaning as it was before.

'Things weren't always in such a hurrry as they are now. Everyone had time to chat a little. Now it's become sort of... *impersonal*. You don't feel properly at home. People leave just when you've begun to like seeing them there when you arrive with your cleaning gear. And the ones who replace them are often foreigners. I mean, you can't talk to those. They just shake their heads.'

Desirée has never 'curried favour and asked for a rise' so she cleans for 10 kronor an hour. That is 2.50 kronor under the old low-income level set by the Metal Workers' Union. Most benches and machines where she cleans are manned by workers who make a great deal more, although many of them could be her children. How does she feel about that?

'I don't care about wages. As long as I have enough to manage on. Money isn't all that important. Envy and lack of comradeship amongst the workers are far worse. The workers are divided into classes too, that's one thing you learn when you do cleaning work. That old boy who drives the cases around, just imagine, he went up to the Turkish woman who cleans in Department 17 and said, 'Bloody foreigner', yesterday! That sour old man who never so much as smiles. One day he went and opened the window right in front of the sick old lady who can't stand draughts. There was such a dreadful draught! He has his own problems, the old boy, they say he lives in one of those working men's hotels and so. But he can't go on like that. We're going to complain about him.'

She says 'we' and she says 'complain' so resolutely that I can see her in my mind's eye leading a demonstration march. But in the very next breath she says something quite different.

'I want respect upwards, for salaried employees and that, that's what I've learned. That there are different sorts of people. But there should be equality amongst the workers, and there isn't.'

This seems contradictory but so does so much else about her, including her royal-sounding Christian name of Desirée and her common Swedish surname of Jonsson. She reads *Svensk Damtidning*, travels to Versailles and distinguishes between classes of people when she feels like Desirée, I thought, and it is only when she feels like Jonsson that she says 'we' and 'upper-class hussy', marches to Gärdet or talks about the 'reality' at Ådalen. The reality which prevails at LM has undoubtedly reminded her to her cost that it is her surname which counts – and yet it is as Desirée she is known in the factory. How did she get this unusual name anyway?

'It was almost certainly my dad who'd heard it. He worked in the garden on an estate when I was to be baptized, and the gentry's children had names like that. Sometimes I was allowed to play with the children and my dad probably thought I was just as fine as they were. That was before I started to serve as a maid. The master and mistress there were fine people. I mean *really* fine. Not like the bullying types you can find here. Fine and considerate...'

Desirée Jonsson has a remarkable capacity for sharing her good humour. The atmosphere in the department grows immediately lighter, and the stress is reduced whenever she comes in and cleans. Smiles light up in the most unexpected faces, but then her ways also remind everyone of something deeply joyful: man's ability to act in the centre of oppression as though oppression did not exist. Even those who are most gloomy sense for a moment that this possibility exists.

Sorrows do not *remain* with Desirée. They simply visit her occasionally. She moves easily. She moves just as easily between her Christian name and her surname, as though there were no chasm between them.

Svensson

is the nickname collectively given to Swedish men but in this case it applies to someone who is neither a man nor Swedish. But then nothing does add up here at LM Ericsson. Before she came to Sweden and married the foreman in Department Vt 32 (whose name is Svensson) she was called Becker and lived in Essen in the Ruhr area. That was more than ten years ago, but if one listens carefully to her impeccable Swedish one can catch the German accent.

Svensson is in her 30s, small and light-blonde and rather pretty. She gives the impression of being in excellent physical and mental trim. Her steps are resilient and determined as though she constantly led a gymnastic group. Her smile, too, radiates energy and purposefulness. When I had been sitting soldering tags for four days at LM, she came up to my bench, greeted me warmly and gave me forms to fill in so that I could become a member of the Metalworkers' Union in plenty of time before the May meeting. Svensson is the contactman for our department.

This was in the spring of 1970 so I could not resist asking her if the wave of strikes had also left its mark at LM.

'No, luckily we've managed to avoid strikes here at LM', Svensson answers cheerfully. 'Occasional incidents have occurred, of course, but we've dealt with them locally. Fortunately. You can give the papers to me directly when you've filled them in. I sit over there.'

Yes, in principle, Svensson sits over there and does assembly work, but when I or anyone else go to see her she is seldom there. If she is not at home or at a meeting, she is away on a union course. She is often away on courses, it turns out. How does she have time to deal with her contact work then? I used to wonder – before I learned what a tremendous amount she has to deal with and has to find time for.

In the trade union movement, as in other organizations, one responsibility usually leads to another, and this is what has happened to a considerable extent in Svensson's case. Not only is she the contactman for the department, she is also the industrial safety officer; but her most important responsibilities are located more centrally. She is the only female committee member, both of the social democratic club and of the shop union. In addition, she is a member of the leisure-time committee and of the study committee, she is a member of the joint industrial council, and she is active on the house magazine *Kontakten*, and usually reports from the representative assembly meetings of the Metalworkers' Union. All in all, this makes a total of about ten permanent posts of trust, to which must be added a long series of temporary undertakings and courses. Finally, she is also a social democratic council member in her municipality.

How can she find time for all this? Her small responsibilities in the department seem to suffer.

As I have indicated earlier, a top level in the union seems to rule the roost at LM. Three or four workers seem to share all the important responsibilities between them. Whenever new positions and consultation functions are opened for the labour sector, e.g. in sub-committees to the joint works council, outsiders easily get the impression that more and more workers are being given the chance to acquire new useful experience. But what actually happens at LM, for the most part, is that the same three or four people take over the new responsibilities as well. Exactly the same names recur on almost every committee and board at LM. But what is surprising is not the centralization in itself, which partly depends on a lack of candidates, but the fact that an immigrant woman like Svensson has managed to penetrate this closed circle. The general opinion amongst the members of the shop union seems to be that women and immigrants may, by all means, receive union posts as long as Swedish men are in charge. In other words, Svensson has managed to break through this wall of prejudice.

How? I am not quite sure, but her go-ahead spirit and competence are unusually well-developed. Her network of influential contacts has been very useful for several of the workers in Department 36, not least those in search of dwellings of their own. In addition, she has a rare ability for smoothing over any conceivable conflict with the aid of smiles and a jaunty manner. Svensson seldom if ever goes around the department asking about causes for dissatisfaction. She prefers to go around selling picture books for children at reduced prices.

Her basic union idea, which also ties in with her constant lack of time, seems to be that everyone who works at LM should keep on good terms with each other, solve conflicts with the aid of consultation and should, as far as possible, avoid trouble. When dissatisfied workers direct her attention to a low piecerate, she usually points out that it is a pity that the price is not higher but that unfortunately nothing can be done about it, that there are others who have been able to make money at that price or, alternatively, that she will see what she can do about it.

As a result, nothing happens after that.

It is not until Svensson is away at a union course which is so long that a new contactman must take her place, a contactman who is willing and who has the time to speak up on behalf of the workers, that it emerges that many of these low piece-rates can easily be raised if only the workers stand firm, demand new time-and-motion studies and refuse to accept unfair prices. But things become unsettled in the department as a result of this – those in charge run about more and there is more open discussion (two clear signs that spirits are beginning to awaken) – and the thought strikes me that an atmosphere like this has not prevailed in the department during all the months I have seen Svensson work alone as contactman.

She seems to like things better when nothing happens.

We sometimes wonder why she does not resign as contactman since she so seldom is on the spot and must have quite enough to do with the other tasks with which she is entrusted. But everyone who wants to make a career within the union or within the company usually finds it a valuable qualification to be able to refer to assiduous and lengthy work at grass roots level, 'in the midst of ordinary workers'. And if Svensson persuades herself that she is better qualified for the post of contactman than anyone else in the department, she does have some justification for doing so.

We wonder how long it will be before she is promoted and whether it will be the Metalworkers' Union which promotes her to union representative or whether it will be LM which promotes her to salaried employee. Her way of saying 'we' about the company indicates that the latter alternative is the more likely. When one of the major meetings of the shop union is attended by a journalist with a camera, I am naive enough to assume that the journalist comes from the union magazine or belongs to the local union. But after a week the journalist appears at my bench with a photograph in his hand and introduces himself as the editor of the house magazine *Kontakten* and asks me what the other worker in the picture is called since he too had made critical remarks at the meeting. I walk indignantly over to Svensson and ask how the house magazine could have gained admission to an internal union meeting without the members who are present being as much as consulted. But Svensson does not understand my indignation. Not in the least.

'But *Kontakten* is *our* magazine', she just says cheerfully.

And she is not without official party support for this 'we' feeling. 'It is in the interest of all of us that the production results be as good as possible. They won't be if we just fight with each other

– but they will if we collaborate with each other – society and
industry, companies and employees.' I read this in a mimeographed information sheet which was distributed to 'opinion-
formers' in work places by a political party in plenty of time
before the 1973 election.

The only snag is that it was the wrong party which gave
Svensson its support in this manner. The mimeographed sheet
goes on to say:

> The counterbalance ideology of the social democrats
> is a mistake which has hindered the best possible pro-
> duction results. The Centre Party has put forward the
> the idea of collaboration instead – collaboration be-
> tween society and industry, collaboration between
> everyone in their places of work.

I do *not* say that the idea of collaboration would be foreign to
the social democrats. There is no shortage of collaboration agreements between the Confederation of Trade Unions and the
Employers' Confederation. I only mean that the unrestrained
conflict-dampening spirit of collaboration which Svensson so
unquestionably gives voice to can only aid a party which seeks
compromise solutions without any union or political reservations,
a party which says 'we' without even deducting the large-scale
employers. Help the Centre Party and hinder union solidarity.

Consequently, I find it difficult to join the ranks of the mourn-
ful when the message finally arrives that Svensson has left the
union and LM's workshop for good. Has she finally become a
salaried employee at LM instead? No. She has become information secretary in the Physical Culture Movement. I feel convinced
that everyone at LM, particularly those who are active in Union
matters, genuinely hope that her unquestionable competence and
energy will find full scope *there*.

The truck driver

is the only one of her kind at LM. She suddenly appears one day,
pale, thin, 17 years of age, dressed in jeans and a duffle jacket,
sitting on a fork-lift truck, a position occupied only by men up
until now. One can sense that many of the women in the depart-

ment silently cross their fingers when this pioneer approaches with her truck, the first girl who has dared to enter the most masculine of all LM's areas of occupation.

But for a long time it looks as though she is going to come a cropper.

Everything seems to indicate that the girl never drove anything bigger than a moped before. Or rather, it would seem that the careful introduction LM is obliged to give each new employee, particularly with regard to work which can entail danger to life and limb, has been omitted once again.

Although she drives at snail's pace, for safety's sake, so that she soon has a queue of angry truck drivers after her, she manages to make most of the mistakes one can make with a truck during her first week at work. She accelerates when she should brake, she lowers when she should raise, she backs into the walls, gets stuck in the door frame, pulls down rolls of corrugated cardboard, gets the fork crooked or drives it into the pallet so that chips fly in all directions. The number of near-accidents does not decrease. Instead, more and more of her male colleagues do everything they can to tease her. Perhaps they feel that this female encroacher is threatening to bring ridicule on their craft, so they toot on their horns, bump into her, offer her snuff or call out 'just like a woman' and shake their heads as soon as they get a chance. And each time they do, the truck girl blushes all over her face.

But she does not come a cropper. She grits her teeth and by the second week she is already driving considerably more assuredly. After three weeks she no longer blushes, and after six weeks she is even beginning to get a taste for frightening the life out of the old packers and cleaning women by accelerating through plastic doors and intersecting corridors at top speed. The strange fascination of power which lorry drivers and crane operators who reign high above the common populace can bear witness to in moments of honesty seems to have gripped this thin teenage girl too, even at the lowly fork-lift truck level. When the elderly men and women she almost knocks over raise their fists angrily after her, she waves cheerfully and triumphantly in return, just like the cheekiest of the male truck drivers, the tall curly-headed, constantly whistling Greek from Thermopolos. Gradually she realizes her own competence and can change over to the safe, gentle driving which fortunately characterizes the experienced truck drivers at LM.

And with that she also becomes accepted in the truck driver's circles. And her sister workers, those who kept their fingers crossed anxiously all over the departments, can breathe a sigh of relief. One more victory can be entered in the long struggle for freedom.

'Why did you take this particular job?' I ask her one day when traffic is low.

'I needed money after school, and this was the only job available. Apart from standing at a machine, of course, and boring stuff like that. Driving a truck is a gas. Except in the beginning, of course', she adds a little embarrassed.

Her name is Ylva, and she has lived all her life in Fruängen, three underground stations from LM Ericsson at Telefonplan. An original Stockholmer of the new suburban generation. She has two emblems on her jacket lapel, one with the lettering (in Swedish) A GREENER CITY and the other with STOP SMOKING. And right enough she waves away the smoke from my cigarette in irritation. She seems more than usually clear-headed. Her marks at school were enough to get her into the *gymnasium*, but she herself chose the practical stream and a vocational school instead. She wanted to get out and start working as quickly as possible.

'Are you thinking of staying on here at LM now?'

'Here? Not on your life! Work in a factory...noise and fumes...that's *unhealthy*. I heard that there were only 18 applicants for LM's apprentice school and that they had 30 vacancies or something like that so I could get in straight off. *Despite* being a girl. But I'd never dream of it! The surprising thing is that as many as 18 applied, 18 of them, they must be crazy. Spend three years hanging about there with almost no pay at all and then sit in a long line and put things in a machine. Or teach others who are just as crazy to put in the same things. What sort of a life is that? *Meaningless*. That's what I think anyway.'

'But making telephones isn't meaningless, is it? Telephones are useful things.'

'Yes, of course, they are. So you can ring people up and that. But have you seen anyone here at LM being allowed to make a telephone then? All everyone does is make small bits or assemble small bits like you do, isn't that right? Anyway, I wouldn't stay here even if they let me make a whole telephone exchange by myself. I want to work out in the fresh air.'

'Is there any fresh air left outside then?'

'Yes there is, smarty. Out in the country. Out in the real country where they haven't managed to destroy everything yet. So we're going to move from here, me and my friends. There are eight of us, and we're going to buy an old farm in Småland. Or two farms, rather. Two small abandoned farms with some forest which we can combine into one bigger farm. Otherwise it won't pay. That's what Anders says anyway.'

'Anders?'

'Yes, my bloke. He's the one who knows because he's worked on a farm for several summers. His parents own a farm. I can see just looking at you that you think we're romantic. That's the way they look at home too. But we've talked this through, *carefully*, those of us in the group. We've talked about getting fine qualifications and making money and building a house and all that, we could do that too, every one of us – but none of us *wants* to. We all think it's crazy chasing status symbols and that. We want to live differently, simply. . .have just enough to manage on. . . cultivate organic food. . .have horses and hens and lots of children. . .*not* group sex if that's what you think but live collectively anyway. . .share everything we get.'

I think about the green wave and wonder if Ylva is going to be yet another of those young rural dreamers nowadays who has begun to be crushed one after the other by large-scale operations and empty decentralization promises. But she seems no more dreamy now than she did a while back when she almost ran over old Desirée with her truck, so I pluck up my courage and ask her straight out: 'How do you think that a group of youngsters from Stockholm is going to get a farm to pay its way when two Småland farmers haven't been able to manage it?'

'Of course we can't; we're not as naive as all that. We're only going to live off the land to a certain extent. Bake our own bread and make our own porridge and maybe sell some vegetables and eggs and that. But we're going to take *jobs* when we need money. Temporary jobs. Anders already has a driving licence for public service vehicles so he can work as a taxi driver or for some haulage firm. Ulrika, my best friend, she'll soon be a qualified nurse, she can work at the Central Hospital sometimes. And her boyfriend, Christian, is a qualified teacher. And then there's another of us who can paint and that and three of us can play instruments, really well, and they may be able to play at dances in the area. And we can all donate blood or work in shops or... drive timber maybe.'

'And you?'

'Well, I wanted to go down there straight off when I saw a picture of the horses! But now I've promised the others that I'll finish a rural domestic course this spring. And maybe I'll be able to drive a tractor after what I've learned here too! If we can afford a tractor, that is.'

Just before Christmas she parks her truck at my bench again. She is not pale any longer but just as deep a red and just as sweaty under her fur cap as all the other truck drivers are.

'Do you still think the whole thing seems naive?' she asks with a smile.

Not any longer, I don't, so I wish her and her mates good luck instead. Anyway, they are probably quite capable of dealing with a failure if casual work should dry up in Småland. Then she drives off with her truck, and it occurs to me what an asset she would be in trade union work if she stayed on at LM. She was not the type to allow herself to be silenced or to swallow any lies. She would probably start a campaign for heating the yard so that the truck drivers did not have their bronchial tubes destroyed by running a shuttle service between the freezing yards and the heated departments during the winter months.

But, of course, she does not stay. Like myself, she leaves for a more independent and creative working life. The only difference is that she and those like her do actually make a contribution to working conditions simply by turning their backs so demonstratively on LM and its apprentice school. The recruitment of new labour is a major headache for top management at LM. If they do not succeed in attracting alert youngsters and can only get those who have no choice, they may soon be forced to improve the working conditions at LM radically.

And may even have to use their own money to do it.

The next day a male driver sits once again on Ylva's old truck, and the entire conservative brigade amongst the shop workers can finally breathe a sigh of relief. Until the next pioneer shows up.

Roland

was dissatisfied with the television programme about Säpo (the Swedish security police) which was shown last summer, he tells me one day during the industrial holiday of 1972. We are sitting at home in his kitchen with a tape recorder on the table and at least ten flower pots in the window. 'Who threatens the nation's security?' was the name of the programme.

'Why didn't they include any workers, the ones who really threaten the security of the nation according to Säpo?' Roland asked. 'Säpo's working hours always seem to be devoted to the registration of left-wing workers while old Nazis and right-wingers have been left in peace and have been given top-level positions in society. I rang up the television people myself and wanted to be included in the programme, but they never got in touch with me. It was the same thing when one of LM's small house magazines, *V-bladet*, was supposed to introduce me. You know what those house magazines are like, guaranteed *free from problems*, but the editor asked me anyway if I had ever felt persecuted. You're bloody right I have, I said. People followed me home from work. I had people sneaking after me, at the barber's and everywhere. If I took a bus or a tram, there they were. Above all during the war and when I was on the Metal-workers' Union council. But none of that was ever included in the house magazine.'

'Did LM have anything to do with that supervision?'

'Säpo is a sensitive point for LM, you know. The Swedish Telecommunications Administration is one of the enterprises checked by Säpo, and the Telecommunications Administration is one of LM's most important customers. That's what it means in concrete terms to have Säpo as a state within the state. A whole series of enterprises and authorities, they were listed in the TV programme, are obliged to provide Säpo with information. The extent to which these bodies help Säpo with underhand information depends, of course, on who pulls the strings. I don't know, for example, if LM have espionage police of their own, but you can't rule out the possibility.'

'Was your telephone tapped too?'

'Of course it was. You could hear it clicking in those days. The cops were lazy too, sometimes they didn't switch it off. One evening I tried to make a call for two hours but every time I lifted the receiver I heard the same police. They seemed to be having fun, playing cards and talking about their investigation exploits. He's not worth bothering about, he's pretty harmless, that was the sort of thing they were saying. Pity I didn't have a tape recorder then.'

Roland Tyrell, born 1910 in Västergötland, metalworker and son of a metalworker, employed at LM Ericsson since 1926, first as a messenger boy and now as a relay adjuster, dismissed 1931, re-employed 1937, contactman in Department Vt 39, active in the Communist Party (VPK), active as a sports organizer, holder of LM's gold watch for long and faithful service – this Roland Tyrell is not only one of the many communist workers in Sweden whose telephone calls have been monitored by Säpo, he has also monitored Säpo's conversations.

'But didn't you find it oppressive in the long run being watched over like that?'

'Above all I thought it was so bloody stupid, the whole thing. The top-level Säpo bosses can't have ranked me as very important because the nits I had watching me must have been amongst the most amateur idiots the Swedish people have ever had to pay for with their tax money. Once for example, someone unknown to me rang up and said he knew me well, that he worked at the Arenco workshop and that he wanted to interest me in a completely unique project. Scania-Vabis in Södertälje was to take over a small abandoned workshop in Ulvsunda, and a Russian car was to be introduced on the market from there. All I had to do was contact the Soviet Embassy and clear up a few formalities, After that I could count on a directorship in Scania, and my future would be secure.'

'But you never became a director?'

'Not even in my wildest dreams can I imagine that there are large-scale enterprises which are run by total morons who let an ordinary metalworker deal out leading positions to people they know nothing about. Anyway, there were severe import restrictions for cars then, so the whole idea was as stupid as it could be. There was another case, a colleague of mine, who happened to work in the same LM department as someone who had been charged with espionage. One evening two pleasant gentlemen who say they are members of the Social Democratic Association

in Midsommarkransen visit him and want to invite him to a
luxury restaurant, I think it was Berns they mentioned, to have a
chat about the evils of the day. But being a social democrat in
Midsommarkransen and inviting unknown people to Berns just
doesn't add up.'

The May 1972 issue of *V-bladet* has an article on Roland but
says nothing about Säpo. But it does say something else. It says
that Roland was in such a bad way due to being a communist in
1940 that the workers demanded his head on a plate, but that the
LM bosses saved him. How much truth is there in that?

'Well, the lads put me up against the wall. Reactionary agitators incited them. Dissociate yourself from it, you bastard! they
said. Dissociate yourself from the pact! It was the Russian–
German pact and, later on, the Finno–Russian war which made
them furious. Just as though I personally had anything to do with
the overall political development. Of course I realized that any
collaboration between Russia and Hitler's Germany was out of
the question, but I couldn't dissociate myself the way my mates
wanted me to. So my clothes and tools were covered with filth,
and they wanted me kicked out as well. There was a fantastic
feeling of hatred. Then my old foreman came out a little jittery
and said that he didn't want me to be fired but that some of them
had requested that. He was an honest sort. Then the agitators
decided that everyone should work free for Finland. I thought:
like hell. I never work free on principle. Suddenly there was no
problem about arranging union meetings during working hours,
something which has never happened since then. They wanted
to get a clear view of those who were against working for nothing.
There was a group of us who said no and who stayed at home
that day. You have to *hold your ground*, too, you know. Show
that you have courage. But there was a hell of a row about it.'

'And yet you were allowed to stay on at LM?'

'Yes, I never got the sack. But I was transferred.'

Four years later the enmity was forgotten and forgiven and
military–political developments had taken a different turn. Roland
was elected to the Metalworkers' Union, and the workers joined
forces to do something more sensible than covering a communist
mate's clothes with filth – they struck for higher wages; 130 000
workshop employees went on strike. This was the famous metalworkers' strike of 1945, and it is usually said to have cost more

than it was worth. Five months of strike for a few öre an hour. But Roland, who was a member of the negotiation delegation and who was one of those behind the strike, will agree with this description only to a certain extent.

'Neither the union leadership nor the Trade Union Confederation believed in the strike. They went out for wage demands which they later said were impossible to achieve. An unsuitable situation, they said. Europe is torn apart and there is a crisis round the corner, so the situation is unsuitable. That was the atmosphere in which the Russian loan came about. But I held a different opinion. There are no unsuitable situations for a dispute, because the dispute simply comes, it comes rushing in. Is one supposed to say no, we'll strike next year, or on Monday when there isn't so much snow – that's obviously impossible. Where is it written, I said, where is it written that history repeats itself? I've never noticed history repeating itself. Where does it say that? Maybe in the capitalist constitution, but are we supposed to follow that when we strike? You can't talk about unsuitable situations, you have to take a dispute when it comes. And a dispute comes when the lads become angry collectively and can't gain a hearing for their just demands in any other way. That was what happened recently in the ore mines, and that was what happened in 1945. The end of the war wasn't an unsuitable situation for the *workers*; it was the only possible situation. Anyway, the strike was worth while economically, in the long term.'

'You mean that one must include the subsequent wage negotiations when one assesses the metalworker's strike?'

'Of course! In 1946–47, a record wage rise was negotiated for the entire industry, 6–7% in one year together with a new agreement and over-time compensation, there were improvements everywhere. Lindberg, the Confederation Chairman, was suddenly prepared to say that if we don't get 6–7% we'll start a new dispute – despite the fact that the union strike funds were at rock-bottom at the time. That was how fast things could swing from one year to another, but then, of course, the postwar economic development had put the government's expectations of a crisis to shame. Before that, it was impossible to get out a single öre above the agreement, it was just wage-freeze after wage-freeze. But now the employers were as amenable as you could wish, they offered 25 öre – that was a lot of money when you

earned two kronor an hour. None of that would have come
without the strike, none of it.'

'But there has been no metalworker's strike since 1945, and
there have only been small individual disputes at LM. You are
almost the only one who takes up controversial issues at the
union meetings. Is everyone satisfied now or is there a poorer
spirit of solidarity amongst the workers?'

'There's a poorer spirit of solidarity. Definitely poorer. Everyone is rushing off to look after his own interests. Formerly union
meetings were fairly well-frequented, most people lived near
their work places. If a boat excursion was arranged for union
members in the summer, you could count on six or seven hundred
participants. That sort of thing is impossible today. Now employees are spread over wide regions and are always in a hurry
home. And if your economic situation is better, if you have a TV
set, car and summer cottage, you have more to rush home to as
well. Formerly workers often mixed during their leisure time.
But other things play an even more important part, of course, in
dividing them.'

'Such as?'

'Piece-work stress and monotony at work. Before it was always
the agreement negotiations that gave most money, but today
they only correspond to a small part of the shop workers' wages.
Prices and rents and taxes have run far ahead of the agreement
wages. As a result, there have been real wage reductions. The
workers are forced to find solutions of their own and that means
increased pressure in piece-work jobs without regard for the
consequences. There are innumerable examples which show that
the rank and file on the shop floor take things into their own
hands, force up the pace and build up pressure behind the wage
drift. But this is done at the expense of the collective spirit.
A chap who is used to getting out most of his wage from piece-
work loses all interest in collective and central agreements which
anyway give *him* only a small proportion of his income after six
months of difficult negotiations. He sticks to the piece-work
instead. At the same time, the work takes all his energy so that
he simply can't manage union activities during his leisure time.
Formerly there were plenty of fine jobs which could engage one's
interest because of their versatility and if your interest is engaged, you have energy for other things as well. But many of

those jobs have been broken down into small piece-rate jobs nowadays. Pull a lever, fasten the same screws, it makes for a deadly monotony. If you add this to the piece-work stress, you have the explanation to why many workers can't stand the strain purely physically. And when that happens, there's no energy left for solidarity.'

'Do you think the trade union movement could have prevented this development?'

'Both yes and no. A small circle of people are associated with the committee work in the factory. They deal with complaints. They deal with the study work which is necessary. They try to get a grasp of the various language groups and their evaluations. A tough and difficult work, but essential. That's the positive side. But take a look at how the Trade Union Confederation acts in the wage negotiation. They control the entire agreement negotiation from the top under the new name "representative democracy". The workers are placed outside of it all, they never get a chance to vote on a new agreement, and even less of a chance to participate and discuss the agreement. It's just like a one-armed bandit, as a mate of mine said, you push in 40 kronor a month and see if you win anything. And so things end up the way they do – the entire movement becomes passive. Not even the shop stewards are allowed to participate when the Confederation big-wigs reach a decision at the conference table.'

'But what chance does solidarity have then?'

'Down at the bottom, you see, down at the *bottom* you'll still find what the workers have in common. That's where you'll find the life blood of labour. You mustn't forget that. The fact that everyone wants as much of a return from his or her work as possible still remains. It doesn't appear so much on the surface when there's plenty of work. Then it may be worth while to hunt on your own. But when labour force reductions begin and the jobs are moved out into the country or abroad, that's when everyone realizes you can't just go it alone. That's when the workers have to turn to each other. The most important thing, I always say, is that there's a *movement*. How does a movement arise amongst the workers? You don't need major issues, like the Collective Agreement Act, it's enough to have small issues on a department level. As long as the issues are *serious*. Where the lads stand from the point of view of party politics is completely beside the point; the main thing is that they join together around a common union demand. You'll never get a movement if you're obsessed with party membership, things get too *careful* then. Everyone must join in, whole departments must stand like one man.'

'Have you succeeded with that in your department?'

'At least we've got part of the way towards it. The new arrangements at 39 were discussed last spring. There must have been 150 of us at a meeting, mostly immigrants. So you can get them to join in too when the wind begins to blow cold. Almost the whole department came along to discuss the rebuilding sketches the bosses had made. We forced them to accept demands that the new machines be enclosed so that they didn't make such a bloody racket and that the drawings be changed and then presented to the entire department before any construction work started. Otherwise, they just start straight off, you know. Now they tried to push through sketches showing that those of us who adjust relays and do other precision work will have to sit in pens like sheep – and have the new machines practically on top of us as well. But why not put the office workers and salaried employees beside the machines there instead? The salaried employees have taken almost one third of the department up there for themselves and made themselves comfortable. Why shouldn't *they* be there beside the machines? Why should *they* have rooms of their own with armchairs and flowers and carpets, fitted carpets – put them out here so that those of us who do precision work can sit in there! This isn't just being envious, I said, I only want to know what it is that decides that we should be the ones to sit out here. What is it that decides that? Is it written in the sky that those who work with their hands in the factory here must be the ones who have such a bloody awful work environment?'

In many ways Roland is reminiscent of an old-fashioned popular speaker when he gets going. He charges his agitation with striking images and has little use for understatement. Even the dullest of trade union meetings becomes lively when he goes forward and takes the floor. His voice is much more powerful than his rather plump figure, and some members are horrified at his colourful language – particularly those who are religious. But most of them approve of the fact that he dares to do what they themselves have seldom dared; he says exactly what he wants to say and he says it to the people he wants to say it to, whether they be party comrades or opponents. Roland, too, has had experience of the increased work pace at LM. At the age of sixty he adjusts twice as many relays a day as he did when he was forty. But not even recurrent heart trouble can make him leave piece-work or bury the union hatchet. He continues to say exactly what he wants to say. He has never been accepted, however, in the shop union committee, not even as a deputy. Better a weak-kneed social democrat than a competent communist seems to be the motto. So Roland is confined to participating in decision-making in Department 39. But if he were allowed to participate in decision-making all over the workshop, how would he arrange things then?

'Nothing would be permitted to take place within the company without first discussing any changes which might result from it with the employees. Why in God's name should it be so impossible to discuss, for example, transfers and moves with those who are directly concerned *in advance*? It's as though the workers were some sort of packages that can be tossed all over the place. And yet anyone who's become rooted in a certain job can't be moved just like that. All sorts of problems can arise – and those are precisely the problems that must be gone through in advance. I mean to say, we must act as though production serves mankind and not the other way around.'

'But surely that's difficult to do with the production system we have now?'

'Yes, the snag is that the system we have makes a product out of labour. Pursuing the greatest possible profit means that those who purchase the product known as labour only accept first-class products and ruthlessly reject the rest. Then society intercedes and offers handicap grants and training grants and transfer grants and grants to establish enterprises in an effort to get industry to show mercy to those who have been rejected. There are already a hundred thousand to show mercy to today and industry sees to it that this number increases the whole time. You know what the employers usually say, that they're not running any social welfare institutions that we must produce and not go hunting welfare benefits – but who is it that goes hunting welfare benefits on a large scale and never misses a chance to get a grant if not the employers? First they pump out all kinds of filth and muck in the countryside, and then they demand tax money to clean up; first they exploit human beings to the point of madness, cripple them, make them nervous wrecks and then they say it's up to society to take care of the pieces. The biggest "social welfare case" in the LM Group is the Group itself! You can't deny that something's gone wrong in the good old capitalistic "people's home"* when things like that are possible.'

'No, of course not. But what can one do about it all? Where can one begin?'

'A more human production system must be adopted, of course. A socialist production system. And only the workers themselves can bring that about. It'll take time to bring it about, but one has to start somewhere and I, for my own part, don't believe you can start at the top. You have to start at the bottom, on the shop floor. It's more important, in my opinion, for the workers to gain influence in the places where they work themselves rather than be represented on company boards. It's more important for them to gain influence on a department level. If you begin by establishing elective department councils you can extend your demands from there.'

* The 'people's home' is a popular term for the democratic, welfare state which has long been a political goal in Sweden. (Trans.)

Prejudices

We live in a society in which industrial life is subdivided and surrounded by walls to such an extent that large groups of those who sell their labour seldom meet.

They catch glimpses of each other during their leisure time, in parking lots and in the state liquor stores, but few of them are acquainted with any work place other than their own. And not always with those either. Factories, state agencies, vocational schools, regiments, office blocks, universities, stores, they all comprise closed worlds. Locked working worlds. No entry for unauthorized persons.

And that is precisely why unauthorized prejudices about others are always permitted to enter. They eat their way into the very walls. In the same way as they eat their way, at the end of the day's work, into all the visible and invisible walls which have been raised between blocks of flats and rows of terrace houses, between attractive neighbourhoods and scruffy neighbourhoods, between houses where immigrants live and houses where honest Swedes live.

What would happen if there were no such walls in society? Prejudices would probably die from lack of sustenance. There would no longer be *other people* to point out and call 'them'.

Them.

But there are so many walls today that every work place is doubly closed to any form of insight: closed from the outside and closed from the inside. How many of LM's workers have ever taken the lift up to the directors' floor or entered the new office complex? How many of LM's office workers have ever looked in at the Low Block or even been down to see where the orders they give or write out usually end up? Outside the gates there is a sign saying that the premises are guarded by an industrial security service and another sign saying 'no photographing within the factory area'. Inside the gates there is a large number of signs saying things like 'no entry', and most of the employees seem to feel obliged to obey them. Most of them know, quite literally, their place.

And so the wall of prejudices grows.

What do the workers usually say about the LM salaried employees? 'The office employees have it made.' 'The office employees look down on us workers.' 'The office employees let themselves be used as a buffer between us and the employers.' 'Why should the office employees have all the benefits?' 'The office employees think themselves better just because they can keep away from the filth.' And there is no denying that the salaried employees do, in essential respects, have it made. But it is scarcely a passion for truth that makes the workers pass judgement on the office employees as a single group, without even distinguishing between upper-level and lower-level employees, and only to take those differences which are disadvantageous for the workers into account when passing this judgement. Suspicion and prejudice creep in here. Otherwise one would surely hear more workers say that they feel sorry for the office employees who get such a poor deal when it comes to overtime compensation.

It is just as rare to hear the workers say that salaried employees and workers are dependent on the capricious favours of the same management and should, consequently, have powerful reasons for joining their union forces; I do not mean centrally and on a director's level but locally. This does not occur because the fundamental similarity is not visible. Nor can you feel it close to your skin. But it would emerge if the two groups started to meet and exchange experiences. Only the dissimilarities and the distance are visible and are felt today – and what else is there for the groups to go on as long as they are forced to live and work separately from each other, with closed doors between them?

There are undoubtedly many lower level office workers at LM who go around frightened that they will be laid off or that they will 'end up amongst the refuse collectors', as the unpleasant expression has it. But the common workshop cliché still portrays all salaried employees as secure, favoured and buoyant – as though the chasm of unemployment which constantly threatens to open beneath the feet of the workers never threatens those who work in the office sector.

And yet every worker *knows* that the brooms of competition and large-scale operations have begun to sweep through all groups of employees. The fact that they do know is strange. Does it mean that knowledge in itself is not sufficient to wipe out prejudices?

Unfortunately I know nothing of what the salaried employees usually say about the workers at LM. Since I myself was confined to the workshop sector, I saw few salaried employees other than the 'semi-office-workers' who earn their livelihood amongst the workers and who seem to find it heartbreakingly difficult to be accepted by either workers or salaried employees, e.g. foremen and supervisors. Their opinions cannot be representative for the group as a whole, even if they have probably influenced the general views on the workers held by many salaried employees who are cut off from the workshop.

But the cocksure and sweeping manner in which university students – as a rule, those who are trained to become salaried employees – can express themselves about workers is often striking in the academic world. In other words, they express themselves thus about the social class which they, as students, particularly seldom come in contact with since universities are still mostly populated by middle-class and upper-class children.

One can hear conservative students say things like: 'Only those who can't manage to get into the *gymnasium* become workers.' Radical students are, as a rule, less patronizing, but not always: 'The workers do not have the awareness required to stand up to bourgeois indoctrination, that is why they become so subdued.'

It is not my intention to moralize but only to produce clear examples of the capacity which the social barriers have for creating prejudices. During my time at LM, it struck me that as many workers expressed themselves in an equally cocksure manner about students as students do about workers. But then, of course, a B.A. is a rare bird indeed in a factory. 'The students yell and demonstrate instead of going and cutting their hair and keeping up with their studies', I have heard conservative workers say. 'The students protest against the capitalist system and that is exactly what we should do here at LM', I have heard radical workers say.

Radical workers? I mean workers who go to the root of things before taking up positions.

In reality only a minority of university students demonstrate and/or have long hair, every student knows that. Every student can see that with his or her own eyes. But the social class which is, through its production output, the main contributor to keeping the universities afloat, has never been invited to look at, and even less to participate in that particular reality – only to finance it. The workers' taxes have the right of entry to the strongholds of learning, but not the workers. Except in occasional cases by way of dispensation. To the best of my knowledge, no delegation of ordinary manual workers has even walked around any university inspecting their creation with haughty expressions, something which is quite common amongst financiers in Sweden.

In any case, there would not be any universities, nor would there be any schools, office blocks, directors' suites and factories nor any gates with the sign 'no entry to unauthorized persons', nor any towns and buildings, nor *any walls of any type* if the manual workers had not been kind enough to build them.

The only constructions they have not had to build are the walls of prejudice. And this is because those who have paid the building workers for putting up any number of walls between people and animals know that the walls of prejudice grow by themselves once the other walls are in position.

What I am trying to get at is that none of the ingrained misconceptions about other social groups which the social barriers have created can be removed without direct contact amongst the people who belong to the social group in question.

If one wants to rid oneself of one's misconceptions about workers, one must seek out an environment where workers live and work. One can only remove a small part of the prejudices through *reading*. One can only remove a small part of the prejudices through *reasoning*. One must seek out the scene of the crime. It is not until one is inside the walls, face to face with reality, that one *uncovers* many of the stereotyped ideas one carries around.

At least that is my experience.

One can retain the most ridiculous concepts about workers as long as one keeps a safe distance away. For example: a worker's hand must be calloused. One quite simply cannot understand that one could ever believe anything so stupid – as long as there is no one nearby to force one to understand it. And no one nearby will force one to do so if no one nearby has any regular contact with workers. Particularly amongst students one can find circles which believe themselves to be free of prejudices precisely because the members of these circles all live their lives at a safe distance from the points in society where *their* particular prejudices would be uncovered.

If one mixes mainly with people of similar outlook one can always retain quite a few prejudices without difficulty and at the same time persuade oneself that one is free of prejudice. Prejudices, one tells oneself, are things *other people* cultivate, e.g. about blacks, about immigrants or about workers. But one sees oneself as regarding all classes and all peoples with the same unbiased look, from Swedish generals to Guinean headhunters.

As though anyone could limit his or her social contacts with impunity!

Before I went into industry I was unwittingly convinced that my own view of the workers in Sweden was pretty free of prejudice. 'Workers are much like other people', I told myself. Not even three months of toiling and observing at LM were enough in my case to demolish this protective wall. It was not until I had been faced, on the spot, with workmates who maintained *other* protective walls that all sorts of sterotyped concepts floated up to the surface. My prejudices about workers collided, so to speak, with the workers' prejudices about people of my type – and this made it possible to get a grasp on them.

And that seems to be the decisive step – the step from regarding social prejudices as things which others hold to regarding them as things which one also holds oneself. The step from regarding a social class from the outside to sharing, at least for a time, its conditions.

A *catalogue of prejudices*

Workers are people who can take knocks.
Workers are strong, taciturn and weather-beaten.
You can tell a worker a mile off.

Workers must be stupid not to realize how bloody
   awful their conditions are.
A worker is not easy to push around.
Automation has turned workers into robots.
Workers are practical and extrovertive people.
Workers are patient and submissive.
Nobody can put his foot down like a worker.
A worker can put up with anything.
Once they were human beings, now they are machine
   slaves.
Once a worker always a worker.
The workers have it too good.
A worker is only a number in modern industry.
Workers do not want to take responsibility.
Workers prefer to follow the herd.
A worker always thinks for himself.
Workers are unintellectual people.
Workers swear like troopers.
You can depend on a Swedish worker no matter what.
The workers comprise an anonymous class.
Workers are all cast in the same mould.
Words and actions are the same thing to a worker.
Workers prefer to jog along at the same pace year after
   year.

Some of these sweeping judgements are so obviously out-of-date
that they can only be whispered in secrecy nowadays – for example 'A worker is not easy to push around.' or 'Once a worker
always a worker.' Nowadays, workers are the *first* to be moved
and they do not always remain workers either. 'Once a worker
now a case for reschooling', would be a truer description. But the
other clichés are more tenacious. Despite the fact that they too
can be refuted with powerful and rational arguments or can be
rejected as far too sweeping, they continue to breed in all sorts
of human souls, not least in those souls which regard themselves
as rational. As a rule, they are also allowed to breed undisturbed
since those who are rational find it particularly difficult to imagine
that their minds contain such irrational elements. Until they
become reminded of the fact.
   I shall provide one example.

'Workers are people who can take knocks'

What sort of slave mentality dominates so many of the
workers? Are they completely broken by the poverty
of their childhood or by their memories of the depres-
sion during the 1930s? (Elsa Appelquist: *Krig med
räknesticka* (*Slide-rule War*) published 1949.)

Beneath the apparently calm surface lie forces which
can be triggered and can change society. (Walter Korpi:
Varför strejkar arbetarna? (*Why Do The Workers
Strike?*) published 1970.

The traditional picture, which is still produced at regular intervals, depicts the Swedish worker as Tough, Strong, Straightforward, Brave, Simple, Slow, Secure and Thoroughly Sound. How
does this picture correspond to the actual situation of the workers
in the poisonous, efficiency-afflicted, complicated, supervised,
scheming, wage-splintering, clamorous, machine-controlled, back-
breaking, nerve-tearing industrial world of today?

In a word: Poorly.

One soon gets the impression at LM that nowadays only the
machines are tough, strong and secure – although they too break
down or are laid off at regular intervals. Thoroughly sound
workers seem to be as rare today as thoroughly fresh air.

Sometimes the old navvies and the old foundrymen are
quoted as the real strong men of the Swedish working class
history. '*They* could take knocks.' Meaning that today's workers
are worthless. But one can, of course, meet splendid physical
specimens in our industries today too, giants with hands as big as
cupboard doors and voices like foghorns. The only snag is that
appearances are often deceptive. One of these giants cannot lift
heavy weights because of his back, another has had two heart
attacks, a third is an out-and-out alcoholic and a fourth pads
silently around with an averted gaze like an old pinioned eagle.
One is often tempted to think, though the very thought seems
blasphemous, that the appearance of the navvies and the old
foundrymen was just as deceptive.

And yet the concept of the workers as a group which can
withstand knocks cannot be dismissed as easily as that.

Despite all, the workers *have* demonstrably stood quite a lot of
knocks through the years. Spiritual knocks if not bodily knocks

and collective knocks if not individual knocks. Industrial workers, to take just one group, stood the compulsory move from the countryside to the town, from one way of life to another, with everything which that included of cultural violence and physical suffering. And then they have had to stand the *stick* in the form of a constant obligation to obey or lose their livelihood: 'If it doesn't suit you, you can always go.' And they have stood the *carrot* in the form of the piece-work system which entices them on the one hand and hounds them on the other and thus has a nerve-rending effect. And today, when wages are higher, the working week is shorter and social security is greater, they have to stand the infernal cross-breeding of the *stick* and the *carrot* which 'structural rationalization and the stiffening competition on the world market', to quote the employers, has managed to bring about, viz. the striving for constantly increased performance combined with a built-in threat of being laid off.

A carrot-stick.

In other words, the heaviest burden in the industrial society is still being laid on the slowly shrinking group of manual workers. In fact, the burden may well be even heavier today, in essential respects, than it was during the 1940s when Elsa Appelquist wrote her book about LM.

That was when the wooden partition around the supervisor was replaced by a glazed partition which permitted the direct supervision which has been employed since then. That was when the engineers came from America and said that the work rate over there was twice as high as it was in Sweden and that things were going to be changed at LM. And from that came the time-and-motion studies, from that came stress at work, from that came the gold fever which undermined solidarity, from that came the wage gaps, from that came carelessness with regard to quality and carelessness with regard to industrial safety arrangements, from that came the increased sick-leave absence and the increased employee turnover, from that came the individual negotiations which pushed the union to one side, from that came the breakdown of jobs into monotonous operations, from that came the rejection of less high-powered labour, from that came the new supervisory staff, from that came the compulsory transfers within the factory and from that came all the killjoy prohibitions: 'Speaking during working hours prohibited, leaving

places of work other than during set ten-minute breaks prohibited, entering closets more than one at a time prohibited,
purchase of pilsner from outside the factory premises prohibited,
taking a break and making coffee during work prohibited, washing oneself before the bell has rung prohibited' – nothing but
prohibitions which still apply at LM's workshop.

The working *week* has become shorter in the engineering
industry since the 1940s, but the working *day* has become longer
in practice – partly due to fewer breaks, partly due to far longer
travelling times for many of the employees.

When LM moved out to Midsommarkransen in 1938–40, half
of the labour force moved into owner-occupied flats in the area
but today only a small and aged minority lives so close. The
national supplementary pensions scheme and health insurance
have increased social security for everyone, but inequitable piece-
work earnings, debts due to loans and hire purchase, intensified
rejection of elderly labour, the threat of rationalization and increased unemployment have *reduced* social security for many at
the same time. Wages have improved considerably and the work
environment has improved to a certain extent, but rents and food
prices are now increasing faster than the agreement wages at the
same time as accidents and collapses become more and more
common. To this must be added the fact that large-scale operations have done away with many of the smaller workshops where
the workers enjoyed a certain amount of job satisfaction at the
same time as the profitable companies have grown so imperson-
ally large that few workers have any satisfaction whatsoever there

Only if today's industries are compared with the poverty, dirt
and boss rule of the pre-war period can one claim that the
workers' conditions are better today. If, instead, one compare
conditions with the 1940s and the early 1950s one cannot possibly
claim that the workers have essentially bettter conditions today
There are too many obvious deteriorations for that. Today's
industrial workers have to stand worse knocks than they did 20
or 30 years ago, that is the bleak truth of the matter.

However, not only medical history but also strike history shows
that there is a limit to what the proletariat can stand. A limit which
says thus far but no further although this limit is obviously flexible
and difficult to lay out in advance, both individually and collectively.

Just when those in charge of a department, which has gone through a series of accidents, time-and-motion disputes and nervous collapses, are prepared for a full-scale confrontation with the workers, everything slips back into the same old rut, those who are dissatisfied calm down and the hatchet is buried. Or, conversely, just when management is beginning to relax in the belief, after a long period of 'calm' in the factory, that the workers are, despite all, 'too stupid to realize how bloody awful their conditions are' or that the workers *are* fairly satisfied no matter how much talk there is about the hell which industrial work comprises – just then the entire production is paralysed by a violent wave of strikes which makes the whole corps of decision makers jump up out of their beds like stuck pigs.

Then – but only then – another saying is confirmed, namely 'no one can put his foot down like a worker'. It seldom happens in Sweden that factory workers, transport workers or municipal workers come forward and say that they, in particular, make a specially important contribution to society and should, consequently, have better pay than others. What is usual is that secondary school teachers, architects or County Councillors come forward in this way. But if, for example, the teachers put their foot down by striking, it soon emerges that a nation can manage quite well for quite a long period of time without teachers. The situation becomes more difficult for the country if the farmers strike, but food can always be imported. If the salaried employees strike, dreadful confusion will no doubt result in many offices, but production will not stop. It is not until the workers put their foot down by proclaiming a general strike that it emerges which group of employees Sweden (or any other country for that matter) cannot do without at any price. Products are no longer manufactured. All means of transport stand still. No leaks are mended and no refuse bins are emptied. No food is delivered. Society is paralysed.

The most powerless class suddenly emerges as the most powerful class.

The expression 'take knocks' has two meanings, one gentle and one tough, one passive and one active. It can mean 'endure' and 'patiently suffer', but it can also intimate 'pit force against force'. When the workers go berserk individually or cease work collectively, they stop suffering patiently and pit force against force instead. But they go on taking knocks. In most industries the workers seem to be able to take a beating for long periods without more than muttering in protest, but sometimes they hit back violently. In this way life in a factory seems to be constantly and irregularly – *dialectically* in other words – switching between the passive and the active sense of the expression 'taking knocks'.

Is there anything prejudicial in this point of view? Not as far as I can see. Those who have power over production cannot be dismissed as prejudicial when they regard the workers (and not the salaried employees) as a particularly dangerous opponent or as a potential threat. On the contrary, they can be said to be unusually clear-sighted when they do so. Somewhere inside himself, every employer knows that he can retain his power and his privileges only as long as those whom he has employed permit him to do so, no matter how much he may avow his fear of the 'state'. Those who carry out the work can pit their force against his force at any time. In other words, he has every reason to be careful of and afraid of his workers.

'His' workers.

But what about the rest of us, those of us who lack these particular reasons; how is it that quite a few of us also experience a vague and obscure threat, an anxious feeling of exposure, a creeping fear as though we ran a risk as soon as we approached a factory or a building site, a risk of running into a hard wall or perhaps, even of getting beaten up? This is a more sensitive question. And this is where the prejudices come in.

When I was small, around the start of the war, I sometimes saw photographs which represented Negroes. No one said 'coloured' or 'African' or 'Afro-American' in those days. On the other hand there was a type of liquorice toffee available which was called NIGGER. These Negroes in the photographs carried out various activities – one ran, another played the trumpet, a third boxed – but no matter what they did they all looked strong and danger-ous. Bundles of muscle with dogged faces and flashing eyes. Consequently, I long believed that it was the blacks who decided things in America and Africa. Who else could have power? After all, no one could knock down Joe Louis, 'The Brown Bomber', according to *Rekord-Magasinet*. Around this time workers were pointed out to me in the street. 'Workers' were, as far as I could see those who dug holes in the street, who hauled gravel, who heaved coal, who drank pilsner in doorways and cursed with deep voices. They, too, were strong and dangerous men. Real he-men. No clear distinction was drawn between workers and winos as far as I was concerned, nor did I ever have any female workers pointed out to me. Workers were men.

Did this mean that it was the workers who decided things in Sweden just as the blacks decided things in America?

I never asked anyone about this because it seemed so obvious to me that those who were physically the strongest must also be those who held power. That is what things were like in the yard where I played, that was what things were like at school, that was usually what things were like in fairy tales and who was it decided things at home when the chips were really down if not Daddy. Could there then be anyone in the 'outside world', anyone who might even be physically weak, who could go up to a black professional boxer or a Swedish stone-mason and deal out orders and then give him a dressing down if he did not obey?

I was genuinely surprised when I finally understood that things were not run quite that way in the grown-up world.

It is possible that these deeply rooted boyhood memories would have remained forever in the shadows of childhood if I had not worked for a fairly lengthy period of time in one and the same industry. They did not return until, after a certain length of time, it grew incontrovertibly clear that most of those who worked at LM were neither particularly strong nor particularly dangerous. How did they return? I found I could relax. I felt a sense of relief. I felt relieved when I discovered that so many of the workers were, in fact, weak and anxious, that so many of them were unsure and entreating, that so many of them were hypersensitive and preferred to hand in their notices or withdraw into their shells rather than protest against an injustice, that so many of them were blocked mentally and were full of complexes, that so many of them were so remote from violent outbursts, that so many of them were contentedly or repressedly diffident and that there were so many cautious people in the factory, people for whom the step between word and action seemed insurmountably great. On the whole, it seemed as though most workers were roughly about as decent as most other people.

This was what I experienced as a relief – that *the workers* were just as docile and submissive as most other people without power. This was not a particularly encouraging insight from the political and union point of view, but on a private level I felt a sense of relief. A vague and obscure figure disappeared. Obviously I had been afraid, deep down inside, that the workers at LM would beat me up.

Not the salaried employees – absolutely not the salaried employees – but the workers. The he-men.

Those of you who read this may have avoided such naive stereotyped concepts from the beginning or may have grown out of them so long ago that you find my presentation of them here a little embarrassing. Or perhaps very embarrassing? Well, in that case, you should find it even easier to realize how simplified and hollow the old heroic picture I had of the tough, strong, straightforward, brave, simple, slow, secure and thoroughly sound Swedish worker was. The Proletarian with a capital 'P' as Albin Amelin has so powerfully portrayed in his fiery paintings, one of which hangs in the LM dining-room. In the form of a faded reproduction. You know how different the worker in today's industrial reality is, both in the sense that he or she is less heroic and in the sense that he or she is more difficult to define. You know that today's worker is no better at taking knocks than many other groups of employees.

Don't you?

Metalworkers of the old sort do occur at LM, as do compulsarily proletarized farmers and craftsmen who never budge an inch no matter how much those in charge try to coax, threaten or entice. Not so much as a trace of self-seeking or slave mentality can be got out of them. But there are just as many old metalworkers and former smallholders who have a Lutheran respect for superiority so thoroughly implanted in their souls that even their bodies act accordingly. When an engineer passes, their gaze automatically drops to the floor, when a foreman approaches their work bench, they tense every muscle, when an admonition is given their voices dry up and when the great boss hands over a gold watch on the last day, their backs bend automatically even if they long ago decided that they would *not* bow at that moment.

I saw LM veterans of 60 years of age who hid behind the nearest cupboard or who dropped below the nearest bench when their foremen came by at an unsuitable moment. When the danger was over, they might titter like schoolboys. I heard low-income women complain that some supervisors behaved too 'common' and did not maintain their dignity. 'One must be able to look up to a superior.' Fortunately, respect for authority was at an altogether lower level amongst the young at LM, those who had received a less authoritarian upbringing at home and at school. Not that there was any shortage of timid apprentices and repressed wiring girls at LM, youngsters who disliked starting conflicts, but even the shyest of them were usually able to ignore the domineering attitude adopted from time to time by the supervisors. They merely shrugged their shoulders. The apprentices laughed when they saw me sit reading the LM workshop rules and when I asked them why they explained that 'the directors can take that rubbish and push it up their arses'. But in the middle-age group to which I belonged, there were many who infallibly gave a start and cast timorous glances as soon as anyone grasped the toilet door from the outside, almost as though they expected a slave driver to rush in, whip in hand. And yet they *knew* that the LM supervisors almost never visited the workers' toilets.

Wherever there is respect for authority, there too will be found that unceasing fear of being caught, of making mistakes, of not being good enough, which bullies so many employees all day long. Wherever there is respect for authority, there too the un-comradely tendency to play up to those in command will be found, to smile for advantages, to climb at the expense of others, to scheme. Wherever there is respect for authority, there too the furtive tendency to say one thing and do another will grow.

If one is overfed on theory and underfed on practice, which is particularly common in an academic environment, one can sit at innumerable society meetings where radical left-wing comrades decide that the only solution is for us all to 'enter the manufacturing industries' without quite realizing how ridiculous it is that this can be decided week after week without anyone ever doing so. This is like sitting at the Opera and hearing a soprano say time and time again 'I must flee, I must flee' without ever seeing her do so.

I had assumed that things would, in this particular respect, be different at LM where there is so much practice and so little theory. But this was not the case.

Scarcely an hour or a day passed without someone of my work-mates, or I myself, making one of the following remarks: 'Things have got to change.' 'We can't have those steps there.' 'We'll have to say something about the cupboards.' 'The girls' rates should have been raised long ago.' 'Things can't go on like this.' But things *could* go on like that and that is usually exactly what they did. Words were seldom followed by action.

There were a few of us who went around with a protest list against the food in the canteen and most of the others signed it immediately since they thought the food was poor and our initiative was good. 'Well done, lads.' But as soon as there was any question of they themselves taking the responsibility for a new list or of handing over the old list to the next department, almost all of them shied off or shook their heads. 'Ask someone else.' The same thing happened when the annual shop union meeting was due. Many of those there had heaped abuse over the union for months and had said that the present committee would have to be replaced. But when the day of the meeting approached and the practical questions had to be put – who would stand as candidates, who was willing to propose candidates, who was prepared to present the criticism at the meeting and how many could promise even to *come* to the meeting – the ranks were thinned out at a disastrous rate. 'Ask someone else.' A remarkable number said quite definitely that they did not intend to come. Not on any condition. Why not? Because at the last union meeting they were snubbed or they had a mate who was snubbed and since then they didn't want to have anything to do with the union. The event may have occurred several years before, but that makes no difference. They could not take the knock.

And if one thinks about it, there is nothing particularly sur-prising about this. On the contrary.

No one needs to be well-muscled or even particularly strongly built to manage the jobs which are normally offered in modern engineering industries. The machines supply the muscle today. If there is room for dreamy workers at LM, it follows that there must also be room for thin workers, big-bellied workers and frail workers. As well as for mentally handicapped workers, blind workers, workers who tipple, painters who can no longer work at their trade due to eczema, or diabetic housewives. Besides, every industrial worker runs the same decisive risks whether he or she be strong as a bear or delicate as a flower. The noise damages ears without exception, the air damages lungs without exception, the stress damages nerves without exception.

It is just as easy to understand why most workers think twice before they shout out their dissatisfaction or take part in collective protest actions. They may have to pay a high price for extravagances of this type. They may be transferred to a worse paid job, they may be branded as troublemakers, they may even get the sack. The risks I took when I asked for the floor at union meetings and when I wandered off from my own department, with or without protest lists in my hand, were minute. I could always return to my ordinary work. But most of those who work in factories have nothing to return to and seldom have anything they can switch over to. Skilled workers or teenagers still have their options open, but the others have to play with their working lives at stake. Who wouldn't keep his mouth shut under conditions like that?

In addition to this, it must be remembered that social self-confidence is a rare guest in the lower regions of the class society.

Fortunately, everyone who has realized his or her own basic human dignity and who feels assured of this dignity independently of whether he or she has climbed high on the social ladder or never climbed at all, can acquire a fundamental self-respect. Admittedly the browbeaten low-income female worker constantly risks hearing that she is worthless, something which her despotic boss does not have to listen to. And yet the low-income female worker may be able to defend her self-respect, her basic moral security, her 'peace with herself' as the Christians express it, better than her boss. As Vera, who works in the sorting department, put it:

'When I see a full waste-paper basket, I empty it. But when I do, the others say that I lose my prestige and that I'm regarded as a scrubbing woman. But I *know* that I have a human dignity, and it doesn't depend on whether I empty waste-paper baskets or not. Those who are only interested in what others think don't understand that. They can't see their own human dignity, like.'

But social *self-confidence* is something else again. Here social position and performance evaluation play a clearly decisive part. Social self-confidence is nourished by things like success in one's occupational life and one's social life; it is nourished by the appreciation of those in power and the respect of those around one. It is difficult to create an enduring feeling of self-confidence through one's inner strength alone. Without external success, it wavers; without any form of appreciation, it breaks. My own self-confidence as a writer has been formed in precisely that way and I recognized the phenomenon amongst the tool-workers and repair mechanics who enjoy a special standing at the LM workshops. Before they learned to master their tools and won recognition for their skills they were probably as unsure of themselves socially as I was before my typewriter began to obey my hands – but now they knew that they had mastered a craft which is much in demand in the engineering industry and which not everyone can learn, they had won appreciation and respect, they had increased their earnings and they were confident that there would always be a demand for them on the labour market even during recessions. This left its mark on everything they did.

They seemed more cocky than the other workers. They dared to do more, even outside their work. If they were interested in union matters, they seldom hesitated to ask for the floor at shop union meetings. They made more determined wage demands. The tool-makers in Department Vt 15 carried on their own collective negotiations, for example, with the management.

But most of those who work at LM do not sit in this secure boat, and they have little chance of ever doing so. The ordinary piece-rate workers, like the truck drivers, like the packers, like the store assistants, like the constantly transferred unskilled workers – what are they to do to win that measure of social self-confidence required to enable one to say what one wants to say, to enable one to take the initiative, to enable one to put one's foot down and struggle for one's rights? These workers know that they can easily be replaced. They know that any schoolboy or schoolgirl getting vocational orientation practice can manage their jobs, at least passably, after a week or two of training. There is little self-confidence to be won from the work they do; still less from the low incomes they earn, unless they are lucky with their piece-work rate; and there is practically none at all to be won from the status and future prospects connected with their work.

No matter how much they may differ in other respects, their occupations all comprise the dregs of the labour market.

We talk about administrators 'making a career', about gradu-ates and artists as being 'talented' or as being 'successful', about small businessmen as 'getting on', about craftsmen and special-ized workers as being 'skilled', etc. But who ever heard of an assembly line worker who 'made a career', I mean just precisely as an assembly line worker? Of a truck driver who 'is successful' in his occupation? Of a store assistant who 'gets on' without leaving his or her store? Of a packer who is 'talented' or a dust-man who is 'skilled'? The exercise of occupations like these is so poorly valued that the degree of competence and ability applied to them seems to make no difference whatsoever.

Here, silence prevails.

Instead, the workers in these categories – and they comprise a clear majority in most factories – are given praise of a different kind. They are told, for example, that they are diligent or careful, that they have a 'responsible' job, that all of the cogs are equally important in the great machine or that the fact that they keep their spirits up is 'invaluable'. Cake for the starving, in other words. Cake instead of food.

Even if these workers slave like horses, they seldom manage to cross the low-income threshold, and even if they master their jobs and do everything they are asked to do, they never manage to cross the wall of suspicion and pitying scorn which has been raised around all workers in our society who lack both training and sharp elbows.

They can always win self-respect, just as they can always win the appreciation of their workmates – and their workmates' appreciation can be worth more than all the small wage drifts and other patronizing claps on the back put together. But as soon as they catch a glimpse of a piece-work artist, of a fitter, of a mechanic or of a salaried employee they are immediately re-minded of their lowly position.

Of their *objective* inferiority.

Those who have not received enough nourishment to build up robust self-confidence often lower the level of their demands, limit their territory, keep out of the way when things begin to get hot, satisfy themselves with accepting what is offered, reduce their ambitions and transfer their remaining hopes from their work to their leisure time.

But don't get a false impression of this neglected workers'

majority! Don't conjure up a picture of a group of similarly repressed Uncle Tom figures before you. The full human scale is represented here too – aggressive xenophobes, gentle Quakers, exuberant storytellers, reserved brooders, eager scandalmongers, fanatic football pool fans, dedicated Maoists, loyal middle-of-the-road social democrats, well-dressed churchgoers, unshaven seadogs.

Think of Jaroslav, think of Kent-Åke, think of Desirée. All they have in common is that they get out of the way when things start getting hot quite simply because circumstances have not granted them a social self-confidence which prevails in the face of adversity. If they take knocks, they seldom if ever do so in the active manner, by pitting force against force so as to damage at least part of the unjust system they are subjected to. If they take knocks, they do so in the passive manner as long as possible, by suffering patiently so that only they themselves are damaged. I say 'as long as possible', because all strike experience shows that even these oppressed people join in when a dispute is around the corner. But they let others take the initiative, they let others take the risks, they let others organize things.

All of this becomes fairly obvious when one considers it. No one voluntarily saws off the branch he himself is sitting on. Only prejudicial thinking demands the impossible – that the workers should take knocks to an extent which neither their social conditions nor the human soul permits. I am thinking now of the innumerable radicals who demand that the workers should *constantly* pit force against force and who dismiss them disappointedly as beaten or tricked as soon as they refuse. Above all, I am thinking of the spirit of the ratified labour agreements which demand that the workers should *constantly* be satisfied with suffering patiently – even when everything inside them and around them rises in protest.

Only as long as the workers are regarded as robots and not as human beings can any of these demands be called reasonable.

A requirement commonly made on me and on others who attempt to portray the conditions of the workers is that we should rapidly get our descriptions over with and offer constructive proposals for reforms straight off. But what can one base such proposals on as long as prejudices and blind spots of the type I have mentioned here prevent a precise definition of position?

After all, only stereotyped proposals can be based on stereotyped descriptions.

From without and from within

If one pays a study visit to a large-scale industry and rapidly goes through the departments, one seldom has time to catch a glimpse of what distinguishes one worker from another. The work operations, the work benches, the machines, the corridors and the workshop landscapes all look as similar and gloomy as the mine galleries in a television film from the northern Swedish ore fields – and the workers thus merge together to a similar mass. By the time one has reached the exit, one has one's picture drawn up – a clearly demarcated class of people who all suffer under the same tough production conditions and who all crouch down in much the same manner under this oppression.

One knows, of course, that each worker is a unique individual but what one *sees* is the joint labour collective, the oppressed class.

But if one sits down at one of the work benches and starts to work in the same way as the others, one's picture quickly changes. The massive impression of the collective is quickly dissipated. The massive impression of common glumness is dissipated just as quickly. One begins to notice how different many of those occupations, which seemed depressingly alike at first glance, are. One begins to notice the different ways in which they can be carried out and the enormous difference with which they are experienced by different workers. One begins to notice that the work rate, too, varies a great deal. Some move jerkily and rapidly as wound-up dolls, others ramble around in the sleepwalker manner of astronauts on the moon. Several times a day smiles break through the hard collective walls of noise and stress which have been built up, and the same smiles are frozen to ice by snubs and squabbles just as often – only to break through again at the first opportunity. Above all, one gets workmates. One by one the individuals emerge from the class, each of them with his or her own face, background, opinion and prejudices.

One knows, of course, that those who work in a manufacturing industry are not only unique personalities but also parts of a collective, a caste, an exploited class. But what one *sees* is no longer the class, the working class, but only the workers – or rather the individuals each in his or her own place and each working in his or her own way.

It is in this situation, when all the clearly drawn lines seem to disappear in a swarm of human beings, that a socialist finds his class standpoint seriously tested. Of course they are comforting, all these rapid study visits which immediately appear to confirm the correctness of a Marxist view of society; one can, after all, see with one's own eyes how the exploited class of wage earners is in fact exploited! But it is not until one remains that one can see how much human diversity and human contradiction one's convictions can stand without giving way. How much splintering and dissension one can stand without losing one's belief in the power of solidarity. How much worm's-eye view and how much unassorted reality one can stand without losing one's overall vision.

It is then one discovers how many different voices one can stand listening to without losing sight of the class for the individuals.

Jaakko has the floor

'It's funny, I think, in those fine dining-rooms they put in LM,'
says Jaakko Stenius one day. 'I mean...it was supposed to be
finished, workers and salaried employers were supposed to eat
together, that was what they said. No discrimination like there
was before. Everyone the same, like. So it's funny, I think, that
they've put a better class, sort of, on the two dining-rooms one
floor up. Not much. Just a *little*. But why one floor up? Little
compartments like where you take your food and little coffee bars
out there in the middle of the tables. You can't mess about with
a thermos and buy *loose* there, I've tried. That sort of invites the
office workers to eat up there, they're used to climbing stairs.
And the worker, he can see right there in the vestibule that *that*
dining-room down there, it's fine too of course but it's like simpler,
big too, like a press shop almost and not high up, no, more down
to earth, more familiar like. So he understands what they were
thinking of, the bigshots, that those of us in the workshop sit
chewing meatballs. No real difference compared with before.
Sound absorption and light, that it *has*. Good view too. Where
I sit I can look at the workshop. But I don't think they were all
that serious about equalization. More a gesture, sort of.'

Jaakko Stenius is fairly young as a human being, 31 years of
age, but he is a veteran as a metalworker. When I meet him in
1973 he has just celebrated his 15th anniversary as an engineering industry worker – seven years in Finland and eight years at
LM in Sweden. All of his grown life has been devoted to industry.

'But it's no big thing', Jaakko continues his dining-room monologue. 'After all, you don't eat with strangers. Not when your
mates are there. That's how it is. But the portions – that's what
really makes you mad. . .'

'The portions?'

'Yes, they're different. . .no justice. But justice is different too! If you have justice down to the last millimetre in food, let's say industrial lunch food like. . .then everyone gets two and a half minced steaks each. A hungry wolf and a little gaffer, two and a half minced steaks each. Stupid sort of justice, I think. A better sort of justice would give the worker three minced steaks and a salaried employee two. Sure! Down on the shop floor, we have the tougher job, we start earlier, an hour earlier almost. We need to eat more at 12 o'clock. Three minced steaks or four. Proper justice. But at LM, they don't have stupid justice and don't have proper justice – a salaried employee gets three minced steaks and a worker two. And the salaried employee gets a slice of cheese, the worker doesn't. A salaried employee gets milk *and* coffee, and the worker only gets one or the other. Salaried employees get seconds too, I've seen them, just wave those ID cards we don't have. . .Yes, that's what it's like!'

'How do they justify that difference?'

'Salaried employees pay more, 7.20 they say. I get three minced steaks and more if I pay 7.20 too, they say. But the salaried employees don't *pay* 7.20, they just get a food coupon, free lunch, it says 7.20 written on it but he only adds four or five kronor to his tax returns, that's all, he doesn't have to pay more. Payment in kind like. Four, five kronor, that's what I pay for two minced steaks, in real money; 4.50 exactly. With none of those extra things. We pay the same but get different. Like I say, I think, it *must* be different for proper justice. But the opposite like. . .not stupid like that.'

Jaakko's broken Finnish–Swedish dialect can only partly be reproduced on paper without making for difficult reading. Above all, it is impossible to reproduce the linguistic sounds and word sequences in the same way each time, since Jaakko frequently changes these himself. The soft consonants easily become hard in Jaakko's mouth. Sometimes Jaakko himself can hear that he uses hard instead of soft consonants, and he then corrects his pronunciation, at least partly. He seems to strive, consciously or unconsciously, to make the Swedish language his own without smoothing over his own verbal individuality – and to cultivate this individuality without permitting himself to be relegated to the fold reserved for picturesque foreigners and to which so many Swedes repair to smile at the broken Swedish and quaint mispronunciations to be heard there instead of listening to what the immigrant in question wants to say. And if Jaakko did not some-times abandon the most charming features of his speech there would be a very real danger that those listening would miss the point of what he was saying. For instance, the point he is making with regard to the portions served in the dining-rooms.

'That's different, it's more important, like, it's more important than the dining-rooms, than what the dining-rooms look like. . . than what different dining-rooms look like. . . but that's the way they do things. At work too. They take away the small differ-ences, keep the huge differences, that's what they do. They change the wrong things!'

Jaakko Stenius and I seldom had a chance to meet during my year at LM. We worked several departments away from each other and mostly had different hours. Now we meet again on a hot July day in Stockholm, and we both have the time and the inclination to talk, particularly Jaakko. He has just read my first book from LM.

'It was right, what you wrote', he says in his contemplative and seemingly mild way. 'Reality, you showed it the way it is, I think. A few things to be discussed there. . .but on the whole. On the whole! A lot of truth. Pretty warm today.'

'So that's what you think.'

'The dot, do you say that?'

'You mean *on* the dot?'

'Yes, exactly, yes. . .some of it is right on the dot, some of what you write. Things *are* like that. I'd like something to drink. Any coffee? HAIRDRESSER, FURRIER,' he says, reading the shop signs. 'You make one of those newsreels, like, of all the problems in the workshop, the induction, that doctor, the wages. . .you don't rub it in the nose either.'

'In the nose?'

'Rub the workers' noses in it, no. Those leaflets, there the workers are told do this, do that! They never ask, like only answer. They know better than the exploited worker, yes. You ask and tell more. . .they say at work, some of them say at work, he don't have any answers in that book, that Palm, no suggestions, like. . .but we're the ones who have to answer, I say. We must answer, not him.'

'We can go back to my place and have something to drink.'

'You live nearby, good. But you go too far a little with the union, I think, what you write. . .party dictatorship. Yes. It *is* manipulated. But they have a difficult job too, in the shop union. Thankless. I'm passive like that myself. But I must say, all in all. . .the book agrees right well with reality. Like it is in Finland at LM too, agrees right well. . .'

When a professional critic writes 'extremely important' or 'highly unsatisfactory' and an inexperienced book reader says 'pretty good' or 'right well', they frequently mean the same thing, i.e. neither one nor the other but something in between. In this case, it is by no means insignificant, of course, that the inexperienced book reader has a thorough knowledge of the reality portrayed – which the professional critic usually does not – but even when talking of other things Jaakko has a remarkable tendency to understate rather than overstate. He calls 30°C in the shade, when the sweat runs down his face, 'pretty warm'. But Jaakko also has a partly contradictory tendency to give everyone the benefit of the doubt. He does not seem to have any factual objections to my description of the trade union at LM, but he still wants to point out that the condemnation comes from me. Similarly, he finds it rather difficult, at least at the beginning, to give words to his criticism of my first book about my year at LM, criticism which one can sense beneath his appreciative phrases.

It almost seems – and this is something very rare indeed amongst professional critics – as though he would have preferred to have been able to say 'right well' about the entire book.

'I think. . .how I should say. . .it's a little *shallow* what you write, I think. Not wrong, not that. Like I said on the beginning, from the beginning, it's fairly correct. But you sort of show most what's on top of, like. Like what can be seen. You don't have anything *extra* to say. It's get deeper when you present the people there at the end, how the worker feels. . .self-confad. . .confidence, and that. That is the best in the book, I think, those portraits. Written entertainingly too. Otherwise, how you say. . .you go around and graze off the tops, like.'

'The tops?'

'Yes, the tops of the potatoes, the leaves. The Swedish language, it is very difficult! I mean like, the potatoes are left in the earth when you have finished writing. Only the tops have gone. Getting hold of the tops, I think that's good *too*. That you get hold of prejudices and tops like that that cover the potatoes. Useful work. I don't need a glass. "Pure, natural products".'

'I hope you don't mind my recording this?'

'That's a fine little thing. "Philips". You deduct it from your tax?'

'Yes, I have a write-off plan over five years.'

'I see. It's not like unnecessary things like workers' clothes.'

'Aren't you allowed to deduct your working clothes?'

'No, but go ahead and record. I'll have to sharpen things in my head. When I read. . .I thought of that unlearning they have at the workshop when you get a new job. The old movements, the old movements from the old job remain like an obstacle first – you must unlearn them.'

'Is it called that, unlearning?'

'I think so. You do the same with them prejuices, no, prejudices. You graze off the tops. Right on the ball there and right on the ball there, I tell myself. Right on the ball about those graduates. Yes. But then the earth lies bare there, ready to harvest. But you don't *harvest*, like. Not real deep. Nothing to get a real bite of, only a snack like. I hope that the next book, that you dig up some of them potatoes. . .will you?'

'I don't know if I can. You'll have to help me, Jaakko.'

'Thanks, but that will be pretty difficult. When you've worked there such a short time. When you worked there a few years, then you know. You don't need to dig and hold lectures, like, because then you have them potatoes right in your soul. "Potatoes in your soul" – if only I could write. It's so difficult to explain to someone who was there such a short time, with talk like this. You live such a different *life*, free. Why you stop so straight off?'

'You sound as if I only stayed there a week.'

'Well, one year, a year. . .but a year is not much if you are *always* in the workshop. For us it is quite short. But only six months there I work, in Department 11. . .if you have been there you'd have understood much more. Or in 19. That easy assembly job you had in 36. . .a pity you never were in the heavy mechanical department. A real pity, I think. Heavy work. A lot of them overalls get worn out in one year that I can't deduct from the tax. Worn out, I promise you! I drive home then and lie on the bunk straight off, I must. The children come and climb on daddy then, lively as hell, they want me to be a boat or a car. . .but I drive them out to their mummy, my wife. Close the door. Must have *quiet*. But I get no rest then because the machinery is there beside me on the bunk, it is there. . .I feel like having a beer then. I sit and stare at the telly and drink beer. . .like cotton wool.'

'Would you like a beer now?'

'Better ten kids than that edge press in the bunk! No thank you. I can't drive out the job like I drive out the kids and close the door, no. The heavy mechanical piece-rate job. . .I mean like. . .it's much tougher than that assembling, much tougher *at home too*. Difficult to relax. You just touch on that difference in the book, I think. You make it dead easy almost, the work at LM.'

'A lot of those working in the mechanical departments have said the same thing. I probably saw things too much from what I myself. . .'

'You did! Them eccentric presses, you only say noise, that it's decipel, I mean decibel, but the operator has to lift several tons of plate each day there, sometimes ten. . ."Picking" it's called. Pick ten tons of berries! And these are not light, rails for the racks you assembled over there, frames you know. I work on the sheet metal, cases and boxes like you had, but after a few hours, sheet metal gets heavy too. Write that this time! I must produce maybe 200 sheets an hour if I'm to make any money. Your arms feel funny in the evenings. . .longer like.'

Compared with the weightlifter types who usually operate the large presses at LM, Jaakko seems almost weak, a slender well-dressed young man whom many probably regard as a white-collar worker when he drives into LM's yard in his Saab Combi in the mornings. But Jaakko bends, punches and shears sheet metal in Department 11, sometimes for extremely small components. And on closer inspection it is only his boyish face which still seems soft. The rest of his body gives the impression of being sinewy and muscular, particularly the lower parts of his arm. His face and his arms do not seem to belong to the same person.

But wasn't Jaakko really after something else, something other than the toughness of the work when he talked about the 'potatoes in your soul'? Didn't he mean that the entire job becomes different after a few years in the workshop?

'No, the job is the same, all in all. It's the person who *does* the job who becomes different, I mean. The worker. He grows used. . .

you say that, don't you? "Grows used". What does it mean?
Uuuused. . .your ears and your back, everyone knows how they
grow used to industry. . .and your chest, your lungs, everyone
knows they are damaged. It is in the public debate. Environment,
everything is environment there, the worker too. Like an "environmental factor". But it's true too. They ask more. You catch
cold more. And a lot of creaking in your back. I have one ear that
hears music differently now. I have to put my hand against it
when there's good music on the radio, to hear with the other ear
only. It gets too loud! My neighbour knocks. But my hands are
even worse, I think. . .They get like the bottom of your foot, hard,
They can stand more, of course, can move quick and determined
without cuts. . .my hands, after a few years you see. . .it's good
for the work that they know like what to do without thinking
each time. But not good at home! I touch so gently, so gently,
I think, but then my wife says that. . .sandpaper. And the children,
it hurts them sometimes when I caress them. "You're not allowed
to bathe me, Daddy", they say. I want to cry almost. When I see
people like you or office workers – there is someone who can love
with his hands, I think. I think that. Hands that can feel, that's
really important! Them old metalworkers. . .workers' hands they
say, almost proudly, real workers' hands. But workers' feet, that's
enough, I think. They haven't thought enough about things like
that, I think, the sort of things that grow on workers in tough
industrial jobs, hands with soles on them. Hand-soles.'
    'Who hasn't thought of them?'
    'Them environmental experts. Can you say that, hand-soles?'
    'Yes.'
    'It's funny really. You master the job after a while, I mean.
More confidently. No one can come there and play the expert to
me about that sheet metal. I know. You also become a well-
known figure in the department in the end. "Ask Jaakko", they
say. That's good, I think – you know why?'
    I am still thinking about Jaakko's 'hand-soles' and I can't find
any answer.
    'But it's obvious, they can't sack me then in a quiet way. There
would be trouble. But it's funny, I mean, funny that you sort of
shrink anyway. That after a few years. . .your arms grown but
your soul shrinks.'
    'How do you mean shrinks?'

'You get used to it in that way too. More careful. You're careful about saving your skin. Yes, you do. Afraid that you can't keep up the same pace, like. Afraid of that rationalization they have, things change so fast. Those racks you work on, they already have new ones...not many can feel safe today, not many. Office worker too! Soon he'll be waving that ID card at home in the kitchen instead, and he won't get so many minced steaks then.'

'But *you're* sitting pretty firmly in the saddle, aren't you?'

'You never know. Can change. More plastic and aluminium and Jaakko's out too...But you can see, those secure skilled workers too, after a few years, they keep things more to themselves like... hide their pay packet, don't give their telephone number at home, keep their eyes down, put up a sign saying "Private. Keep out...not all of them but many. Can't be just that...not *just* that unemployment bogie. No. Growing older...maybe is like that growing older?'

'Are you asking me? I probably kept my eyes down more when I was younger.'

'I think that too, Göran. Before you were on *easy* street. No, I didn't mean to be offensive. It's like that, not many in the workshop are on easy street – you get more sensitive, like. Anything can happen, small things you don't notice because of other small things that come. When I was...'

Jaakko stops so suddenly that I lose my voice myself. The tape recorder records the silence for half a minute or more. Then he swallows and continues where he stopped.

'In that department before number 11...in *one* of those departments. The boss there, my foreman...let's say Sköldström...that he's called Sköldström...I'm not saying this to get at anyone, no! Sköldström is a real name?'

'Not a very common one, but it'll do.'

'Say another name.'

'No, Sköldström is all right.'

'I'd like that beer now.'

When I have fetched the beer from the fridge, I try to cool down the room we are sitting in by opening the window. The room grows warmer instead. The beer tastes cold. But Jaakko seems to swallow his the wrong way down.

'Thanks. It was a long time in that department. He was quite decent...Sköldström. With piece-rates and that. The work, the

work itself was more qualified than I have now, quite good.
After a long time, a long time – he stopped looking up and nod-
ding when I came. Looked down at his papers instead at the
table. He has a lot to do today, I think first. But it was the same
thing next day and next. One of those stupid little things, idiotic!
An overseer never kills himself greeting workers in the shop, you
get used to that. . .a nod in the morning and a cheerio in the
evening because he is in better humour then. He can go home.
But it feels funny when those two greetings are done away with
too, like. . .I don't know, cold. First I get angry at that bastard. . .
but we had quite a good con*tact* before, *con*tact, so I went up to
him and asked in a friendly way, like, if there was something in
particular, something wrong or so. But then he pretends he does
not know. . .he pretends ignorance and say "no" easy like that,
impersonal, there was nothing wrong and he held me off with a
long look as though to say that in his department, his territory. . .
no one should try to get cocky. Well. I knew then. The badly
paid jobs came more to me, not so much at first but gradually, a
little at a time. So that only I would understand, not the others.
He greeted me again, but in that other way. It just *happened* like
that, material, and tools, and time off, became more difficult like
then, no time off just *now*, because of delay, someone sick in the
store, good spanner missing. . .there are many ways. Get loaned
out to other boss, get other work bench, worser prices, no orders
any longer on the jobs you like. . .there are plenty of ways! I think
"to hell, to hell with him, put yourself above this, Jaakko". But it
was difficult. I get on well with my mates, the job too, but then
there is the money. Always the money! When I seldom got those
jobs he knew I could earn money on. . .my wage became less.
Too much less at the end. I think I finish then, many do that.
A boss has a lot of power then.'

'A supervisor has even more in that case.'

'Yes, not up there, with the big boys. I mean down below, if he
wants to push us around. Yes, they have. Cheers.'

'Cheers.'

'There you have one of them potatoes that come up after a few
years, suddenly in my case. But it stays a long time down in the
stomach.'

Jaakko is one of those immigrants who have made a success of
establishing themselves in Sweden. He is, for example, married

to a Swedish girl. When he talks about lack of contact, he does not mean lack of contact amongst the large group of foreigners in the workshop only. Jaakko is also one of the early immigrants who never received any organized language tuition, neither during nor after working hours. He has had to make his own way, not only in Sweden but also in the Swedish language – this is particularly noticeable in the order in which he puts his words. But instead of the verbal inhibitions which further reinforce the sense of estrangement which so many immigrants suffer from in Sweden, Jaakko seems to have succeeded in developing something quite different – the autodidact's right, as a beginner, to coin new words and turns of phrase when the correct ones escape him, a sort of joy in verbal invention which, in relaxed moments, stands in bright contrast to the gloomy experiences he recounts. As though necessity really *were* the mother of invention, Jaakko wanders about in a language which is still strange to him much as he might wander in a summer meadow where wild flowers blossom for him alone.

'Comradeship gets squeezed out by that bloody carrot bastard sitting up there on the machine and urging you on. That invisible carrot bastard, on and on and on! Just do ten bits more an hour on this job, and it will be enough to repair the car or for a room for the children, otherwise the children will not have a room of their own. He urge you on like that. It gets to be my fault, like, if the children do not get that room. My fault. If I have a fairly tough job then and someone else has a good job, I want his good job. It gets to be like poison, poison. No one wants to help out, like, only to get that good job, everyone. . .'

'And solidarity disappears amongst the workers.'

'Yes. yes. On the *leaflets*, there it still exists, that fine working class, one for all. . .on the leaflets it is visible. But on the shop floor, where is it there? You don't even have time to look around to see if it is still there because of that carrot bastard. . .I stand and cut and cut like crazy that metal sheet and suddenly – I remember, the children have that room now, they have it! I don't need to hurry, but then I am sweaty already. You get that carrot bastard into your body like.'

'Like a tapeworm, someone has said, that grows bigger and bigger while the worker grows smaller and smaller.'

'Yes, obviously there is less room for the worker, like, when both bosses and that carrot bastard have to have room to sit *on top* of him. I think LM can buy a special chair for that carrot bastard.'

'Or get rid of the whole piece-work system?'

'Good too. But it won't happen. Monthly salary, maybe, but not a *real* monthly salary. They will put that carrot bastard up there, on the monthly salary, you'll see! Like one of those bonus things – 10% carrot bastard. So the piece-work system is still there, only hidden, like. More restriction then too. No wage drift for. . . for us.'

'Perhaps they'll have merit rating instead, like they have at Götaverken.'

'With speed as the first merit, I'm afraid. That will be almost worse! In the public debate. . .I get angry with the public debate when they just play the same record all the time. 'Stress-and-strain", you know how it goes? "Piece-work, what is that? Stress-and-strain, stress-and-strain. And what is it like to work on piece-rate? Stress-and-strain, stress-and-strain." '

"Yes, it was top of the pops for quite a while, "Stress-and-strain".'

'But it's dropped down now. So now they are playing the rivers side instead. It is called that? No, *reverse*, not rivers, the reverse side. . .yes it'll soon be at the top, that other song, "Stop nagging about piece-work". You know how it runs? "Stop nag-ging about piece-work/we. . ." No, "Stop nag-ging about piece-work/now we have a monthly sal-ary." '

Jaakko does actually sing it, or at least half-sings it and the tune sounds like a catchy popular tune. I, too, am beginning to feel the effects of the beer, or perhaps it is the heat, so we sing Jaakko's new hit song together a couple of times. Then Jaakko starts to analyse the text.

'They want to say the opposite now, that stress-and-strain, that the piece-work system is out of date, like, not in fashion any longer, ridiculous almost, like an old two-stroke car, the Saab 96. He can sit there and blow his horn now, that old carrot bastard, because soon he get the sack, he go on relief! So they say in the papers, on the telly, piece-work is almost gone. . .but that *real* carrot bastard, he not get the sack, he already sitting there in the new Volvo and laughing at the worker, he just change cars. . . that wage incentive system. . .movable like. . .merit rating. . .*that* is what he is called now, the carrot bastard. He just change with the times.'

'They're beginning to call him a "more fixed wage" too. A *fixed* wage is the same thing as a salary, but a *more* fixed. . .'

'Just one word with four letters. . .he squeezes in easily, that old carrot bastard. *Real* easily! But I don't understand. . .how can it change, how can the public debate change so fast? Such complaints so long, the whole industry just one big black hole, grimy miners in every paper – and now, everything good come immediately now, monthly salary and machinery that just murmurs, industrial democracy, bosses like mates, no firing people, only security, sit at work smoking your pipe, more holidays too, no low-income groups for women, everything. . .they talk almost like we had it already! But we don't. On the shop floor it is the same as ever. Things don't change so fast there.'

Does Jaakko read poetry in secret? It almost sounds like it when he speaks. No, he says he reads a popular technical magazine. The daily newspapers when he is tired and the technical magazine when he is energetic. No books? Yes, instruction manuals for the machines. There are whole library walls full of living poetry and prose waiting to be borrowed free of charge and Jaakko ignores it all and takes out an instruction manual instead. Strange. But sometimes he sits in the reading room with an encyclopedia, opens a page at random, for example 'PA', and reads everything it says there, from beginning to end, about pantomime, Papandreou, papaw, paper, papyrus, parable and parachute. This seems more like him. And when I put on Paul Simon's latest LP during a break in our talk and Jaakko shows his appreciation by closing his bad ear with his hand so that he can listen with his good one and, at the same time, asks me to increase the volume – this is in the middle of 'Tenderness' – it emerges that he once sent in a poem on this theme to a paper. A poem about tenderness. In other words, Jaakko Stenius belongs to that remarkable majority of poetry lovers in Sweden who do not read poetry but *write* it. Was the poem accepted? Yes. Was it a long time ago? No. But Jaakko will say no more.

'One of those mood pieces just.'

'Do you often write poems?'

But Jaakko prefers to return to the workshop problems instead. 'That distruct – blast it – *disruption* that comes. . .that commerce with human beings, like trading fruit almost, extra fine quality, ordinary quality and then windfall fruit...and that roller coaster with earnings, 100% difference sometimes...more important things like that, you take them up in your book, I think.'

'That's a relief to hear. I was beginning to fear that you included me in your description of the public debate.'

'No, you take up more things. Important things. But why do you forget what is most important of all?'

'You mean that I don't mention the most important disadvantages of the incentive system?'

'No, not that.'

'Well, tell me. I'm all ears.'

'It's like a charge-hand in 11 says, we can call him Malm, not Palm, *Malm*, a strong fellow, spent many years at LM, many years...'

'What does Malm say then?'

'A cheat and a swindle, he says. "The piece-work system? Just a cheat and a swindle!" This Malm – he's pretty red, so you have to make allowances. But it's pretty much a lot of truth, it is. I don't say a cheat and a swindle, but *carelessness* and...what's it called, scheming, such scheming. Carelessness and scheming, no one can say it isn't. You know the piece-work system...It doesn't really *work*.'

'Doesn't it work? I thought it worked far too well.'

'No, only when everything is fine...All the machines are working and the material comes...not too many sick and all the big problems have been discovered, no stops and trouble and that – the piece-rate system – but that is not often! Often you have to wait, the machine is bad, no material – how does the piece-rate system work then? You're tough and you know how to talk, let's say. So you get the boss to write hours when you haven't worked or you get a new job card, a non-existent job, so you don't lose because of the stoppage. Sometimes you gain too! But like I say, the worker is usually not so tough, so he loses when there is trouble. "The breakdown wasn't as long as *that* and it can't be as much extra as *that* and I can't write cards on jobs that haven't been done and of course you can make money on *that* machine" – he just stays quiet when they say like that, the bosses, because he can't prove anything the worker. No one can! That is what I mean. You can't *calculate* all that when you fix the piece-rates, not the breakdowns, not how the machines run, not the bad material...you can't talk about that, but the piecework system... you must be a liar almost, *brazen*, to make money. Fast as a fool or brazen. You wait as long as possible to punch your card, you talk your way into a higher compensation than the agreement says when the machine is stopped a long time...you get a good set-up time, you fix the best job all the time – everything that the one who is soft doesn't get. Scheming. A lot of injustice, I think.'

When Jaakko mentions this aspect I find it easier to understand a section of a newly published study of what happened at the LKAB Mining Company during the years after the miners' strike in the north of Sweden. The miners were asked which feature of the transition from piece-work wage to a monthly salary (*without* any performance rating) they regarded as particularly favourable. Many of them mentioned that they had securer incomes now and that the work rate was more uniform – but a notable number emphasized what Jaakko had said: 'Now we don't have to pay for all the faults which occur.' 'It was impossible to set rates for the piece-work. We had to pay for the inadequacy of the technology involved.' 'Why should a worker suffer because a shaft doesn't operate.' And then it emerged, in plain language: 'You don't have to bluff any longer, that's the best thing about it.' 'You become more honest in some way.' 'The best thing is you don't have to bluff and lie. You can look at yourself in the mirror in the evening.' But payment by results doesn't only force drillers in Kiruna to specify non-existent metres they have not been able to drill and pressers at LM to specify non-existent sheet-metal which they have not been able to press. An aspect which seems even more important to Jaakko is that the payment-by-results system sanctions a more or less systematic carelessness in quality.

'When you're not young and crazy any more, like I said...You want to be more responsible. You want to do a good job, take care of your tools, protect yourself too, check every component you produce, things like that. I want to feel the metal sheet with my hand, to see that it is even. But that is not allowed. That is not allowed! It's not supposed to be a good job, like, only a fast job, a quick job...those blanks we make for the racks, sheet-metal cases, the sort you assembled when you were there...were they always perfect?'

'No, seldom.'

'But you could assemble them anyway?'

'Yes, but somewhere. . .'

'Then that was fine! If I make them perfect, I don't make any money. And no praise, never. Only more that I am slow and stop things, that sort of atmosphere. Like I was being too fussy. Those blanks should only *just* pass through the inspection, that is the best. Maybe I think they are awful. Pang, pang, pang. But they do not think so, the management, they reckon with carelessness. But they don't say it has to be accurate either. Accurate, they don't know what it means almost. With electronics yes, but not anything else. They say: work fast, we must finish this off, a new order is coming, a new order! Always like that. So there is carelessness. Carelessness and rejects. A lot of rejects. No respect for the material like. Sheet damage that is discovered in the painting shop first, expensive to fix, a long job. . .but the worker does not have time to look at every sheet he picks out, then he makes no money. He looks in secret at the inspection instead, he looks to see what they don't inspect so much there, then he makes money. *Then* he makes money!'

'It just struck me that things must be the same at LM in Kristianstad where they make all those plastic components. Sometimes almost every second guide bar we got was so fragile that the fixtures came loose and sometimes whole boxes of cable holders or plastic sections were bent and twisted. We had to send back an awful lot, but when we used that material sometimes the racks were approved anyway.'

'It goes like that when you are not allowed to do a good job. Everywhere! Just look at the construction sites. . .'

I nod and think of painters who skip a couple of coats to make some quick money. Of craftsmen who avoid tax when they do jobs on the side in private flats, of estate agents who make deductions for 'depreciation' on buildings which have risen in value. Of doctors who don't want to give their patients national health receipts for tax reasons. . .a cheat and a swindle outside the factory gates too.

'But you said that management doesn't want to acknowledge the fact that carelessness occurs. . .I wonder if Wahlberg, the chief engineer, didn't do just that, indirectly, during that debate about LM at Midsommargården when he spoke about the "correct quality". He said that many workers produce "too high a quality" at LM and that this does not result in any "surplus value". The quality mustn't be too high, Wahlberg said, it should be the "correct quality"...'

'The correct quality, everyone knows what that is. Everything that gets through the inspection. Sometimes good, sometimes bad. Like I said, *carelessness*. I can...I could...'

Jaakko could, undoubtedly, give any number of examples of carelessly executed work which has passed through the inspections at LM down the years, but since he and his workmates are still employed in Department 11 we agree that I should provide the examples. In my case, the 'correct quality' means that the following results, amongst others, are passed: plastic insulations which have been cracked by soldering which has fallen on them, twisted spring washers with deep marks after screwdrivers in them, screws which just turn and turn when the threads have gone, crookedly soldered connection rails, poorly fastened multipoint connectors which will come loose sooner or later and large numbers of cracked or loosened guide rails.

I really hope that my foreman or one of the girls in the wiring sections rectified the worst faults without asking me first. But I never had to redo poorly executed jobs, only jobs which were completely faulty. And, in addition to that, I could sometimes see for myself that the parts which were dangerously loose after they had passed me were still loose when the finished telephone racks were to be dispatched from LM. I saw them being packaged in the cellar. These were no dummies supplied for beginners to practice on. They were the genuine article right from the first day. The racks are, undoubtedly, spotless and shining when LM's successful foreign salesmen travel all over the world and whisper those persuasive words which still retain their magic – 'Swedish quality, you know'. But a few plastic casings and tingle-tangle are all that need to be removed for the beginner's faults as well as the more professional carelessness to become exposed. The 'correct' Swedish quality, so to speak.

'I wonder sometimes. Can they sell? This Swedish quality, maybe soon they know in the world. Who will have that carelessness...I wonder sometimes.'

I immediately recognize Jaakko's description of reality with regard to another important point too. A lot of material was wasted in my department, not least soldering tin. Tin is a raw material which is much in demand. The rich deposits are few and far away (south-east Asia, Bolivia). The world trading price for tin is at least twice as high as it is for copper. But at LM – where a gratifying care was exercised with regard to copper – there seemed to be tin all over the place. Those of us who soldered were never told to be thrifty with the tin, to try to solder correctly the first time or even to finish one roll before we were issued another. On the contrary, it was surprisingly easy to get out new rolls even when there was a good deal left on the old. Respect for raw material and work ethics both drop sharply under conditions like this. Half-used rolls of tin slip down into private bags almost as a matter of routine, and no one says a word about plundering the resources of the earth since no one seems to have the slightest knowledge of what environmental management means.

'It get's like that', Jaakko says again. 'That mentality, like a fast-service supermarket, disposable products...They probably include the stuff wasted and stolen at LM too. They know about it! But they don't give a damn about the morals if that turnover just increase. Fast-service, fast-work!'

Scheming, carelessness and wastage all comprise consequences of the payment-by-results system which are seldom mentioned in industry. Seldom mentioned and even less frequently acknowledged consequences. The only thing I cannot quite understand is that 'cheating and swindling' should comprise the *worst* result of the ravages of the 'carrot bastard', even worse, for example, than the disunion it causes amongst the workers. I think my question is a rather natural one, but Jaakko is first astonished and then almost discouraged.

'Don't you understand?! I see...you don't understand.'

'How do you mean?'

'I'm pretty tired. Maybe best end now.'

'I hope you mean we can continue another day?'

'It's difficult to explain. I don't know.'

'But Jaakko, we can't just break off in the middle of everything now?'

'I have to think. Yes. There is something...wrong.'

'In this last bit we talked about?'

'No, everything. The whole tape. Something *wrong*. I can't say now...pretty warm. I'll ring you. Cheerio.'

A week passes but Jaakko does not ring. Another week passes

and Jaakko still does not ring. It is not until the holiday is at an end that he has finally finished thinking or else it simply happens that the plate shears or the edging machine has broken down long enough one day for him to get around to ringing me. He is at work then, and we agree to meet on a day when he has had enough sleep, in other words on a Saturday. I am eager to start straight off when he arrives, tanned after a week in the Åland skerries, but when I produce the microphone he stops me almost vehemently and asks me to play back the old tapes first.

'From the beginning?'

This would take several hours, but Jaakko is adamant.

'From the beginning.'

He sometimes smiles involuntarily during the playback, almost against his will as though the entertaining sections on the tape served only to disturb his fault-tracing work. Fortunately, he asks me to skip passages of a few minutes now and then, but almost never when the pauses are particularly long and the sentences are particularly difficult to grasp (the material presented here has gone through a great deal of sifting); the jumps are more often made over passages where he is in full stride and rather amusing. He seems to listen particularly carefully to my questions and remarks, and his seriousness increases each time he does so. Not even our combined recording of our pop hit 'Stop nagging about piece-work' manages to lure a smile from him. But after listening for two hours he suddenly seems to be in a tremendous hurry and asks me for the microphone at once.

'It was just like I thought, a lot of whining. The worker shrinks and shrinks, just gets smaller, almost like a little elf at the end, scarcely reaches up to the machine after two tapes like that. . .whining! The way I talk there about bosses and that carrot bastard, you too, everything that is difficult on the shop floor – it is strange that the worker, that he can work *at all*, that pygmy, he can't handle a ton of sheet metal, he's small and weak. He creeps around and is frightened of that *giant* boss the whole time, doesn't hear good either, and has worms in his stomach, tape-worms, the poor worker. . .'

During the entire playback I was struck anew by Jaakko's ability to portray our difficulties without lying about them or allowing himself to be oppressed by them, and now I cannot conceal my surprise over the gloomy summary he makes of it.

But today Jaakko seems to be completely concentrated on the contents of the monologue.

'It's not wrong, not like that, All that is there...everything which destroys, it is there. Yes, a hell! But when I talk it into this Philips, everything that is positive has vanished, like. The pace has vanished.'

'The pace?'

'The *base*. The base, the fact that...I *want* to work, I *like* to work! To work in a manufacturing industry, to manufacture things, I don't want to sit at home or add up tables...I want to work in a manufacturing industry, make things, that is positive! Not guns or rubbishy plastic packaging – useful things...You see that when people are moved around today in Sweden, in Finland, too, that they can always make a telephone call, a little con*tact*, *con*tact, that is important. I am part of that, I think of it sometimes, I am involved in helping them because if we don't cut that sheet metal and do other tough work on the shop floor, they can't ring on the telephones, only *write* like you...it's not that I don't think you do useful work too, but do you often feel...?'

'That I do useful work? Only when I feel I am writing well.'

'I don't feel it always either, not so bloody often, but I know it the whole time anyway. I know! It is so obvious that we do useful work down there, you can *see* it, the usefulness...there must be a lot of jobs in industry, design, writing invoices, travelling around and selling too, otherwise the money does not come in... But to make the thing itself, to stand there in the centre, that is something special, not just noise and decibels but something important...that is the *base* which has vanished from the tape! Bloody work, it always gets lost! It gets lost on telly too, when you said...When they ask you what the worst thing is, typical, what is the worst thing in industry? The "degradation", you said that, "Degradation!"'

'"Did I..."'

'Yes, you *meant* the carrot bastard, injustice and that, but you not make it clear...that the job is not degrading, it is the opposite! It is important that it is not covered over, that difference... almost get mad sometimes at those young people who do not want to go into industry. Or those who leave after their first wage packet, just leave. "Stand in a factory? Not on your life!" It is good that they are critical, I mean that things may be better at

LM, must get better, better environment and that, otherwise only Finns and Turks will come to work there...But how you want to work then? I ask them. Well, interesting jobs of course, preferably nice jobs, maybe professional football player or a hostess on the telly or have a little garage with two employees, maybe a farm in Småland, milk cows there...or study to become an office worker, study and study, many years and then? Unemployed! Because no goods will be produced with office workers only, it is impossible. Sell invoices – who will buy? But...small family factories only, that is impossible too. Pygmy production. Rings to put around the necks of birds. Pleasant little things. I think so too. Rings to put around the necks of birds. But what will happen to the export millions then? You have to have big production *too*, I tell them, big series, how will you get the money for your books and schools otherwise? I ask them. And for your offices too. But they just shake their heads. Probably think I am one of those machine slaves.'

'But it's not just young people who are critical of the working conditions in industry, you're critical yourself.'

'LM is probably big in the wrong way, I think...Impersonal, like an hotel almost, people come and go. *New* all the time. Only less comfortable, of course...Maybe like a youth hostel more. A lot of things should be different, *a lot*, yes yes! But large-scale production, you can't have it in a pretty red cottage in the country, you can't sit there on the veranda and make telephones...you would have to build a hundred red cottages with a conveyor belt between them. A funny little village, a tourist attraction. Sure. But like they say...it's true too, a machine slave...I *am* a machine slave, I know it too, in the sense that I don't decide much. Very little. The bosses decide more. The carrot bastard decides more. The machine often decides more too. But they forget the important thing anyway, these young cocks, because we do what is most important anyway. The bosses and that carrot bastard, what do they produce? No telephones. In that case, the machines do more, I like to work with machines. Good comrades sometimes, yes! But if the worker doesn't stand there and feed and look after and operate the machine, what can it produce? It can only stand there and cough. No racks, only decibels. Automatic machines they call them, they say that they do everything...but the worker must stand there watching it like an idio anyway, otherwise you don't know what the automatic machine will decide to do. And often you can't use automatic machines anyway, too expensive. That is forgotten the whole time, I mean that the worker. . .I forget it myself too, sometimes I must almost shout in my own ear. . .that the machine is not the most important, Jaakko, not the bosses either, nor the time-study engineers either, nor the office clerks either, it is you! That is easy to forget. Things are *arranged*, like, so that the worker will easily forget that *base*.'

'You mean that respect is reserved for those in charge, whereas the work itself and those who carry out the work. . .'

'The *machine* too. More respect. A new worker who comes, he is nothing, he just come, but a new machine that comes, it is such a big affair, then the engineers and bosses, they all come and admire it and talk of how much it costs, how much it produce, how important it is that it be treated properly. . .they never *forget* to say that. But treating the worker properly, no one bothers about that. He walks around there and he is supposed almost to feel *ashamed* because he "only" does the most important work. I have got such fine relatives in Sweden, supporters of the Liberal Party. . .they were curious when I married into the family: "Jaakko works at LM Ericsson, how interesting. Is he an engineer?" "No, I work on the shop floor", I said straight out. Then they were not so curious any more, they sort of lost interest, asked about the baby. It was obvious what they thought, just an ordinary worker, and a Finn too, his poor wife, and I laughed to myself. It was so upside down, like. I don't think anyone should strut about like a cock, not *any one*. But if the *workers* strutted about, I would not be so surprised, since that is the way production is in society, the money for the social reforms and everything must come from export, so the worker is important. But today – the worker is almost the only one who does *not* go around strutting. Instead, the worker goes around crouching. Pretty odd.'

'But how widespread do you think that insight into the value of the worker is in the workshop?'

'Like I said, I forget it often myself! Things are arranged so that the worker often forgets, he is easy to replace, easy to move, easy to fire, and his work is broken down into small operations. The worker is not so tough that he can decide not to give a damn about the respect he never gets. He is human too. So it gets like that in industry that they get more and more workers who *easily* forget what is important. I mean, if you have that carrot system then you *get* workers who only chase money and money and never ask about anything else. And if speed is the only thing that counts, then you *get* fast workers, quick-fingered workers, careless workers. And if you have a lot of moving, turnover, idiot work, scheming, everything, then you get drifters and robots and schemers and...bloody foreigners. You get the wrong workers, like, then, those who are careful and maybe slow, can't manage. Not often. No, I am saying it wrong. All workers *want to*, I think, deep down, want to do something useful, do a good job. But they, the management...how you say, en....'

'Encourage?'

'Yes, they encourage the wrong things in the worker. Only those things that are like a machine, to be strong, to be fast. The other things that are underneath, they cannot come out then. Only the *body* is allowed to grow. A soul never gets work on the shop floor, like, only the body. Not the brain either. A worker should not think, then he only gets crazy. They don't ask the worker what he thinks, how he thinks things should be. They probably don't believe he *can* think, only obey or talk. No work for the brain either! The brain has to stay at home with the kids.'

There are people who make such a completely ordinary impression that one is astonished when they suddenly disclose extremely uncommon aspects and interests. With Jaakko Stenius it is the other way about. His clear-sightedness and quick-wittedness are so strikingly uncommon that it is not until he discloses his quite ordinary aspects that one becomes surprised. For example, the fact that he seems to have a weakness for status symbols or that he is as diffident in public as he is talkative in private. I saw him sit silently through two shop union meetings at LM. Jaakko's sensitivity to pressure, and particularly the pressure exerted through the exercise of power, his deep distrust of all discussion which is not based on concrete reality, his considerable interest in technical details, his dogged sense of belonging to the working class, his passive (with the exception of election day) fidelity to the social democratic environment he grew up in, his suspicion towards students who distribute leaflets, his constant changes from eager optimism to tired resignation, all of these are features which immediately remind me of several others who work at LM.

But how *uncommon* are Jaakko's features amongst the workers there? I don't pose this question because I believe that there are many who have his intellectual and verbal resources (in the Metalworkers' Union *or* in the Swedish Union of Clerical and Technical Employees in Industry) but because *not even Jaakko* gave more than a small glimpse, whenever I met him at LM, of the eloquence which now pours forth when he is free. Nor did he make a particularly vivid impression in the workshop. One wonders about all the others who are forced to live at half-steam during working hours due to the factory machines and the check-ing systems? What funds of human productive power, of the same type or of a completely different type, lie bound and con-cealed and are only occasionally released during leisure time? These powers usually only come to life when something happens at a particular work place, when a door is suddenly opened, a sense of liberation suddenly felt. A door of this type was opened in the mining industry in 1969 and a door was opened in 1973 (and closed again) at the LIP watch factory in France. But even when the door is only opened a little – as when a group of ten workers manage to achieve a change in their internal work order, when a list of names is sent around the factory or when a depart-ment begins to negotiate wages collectively and directly with management – unsuspected funds of energy and comradeship can suddenly be liberated. Like Jaakko, many workers seem to be passive in union matters due to the shortage of, or while waiting for, openings like this.

'I think I'm beginning to understand what you mean now. That the desire to work and the knowledge that the worker is making an important contribution to society lies there at the bottom like a fresh spring which all the negative aspects of the workshop contribute to concealing from the worker. But do you mean that it is the carelessness and the scheming in particular that conceal this spring more than anything else?'

'You haven't forgotten, no. I've thought it out now, I think. Carelessness and scheming...And breaking up the jobs into small pieces...that not only conceals that spring, it *poisons* it too, I think. No, not poison, what is it called. ..you don't see the water clearly...*muddy*. The spring gets muddy then. You have a worker, I say as an example. He stands there isolated with a pretty unskilled job, maybe ten operations, and a sour boss and noise, no respect, just an ordinary example. . .What does he have left then? He makes money yes, but in his work? He knows that he does a *good* job anyway, a *full* job, fairly full and an *honest* job. Important! Pretty important. He can tell himself at home: you are not one of those genius engineers, no bright ideas, just ordinary work, but you make things and you make them properly. He can say that. But when carelessness comes and scheming and breaking the job down into only three or two operations, what has he left then? Money, yes but in his work? He is not *allowed* to do a good job, to do a full job, an honest job. I mean, he loses his desire to work often. He is useful *anyway*, in production, he is a cog, but the spring is not only concealed, it is muddy too, he doesn't want to see it any longer, he doesn't give a damn about it. Only money left then.'

'So you mean that the desire to work and the contact with that spring are so fundamental that the disunion amongst the workers can't be stopped and comradeship won't have a proper chance to flourish until these needs have been seen to, at least in an elementary manner?'

'Yes, exactly.'

'Then I have only one question left.'

'Good, I'm hungry.'

'Even if the "carrot bastard" disappeared completely and everyone in the workshop got a proper monthly wage, competition and profitability would still remain and would probably give rise to new rationalizations and new measures to increase production – aren't you afraid that the elements which conceal and muddy the spring will still remain?'

Jaakko makes ready to leave while he is thinking of this. He gives part of his answer in the hall, part in the kitchen and the last part comes as he is on his way out through the front door. I have to follow in his footsteps with the microphone so as to be able to record what he says.

'Maybe right. I haven't thought like that. . .That profitability, Christ! You see. . ."Basic Cooking". . .you forget. You stand there in the workshop and have the carrot bastard in your body, like I said. . .if only he wasn't there, if only he wasn't there, I've thought about that so much! Then you don't see the rest, like. Bloody hell, the rest is still there. That bloody. . .why can't they understand, increased production, it could be a *lot* if that respect was given to the worker . . .where you have the lav? Here? It's an important step, I think, to remove the piece-work system but only one step. Yes. But you *see* then how important it is that anyone who does not stand on the shop floor and forget all the time – that he not talk about degrading and that, not only whine. He must *point out* instead, point out that base. Clear water that the worker does not see often, it's there. . .you mustn't forget that when you write about that base!'

The flight from work

Working hours – if we take those as the first example – are not the same for everyone at LM Ericsson. The managers have flexible working hours. The ordinary office employees have fixed working hours. The workers in the Low Block punch their cards 12 minutes before the workers in the High Block, who in turn punch their cards earlier than anyone in the office sector. The shift workers clock in earliest and latest of all, depending on whether they have the morning or the afternoon shift.

But what is most important of all is that the working hours are *experienced* in very different ways on the various levels into which the company is divided.

When I sit at home writing I usually think that time passes too quickly. I seldom look at my watch because my work absorbs me. But if I do look at the time I hope that it is earlier than it really is. Almost always! If it is later, I become nervous. If it is earlier, I grow hopeful. As a rule, it is later. Stretching out the time to cover what has to be done is a constant problem.

I should imagine that most of the managers at LM experience working hours in much the same way. As do many salaried employees caught up in their careers, administrators who love administering, engineers who must soon complete a major project, dutiful supervisors, hurried cashiers, skilled workers who are in demand, as well as all employees at all levels who enjoy doing the work they do — and such people can be found in the most surprising places. Even amongst semi-skilled workers.

Whether it be due to stress or to joy, they all find that time goes too quickly at work.

But for the vast majority of workshop and office workers, the situation is quite different. Their problem seems to be to get their working hours over as quickly as possible. It sometimes happened that I myself forgot the time at LM, when a discussion got going, for example, or when a troublesome order had to be filled or when something unusual happened, such as an accident or someone leaving and celebrating by buying a cake for the coffee break and so on. But, for the most part, I often looked at my watch. And when I looked at my watch I hoped it would be later than it was. Almost always! As a rule, it was earlier. Sometimes the hands crept around. Some days they seemed almost to stand still.

And this was by no means peculiar to my watch. Those who sat so that they had a wall clock in view claimed that it was like being subjected to a mild form of torture. Even the second hand terrorized them. During the final minutes before each break the hands moved in slow motion. But as soon as the bell rang, they rushed round like mad.

Most of those who worked near me seemed to agree that the best working days were those when time passed quickly and that time passed particularly quickly when there was a lot to do. Not *too much* to do, which frequently happens in piece-rate work. 'You get out of step both with time and with yourself then', Otto said. 'Moderation is best.'

'What do you mean moderation?'

'An easy flow of work, so to speak. Nothing that stops you up, exactly. You should have time to let your thoughts wander, much the same as when you drive a car. Light thoughts that wander here and there. Nothing *heavy*. If you have too little to do, you easily get depressed. You begin to think about your own situation and so on. If you have plenty to do, you can keep afloat more easily, so to speak. Time rushes past. But it must be in moderation! I want to be able to cast an eye on the paper or have a chat now and then, otherwise the whole thing becomes inhuman. But you must have enough work left to break the backs of the slowest hours. On days like that, you can't complain.'

This makes sense.

Nevertheless, I wonder if Otto and all those who agree with him realize what they are saying. They are saying that the most important thing in work is that the working day should end as quickly as possible. They are saying that the occupation which they have at hand, the work which they have here and now, is seldom good enough and must be put to flight in one way or another. They are saying that time, the time they spend at work, is there to be whiled away.

Minute by minute, day by day, year by year.

The sacred future

When the present is not good enough, one puts one's trust in the future. In doing this, one must find as much as possible to look forward to and to long for so that the present does not overwhelm one. At eight o'clock in the morning, for example, one begins to look forward to the nine o'clock break. At ten o'clock one begins to look forward to the lunch break. At two o'clock one begins to look forward to the afternoon coffee break. After coffee, one begins to look forward to the bell which rings to mark the end of the working day.

Soon, looking forward to small things like these becomes a habit.

Since most of those working at LM have a five-day week, Friday is by far the most longed-for working day. In a different situation, it could just as easily be Monday, but here it is Friday. Many of the employees drink medium-strong beer instead of low-alcohol beer for lunch on Friday, smiles are more common than usual, popular weekly magazines are produced, laughter is heard at the tables where the Swedes sit as well as those where the immigrants sit, even the food sometimes seems to taste better. And during the course of the afternoon one often exchanges small talk with someone who has walked around stone-faced all week, absolutely silent and closed in. Now he is changed beyond recognition and explains, with sweeping gestures, what things were like in the docks when he was at sea or what happened at the Mantorp racetrack in 1968.

Beacons from the future which are extinguished once a week are not enough, however. Consequently, Christmas appears as a mirage on the horizon as early as November. Easter appears in the same way as early as February. And Ascension Day has scarcely pased before Whitsun rises like a morning star above the factory roof. God is seldom spoken about on the shop floor, but the Christian holidays are valued highly, nevertheless. This is particularly true of the feast of John the Baptist, which marks the beginning of the longed-for, endlessly discussed, major event of each year – the industrial holiday. When the Confederation of Trade Unions gave notice of their intention to proclaim a dispute at the end of June 1971, almost nobody at LM wanted to strike since the summer holiday was just around the corner. Much the same was true of most other factories in Sweden.

Since this habit of looking to the future is such a sensitive matter for a great number of people, it is dealt with in innumerable brutal jokes on the shop floor and, in all likelihood, in many of the office corridors too.

'Holiday? You mean those rainy weeks in July when you get eaten alive by mosquitoes?'

'Thank God that bloody camping is over for this year.'

'We'll have to tell the job-satisfaction experts to put up big clocks on the long walls as well, otherwise the time will go too fast.'

'The funny thing about Irja is that she's left LM once a year for the last ten years, but as far as I can see she's still here.'

'Is it half past seven already? Only nine hours left until it's time to go home then.'

'Don't do anything rash now, Brännström. Think about moving to the provinces for another few years. They'll still be there then.'

'Nice that it's Monday again, isn't it?'

These jokes sometimes come from the privileged minority of workers who do not need to take out insurance on the future – and that is why they are brutal. After various transfers or training courses, they may have found something which most people can only dream about, a job which they find so stimulating that time passes by itself. Or else they belong to that rare breed who simply enjoy work, no matter what it is or how much one is paid for it. There are also quite a few that reminisce who prefer to look back rather than forwards and who always slip into talking about how things were before, during the war for example, or last Easter or during the reign of Queen Christina. Or, quite simply, as generally as the word 'before' will allow.

'Things were different here at LM before.'

'When?'

'Well, before.'

The very thought of linking one's hopes to certain predetermined hours and dates in the *future* seems to be as dreadfully or comically foreign to these nostalgics as it is to the impulsive here-and-now people who *can* only live in the present, whether they like or dislike their jobs. For example, Villard Axelsson from Halland. Suddenly he works intensively for an hour. Suddenly he drops exhausted on a chair. Suddenly he rushes off to make a telephone call. Suddenly everything seems hopeless to him. Suddenly he begins to sing. Each moment caught in the grip of a futureless present.

But most of those who joke about the sacred future belong to the group which counts the minutes most eagerly until the breaks, the days until the weekends, the months until the summer holidays and the years until new jobs. That is, so to speak, why they joke.

These rather perennial future goals, which are set up in advance and are the same for everyone, are not enough, however, for daily survival in the lower regions at LM – and I repeat that most office employees belong in this group, perhaps even the majority of them. As a rule, a whole series of auxiliary beacons which one can set up for oneself are also required. One thinks, for example, of what one is going to do that evening. One calculates whether or not one can afford to buy a car radio or a fur coat. One wonders if Ralf Edström will be able to play in the next international football match. One dreams about what it will be like to work in Gröndal, instead, or in Gothenburg or whether or not one would be able to manage a course in civics. One imagines oneself enrolling for such a course at the Workers' Educational Association – or taking one's seat beside the window in a package-tour aeroplane on its way to the sun and the south. Now and then, one sees one's children before one in various situations, for example when they are about to eat Sunday breakfast and there is a pleasant smell from the cooker where the old lady stands with the frying pan.

But the homemade auxiliary beacons of our daydreams are, unfortunately, liable to explode – particularly when the panic of work comes creeping in on one and the unprocessed components pile up around a troublesome machine. Suddenly the children begin to throw sausages at each other, the course instructor ridicules the stammers of the newcomer and one's new car drives straight into a juggernaut in front. Suddenly one breaks out into a cold sweat, convinced that there is not enough money to cover the next instalment. In a situation like this, the only thing one can do is increase or reduce one's work pace until the sense of disquiet disappears or seek out a workmate with whom one can chat until one's head is above the surface again. Until the familiar beacons begin to twinkle again.

But there are also those who adopt a more methodical approach when they stake out the sacred future.

One of my workmates did not permit himself to go and make a telephone call home until he had punched out his job card. Another did not permit himself to buy a mug of chocolate at the dispenser until he had soldered a unit. A third did not permit himself to sit down and rest until he had screwed all of the guide plates into position on his rack. For my own part, I decided at an early stage that I would not smoke more than once an hour, starting at seven o'clock. In this way, I set up nine foolproof future beacons, evenly distributed over the entire working day, bright enough to begin to twinkle strongly by twenty to the hour. And this happened nine times each working day.

Even trivial events can be provided with an enticing shimmer in this way – something which is not without importance when one is completely or partly paid by the hour and has few other fixed points to break up the monotony of the work itself.

Things are different for the large majority of workers, who are employed on a piece-work basis only. For them, this hysterical dreaming of the future is, so to speak, built into the system itself. The carrot with its promises of constantly increasing earnings hangs in front of them as a never-ending reminder of the brightness of the future and the inadequacy of the present. On and ever on! 'That bloody carrot bastard!' And yet there are piece-rate workers who spur themselves on even more with the aid of carrot rules they have drawn up themselves. They suppress, for example, their need to go to the toilet until the next full hundred components have been finished. They refuse to allow themselves to dry the sweat from their foreheads or to change their posture on the chair until the next full 50 components have been finished. Or they deny themselves the right to look up or scratch themselves until the next full ten components are finished. Yes, that's how it is! Jaakko would have added.

The atmosphere of pursuit and competition which surrounds all piece-work seems to invite semi-masochistic devices of the most neurotic type. Many workers who are tormented by the payment-by-results system are also afraid that time would pass much more slowly if they were on a monthly salary.

How innocent a part do all these conjurations play in excluding the present from life and putting work to flight? How innocent, how indispensable, how destructive are they? The answer to this seems to depend on what is at stake.

When temporary workers like myself glance at our watches and count the days, we are doing nothing more serious than what National Servicemen do when they mark off the time left to demob. We have something else ahead of us all the time. Another job, another life, *and we know that both of them are within our reach.* We toss one or two years of our lives into the kitty at LM and then withdraw. But many of the others will almost certainly spend all of their working lives at Midsommarkransen. Or at some other of the Group's factories in Sweden if the work at Midsommarkransen is transferred elsewhere. If they have been working for LM for ten years or more they seldom make any changes. What do they have to look forward to apart from the fact that it will soon be Friday again for the thousandth time?

A better job? Their prospects are reduced for each year they remain where they are.

A win on the football pool? Their prospects are even smaller there.

Wage increase? If they are over 45 they are more likely to get a wage reduction.

Further education? They should have thought of that earlier.

Reschooling? This future prospect seldom holds any enticing shimmer.

Retirement? Yes, many look forward to their retirement. Once they have celebrated their 50th birthday, retirement day is all that remains. And yet there are quite a few who fear that retirement will be the threshold to an empty room, a room where 'that bloody job' will be replaced by something even worse – idle loneliness. When *these* faithful toilers in the vineyard wish that the working day would come to an end as quickly as possible, there is nothing innocent in their wish. They have far too much at stake for that. Their entire working lives usually lie in the kitty. And when retirement approaches, it turns out that many of them want to stay on as long as they can, despite all – despite all!

As a rule, those who are younger satisfy themselves with shorter future perspectives and more modest stakes. But those who are younger are often cheated of their rewards when the longed-for future changes into the present. For it is not just the hopefully lengthy freedom, that mirage at the end of the working life, which entails so high a price that only a few still have the strength to harvest the fruits of the freedom. The short-term freedom which acts as a mirage at the end of each working day, a free evening, as the expression has it – can disappear in the same way.

Hour after hour, the younger piece-rate workers look forward to the moment when the bell will ring so that they can finally do whatever they want to do, and year after year the older hourly-wage earners look forward to the approach of their 65th birthday so that they, too, can do whatever they want to do – and the thought of everything they can do then helps both the younger and the older workers to keep their spirits up during the course of their work. But in order to be able to afford to do whatever they want to do and, at the same time, in order to pass the period of waiting, they are often forced to work so hard that when the gates are finally opened they are seldom capable of doing as they wish any longer.

When they finally have both time and money, they no longer have the energy required. They go home and fall asleep in front of the television set instead.

Both those who gamble on free evenings and those who gamble on retirement can be cheated of their prizes in much the same way as those who place their bets in a more literal sense on future dreams. I mean all those workers who try to keep the future constantly shimmering by backing horses or doing the football pools week after week – and by discussing all the horses and teams involved in the meantime. When they finally strike lucky, it frequently turns out that their wins scarcely exceed their stakes.

Free Saturdays and four weeks holiday a year are more reliable bets. Particularly the free Saturdays. Free Saturdays are probably the most popular reform implemented throughout the entire 20th century. Universal suffrage and supplementary pensions may be fine, but they cannot be compared to one whole day a week which is not succeeded by a working day, a *proper* holiday! When the five-day week was introduced, many lowly workers seemed to be able to 'afford', so to speak, to abandon their hopes with regard to week evenings and began consciously to sleep through them so as to be able to live it up all the more during the weekend, like bear cubs released from hibernation.

'Just wait till Friday, lad!'

And yet, when the present in the form of the working day and the working week remains a darkness which must be banished, the hopes which are linked to the weekend and the holidays are often so escalated that reality seldom lives up to them. The closer the free time comes, the more these expectations are mingled with anxiety. Anxiety because one has not made arrangements for the weekend, anxiety because one does not have anyone to go out with, anxiety because the long-planned journey will be a failure, anxiety because one may not have time to do the things one has postponed so long, anxiety because one's camping holiday will be filled with rain and discord instead of sun and companionship, anxiety because Nerves, Alcohol or Gloomy Thoughts may get a grip on one when one does not have a work bench to provide support.

In other words, if one takes a closer look at the sacred future, it shrinks and disappoints many of its worshippers. When the future becomes the present, it frequently turns out to be as grey as an ordinary working day.

And yet it never loses its sacredness.

A drenched industrial holiday has scarcely passed before the hope that at least the remaining holiday week will be better is nurtured. And a new working week has scarcely started after an unsuccessful weekend before the hope that the *next* weekend will be better is nurtured. And this goes on week after week, year after year. Why? The question of whether free time is unsuccessful or not may not, after all, be the most important. The most important is, perhaps, whether one's *expectations* for this free time can make daily work easier to put up with or not. If this is the case, and I think it is, one's dream of the future is more important than the future itself. In fact, the whole point of having a future seems to be that it never becomes the present.

Free time never appears as attractive and valuable as during working hours. Before it has started.

There is, of course, a limit to the number of disappointments a wage-earner's dreams of the future can stand. And there is a certain turnover on the stock exchange of the future at LM. Those who have staked considerable amounts on discotheques, football pools, Saturday drinking bouts or holiday trips for a number of years gradually begin to invest in more gilt-edged future securities instead. When they set their sights on building a house or a boat, when they study for upper-secondary school qualifications, when they devote themselves to associations or save money for a longer leave of absence, they frequently count on passing their leisure time in a more meaningful manner for several years. Or, at least, their disappointments will be more widely spaced out.

What seldom happens, on the other hand, is that disappointed future-dreamers address themselves to the present on the shop floor so as to try to extract some of the meaning and joy, which their free time so often cheats them of, from the reality around them. It is, after all, there, at work, that they spend by far the greater part of their waking lives. It is, after all, there, at work, that they are forced to expand most of their energy.

They never arrive at their leisure time thoroughly rested in the way they arrive at work.

But the working day and the working week seem to have been rejected from the beginning as quite impossible investment objects from the point of view of joy and meaning. Instead, the working day and the working week emerge as a sort of enormous, unchangeably gloomy burden of enforced dead time which one should push ahead of one and get rid of as soon as the 'bell of freedom' rings. Work does not seem to contain any enticing future.

Down on the lowest reaches of shop floor this manner of experiencing time seems to be so generally accepted that few regard it as destructive. 'The best working days' are those which come to an end in the quickest, easiest way.

The best *working* days.

'That's the way it is.'

'Of course you want that bloody clock to go.'

'Work is work, after all.'

'A workshop is a workshop.'

'Of course you live for your free time, what else is there to live for?'

'Work is something which just has to be done.'

'That's the way it is.'

Most of those who do semi-skilled work, machine supervision, transport work or store work – and this comprises by far the greatest majority of shop workers in the LM Group, particularly in the rural factories – seem to be relegated to such a low level of demand that they expect nothing more of the work they do here and now than that it finance their leisure time in the most pain-less way possible. As long as the sun drags itself across the sky at a reasonably acceptable pace, as long as the taximeter ticks, they are more or less satisfied. Perhaps they pin a few expectations on some of their needs, perhaps they pin a few expectations on the breaks.

But they seem to pin no expectations whatsoever on the actual work.

The very thought of putting up Horace's words as a motto on one of the shop walls at LM – CARPE DIEM! – seems so out of place as to be crazy.

They know of course, all these workers who comprise the majority, that there are tasks at LM too which can be experienced as so fascinating that those who carry them out seldom glance at their watches and even stay on after work without immediately demanding over-time compensation. They can see that lights always gleam in more than one office window when they them-selves are on the way home after a full evening of enforced over-time work. Out in the yard they sometimes see managers who step into their cars with bulging briefcases, and the briefcases seem to be full not of newly purchased liquor bottles but of voluntarily undertaken homework. Even in the workshop they have run into strange figures. Fitters and other professionally proud skilled workers who often use part of their lunch break to finish off a precision job; piece-work aces who become furious or desperate when the bell rings to mark the end of the day because they have not had time to do more than they have; instructors who have drawings in front of them even during the coffee break and not just so as to be promoted to foremen either.

They have seen all this. They see it daily. Highly qualified professionals are particularly plentiful at the main LM factory since the Group development work is carried out there.

But they also know that stimulating occupations like these

seldom occur in that part of the production where they themselves are active. There, only piece-rate jobs are available. And
for most of those who work in the LM workshop, it seems so self-
evident that the working day is there to be passed as quickly as
possible that they can scarcely imagine a situation in which they
would voluntarily work over-time or bring work home. If they
work over-time, they do so for the sake of the money only or
because their supervisor asks them too, and if they can be said
to bring their work home with them, they do so in a sense which
bears little evidence of any particular pleasure in the work and
even less of loyalty towards the company.

'Bring work home? Not on your life! Though there are a
number of things I *could* imagine taking home, of course', I have
heard someone who works at an inspection station, of all places,
say. 'A length of cable and a few screws can always come in
handy around the house.'

It seems so self-evident to most of these employees that the
working day is there to be passed as quickly as possible that they
seldom even think of the fact that *it could be* different. There are
constant complaints at LM workshops but seldom about this
particular aspect, seldom about the fact that there is something
wrong with the work itself. It is almost as though there were no
one to put the blame on here. It is almost as though a law of
nature prevailed.

'Work is work.'

'A factory is a factory.'

'That's the way it is.'

But the very fact that this way of experiencing working hours
is common entails a pretty crushing judgement on those who have
organized and distributed the jobs at LM. And not only at LM.
They have organized these tasks in such a way that those who
have to carry them out do not feel satisfied until the tasks have
come to an end, i.e. when the bell rings. They have organized
these tasks in such a way that those who have to carry them out
concentrate on getting through them as quickly as possible so
that they can go home.

Every day at 6 minutes past four the Low Block employees
rush as one man to clock out. Every day at 18 minutes past four,
the High Block employees rush as one man to clock out. Everyone seems to want to shake the dust of LM from their feet as fast

as possible, and no one ever tries to halt the flow by calling: We have only one life! What sort of madness is it to kill time instead of filling it with meaning? Not a single day can ever be relived!

Instead, each one of them searches silently and feverishly after his or her clock card.

When I say each individual, I am not forgetting that the workshop sector also contains those who devote themselves to their work and sometimes enjoy their work so much that the clock almost seems to race ahead. I have already mentioned the skilled workers, but numerous exceptions can also be found amongst the rank and file. Remarkable exceptions.

Interesting exceptions. Pathetic exceptions.

At LM, too, there are housewives who after many years of isolation in a suburban flat think it so marvellous to earn money of their own and to have workmates other than occasional neighbouring housewives that the lack of freedom and the constant repetition of semi-skilled work does not seem to affect them very much. At LM, too, there are those who long for clerical work to such an extent that their eyes light up with gratitude when they are finally granted a subordinate position in the dispatch department after many years of toil. At LM, too, there are handicapped employees who are so frightened of ending up in a sheltered workshop that they are happy to get even the simplest of store jobs as long as they are allowed to work amongst 'normal' people. At LM, too, there are immigrant workers who find it so fantastic that they can make more than 20 kronor an hour on piece-work that they ask for *nothing* more than to be allowed to pile up the money until it is enough for a new Volvo – a Volvo in which they leave LM for good with a screech of tyres and make a jubilant entrance into their Yugoslavian or Turkish home village after a few days. At LM, too, there are 'convicts' who prefer any sort of work to ending up in an institution again; single old people who gladly permit themselves to be degraded to the most menial tasks so as to postpone, at all costs, that final transport to the old people's home; mentally retarded who are sometimes so proud of managing a monotonous machine job that they do not seem to experience it as monotonous at all. At LM, too, there are work addicts, people who flee into their work in the same way as the majority flee into their leisure time simply because the workshop or the office comprises the only fixed point in a life otherwise filled with confusion or because getting stuck in and working until they drip with sweat, particularly on over-time, is the best way they know of getting away from drink, loneliness, family problems or overweight. At LM too, there are, finally, workers in simple occupations who do *not* belong to any group of outsiders and who do *not* have personal problems and who still like to work. Why? Perhaps because they live close by and have relatives and friends at work. Perhaps because they, like Jaakko, enjoy standing at the centre of the manufacturing industry and knowing that all of society is dependent on the products they help to manufacture. Perhaps because they, like the cleaning woman Desirée, have a cheerful disposition, an ability to see the positive side of everything, no matter what work they are given.

This minority of satisfied and pseudo-satisfied employees brighten up daily life for their more morose workmates, there is no doubt about that. And it is from them that the most spontaneous protests against the gloomy portrayals of industrial work in recent years have come.

'There must be something wrong with those who don't like working in a workshop.'

'It sounds pretty awful the way you describe it, but that drivel about leisure time shouldn't be taken too literally.'

'Sitting doing finishing work isn't exactly a vocation, but all types of work have to be done, and this is the one I'm used to doing.'

'No matter what they say, after fifteen years at the same place you begin to feel at home somehow.'

'Work in an office? Never! I want to work with my hands.'

'When you're tired in the evening, you know you've done something useful.'

'There is no getting away from toddling in to work every day, but on the other hand, it's no worse than sitting at home.'

'It seems to be *forbidden* to like industrial work nowadays.'

Remarks like this probably sound like music to the ears of management. And if the managers close their eyes and open their minds to dreams, they soon see a vast band of workers – perhaps even a majority – whose eyes glitter with job satisfaction.

But more than 240 workers, or 11% of the workshop labour force, are missing each day at LM. And LM recently had to introduce a year-long recruitment halt and call in the support of that ghost from the 1930s – unemployment – in order to get employee turnover down under the embarrassingly high figure of 50%.

A high rate of absence and rapid employee turnover do not exactly indicate that most workers are satisfied with the working conditions which are offered to them. An increased aversion to over-time, an increased tendency to apply for early retirement pension and sudden, long sick leaves due to 'nerve trouble' do not indicate this either. Silent and expensive protest actions of this type do not even indicate that most employees are mainly interested in money. After all, most of them earn less when they are ill, when they permit themselves to be retired early, when they refuse over-time or when they frequently change jobs.

Nevertheless, most seem to find it so important to flee from work that they are even willing to sacrifice earnings in order to do so at regular intervals.

From leisure-time demands to job demands

If one regards union work in the light of what I have said here and in the light of what Jaakko Stenius has said, a strange shadow falls over almost all the reform demands which the Swedish trade union movement has fought for during the 20th century.

The annual wage increases, the increasingly laboriously raised real wages, holiday compensation, over-time compensation, supplements for inconvenient working hours, weekend supplements, transfer grants, severance pay, etc. – all of these are undoubtedly and unreservedly appreciated by those who have benefited from them. Housewives, farmers and small businessmen do not form part of this group but the vast majority of those who sell their work for payment in Sweden do. The successful wage struggle has helped lift the working people out of the poverty, slums and undernourishment which still prevailed well into the 20th century. Tuberculosis has been eradicated, as have the cockroaches. Modern dwellings, comfortable clothes and fast cars have come instead. And yet: are not all these improvements remote from man as a worker, man as a human being who sits at his or her machine or works on his or her components? Are they not basically directed towards free time, away from work?

The eight-hour day, the five-day week, the statutory holiday, the shorter shifts, the lower retirement age – all of these are undoubtedly appreciated by everyone. The reduction in working hours has made it possible for all those, whose travelling distance to and from work has not increased at the same time, to relax during leisure hours and build up new strength, to devote time to their families, to cultivate personal interests and even to travel abroad. But are not these improvements, too, remarkably remote from man as a worker standing at a machine, sitting working on components? Are they not, in all essential respects, directed towards leisure time, a leisure time which is constantly expected to increase, away from work which is constantly expected to grow shorter?

Security in case of illness and accident, security during disputes, security in case of unemployment, security in case of compulsory transfers and security in old age – these, too, are social improvements which are undoubtedly appreciated by everyone They have made it possible to alleviate the old and well-founded worker's dread of falling ill, becoming unemployed or growing old just as they have alleviated the old and well-founded dread of becoming poor again. The knowledge that one belongs to a powerful and rich trade union, that financial support is available and that insurance money will be paid out if anything happens undoubtedly also contributes to increasing the feeling of security enjoyed by individuals even during working hours. And yet: are not these social improvements, too, remarkably remote from man as a worker, standing at a machine, or sitting working on components? The funds which have been built up are, after all, intended to aid men and women when they *cannot* work. As long as they work, they are simply expected to pay their dues to these funds.

Everyday union work, which aims at persuading workmates to undertake commissions of trust and to attend union meetings, to buy tickets in lotteries and to take part in study circles, to acquire occupational training and to fill in consultation forms, all this work is carried out at a range which is closer to man as a worker. The considerably more popular daily union work which consists of persuading management to build better changing rooms and to reduce queues at the medical centre, to improve induction and information, to introduce resting rooms in the departments, to improve toilet cleaning, to provide short-cuts to the dining-rooms, to provide more parking lots, nearby telephones, free laundering of working clothes, more coffee dispensers, etc., all this type of work is also carried on at a range which is closer to man as a worker. If these activities are successful they affect the workers favourably in their work, at least insofar as they no longer become bad tempered at the very thought of, for example, the changing rooms they have to use.

The only snag is that the workers must leave their work to partake of these benefits and to fulfil these union duties. Only in exceptional cases may union tasks entrusted to members be carried out during working hours. Union meetings and study circles may never be arranged during working hours. Books and forms may not lie about during working hours. Not even changing rooms, notice boards or rest rooms (which were non-existent at LM) may be visited during working hours. As a rule, the workers have to use the 9th hour which they spend at work without pay, the hour which must suffice for both breakfast (12 minutes) and lunch (48 minutes) and to queueing and moving in conjunction with these meals. 'May' is, of course, a flexible expression. Sometimes extra breaks can be taken. Sometimes one can wander around the workshop. But if the bosses turn a blind eye to this, the bloody carrot does not, that's for sure. Those who work on piece-rate, and the majority still work on piece-rate, suffer a drop in earnings the moment they leave their work bench. They cannot even go to the medical centre without clocking out.

So the gains are pretty poor here, too, for man as a worker standing at a machine or sitting working on components. The 'cultural' improvements also seem to be turned, in essential respects, towards leisure time away from work. Even comradeship on the job seems to be turned in the same direction; most of the employees work individually and can only hope for comradeship during the breaks. And job satisfaction is usually the first thing to suffer in the decisive trade union battles.

The wage struggle, reduced working hours and social security, these are the three major battle grounds, in that order, for the trade union struggle throughout the entire course of industrialism.

No, not thoughout the entire course. At the beginning a long fight was needed to establish the right to *form* trade unions, to take over the trade unions from the liberals, to force the employers to acknowledge the unions' right to negotiate and strike without immediately being replaced by blacklegs or being forced back by the army. A long and intensive fight. But since then – and, in some respects, even earlier – negotiations for higher wages, shorter working hours and certain of the security reforms have completely dominated union work. August Palm introduced his speech at the very first May 1 demonstration held by the labour movement in 1890, with the following words: 'Shorter working hours, higher wages, civil rights!' And he thus set the key for union agitation throughout the entire twentieth century, not only in Sweden and the capitalist world but also in Eastern Europe, in the socialist countries.

Material security for all – up until now this appears to have been the overshadowing union objective both in the east and the west. The USSR has managed not only to adopt the considerably more far-reaching motto 'work for all' but also to implement it. This is an important step forward, though one which is seldom given prominence, for the entire international labour movement. But at the same time the USSR, like so many other socialist countries, has promoted the basically misanthropic piece-work rule 'to each according to his *performance*' – and not according to his need – to a basic thesis in socialist trade unionism.

The struggle for higher wages and, consequently, economism and, consequently, materialism seems to have been given a self-evident position in the centre of trade unionism all over the world. In fact the very concept of a union struggle has been identified in many quarters with a wage struggle. A constant hullabaloo about percentage increments and small sums of money is the standard concept many people have of what union work consists of. The expression *agreement* negotiation is equated with the expression *wage* negotiation in Sweden, as though the wages one was paid for one's work were unquestionably more important than the work itself.

The agreement negotiations are now called 'the wage match' on Swedish television.

One may well wonder why both reformers and revolutionaries have concentrated to such an extreme degree on the wage struggle. One may well wonder about this even if one regards the wage struggle as important. One may well wonder about this even if one 'only' wants to question the sanctity and special position of the wage struggle. The reformers seem to be particularly powered by their conviction that a mixed-economy democracy requires a flourishing industry to finance reforms and that industry can only flourish if the consumers have considerable purchasing power – in other words what is important is to fill the workers' wage packets. The revolutionaries seem to be particularly powered by the conviction that the working class can only weaken the capitalist system by forcibly obtaining a constantly increasing wage share through negotiation or strike – in other words what is important for them, too, is to fill the workers' wage packets. The motives differ, the conclusion is the same. In fact, Sweden's largest Communist Party (VPK) carries on an even more intensive wage struggle than does the Labour Party (SAP). The further out one moves to the left the higher wage demands seem to become. I saw on one poster that the Trotskyists want 'everyone' to have *four* kronor more an hour and as soon as highly paid employee groups strike in a firm, the Maoists can be seen rushing enthusiastically to their support.

But reformists and revolutionaries of a more traditional type, who may disagree on many union matters, also seem to have a *common* driving power here. A striking number of the leaders in these groups have grown up in poverty and destitution themselves and have been roused to activity in politics and trade unionism when confronted with this destitution. August Palm and Joe Hill, Togliatti and Stalin, Gustav Möller and Arne Geijer, Hilding Hagberg and Sigurd Klockare – they differ in much but on this one point they have all been in agreement: the primary objective is to do away with poverty.

Or, to use Bert Brecht's words: 'First comes food and then come morals.'

And is it not true that food comes first? Clearly those who are hungry must first have enough to eat. Those who are hungry are capable of doing anything to get enough to eat. They are capable of stealing bread on Seskarö or attacking grain warehouses in Bengal. But how far above the starvation level does this rule apply? Is for example pudding more important than human dignity? Is owning a pedigree dog more important than the dignity of work? Is freedom in a house of one's own more important than freedom at work? Or do the old wage-struggle advocates still imagine that self-respect, the thirst for knowledge and political consciousness automatically arise in the workers as soon as their fridges are full?

It is first in recent years that a sudden and much-needed public debate has arisen on issues which directly concern man as a worker in his *work*: work environment, the right to direct and allocate work, industrial democracy, job satisfaction. For a long time, there was general and careful talk about joint works councils, consultation committees and self-managing groups as well as about mental health, but suddenly the striking miners put more weight into the debate by daring to place the word *human dignity* on the union agenda. The last time this was done was probably when Ernst Wigforss,* in his programme for industrial democracy in 1923, demanded 'a dignified human life not only during leisure time but also at work'.

But exactly 50 years later, in the summer of 1973, when the discussions on environment and democracy had already been going on for several years, the Trade Union 75-year jubilee publication 'Tvärsnitt' is issued (and a gratifyingly self-critical issue it is) and contains the following pungent summary by Bernt Schiller, the historian:

> It took more than 30 years for the combined trade union movements to obtain any influence whatsoever over dismissals. It took over 60 years before the right of employers to direct work was restricted. Paragraph 32 (the right to direct and allocate work) and industrial democracy have not been top-ranking issues within the trade union movements. Wage issues have been more important and will, in all likelihood, continue to be so.

'Wage issues have been more important and will, in all likelihood, continue to be so.' Since this can be said about the trade union movements in many industrial countries, both in the west and the east, the strange shadow which falls over almost all the reform demands put forward covers quite a large sector. In fact, it coves so large a sector, both geographically and politically, that it would be provincial to single out the Swedish trade union

---

* Ernst Wigforss, 1881–1977. Politician, linguist, writer; Minister of Finance, 1925–26, 1932–36, 1936–49; for many years regarded as the leading theoretician of the Swedish Social Democratic Party. (Trans.)

movement as responsible for it. The Confederation of Trade Unions and the various specialized confederations have, in the main, done what the trade union movements have done elsewhere, they have followed the same pattern and the same lines of action.

It is considerably more important to define the shadow and try to interpret its import. And the most easily discernible import would seem to be that those union demands which have been pushed to the fore decade after decade can mainly be regarded as *leisure-time demands*.

Not work demands but leisure-time demands.

If this is a reasonable interpretation, then something alarming has happened. The international trade union movement has, throughout this entire century, ignored or relegated to a subordinate position values and needs which must reasonably be regarded as quite fundamental for every working human being, no matter whether he or she sits on a tractor, in an overhead crane, at a kitchen table, in an office module, behind a counter or in front of a machine. I have mentioned several of these values and needs before, but it is high time we listed them in order:

> freedom at work
> the right of decision at work
> independence at work
> quality in work
> training opportunities at work
> a future at work
> variation in work
> responsibility at work
> the right to be undisturbed at work
> personal engagement in work
> meaning in work
> integration in work
> health at work
> companionship at work
> profit-sharing at work
> respect at work
> human dignity in work

Taken at a surface level, all of these values and needs can be compiled under the common heading 'job satisfaction'. Taken at a somewhat deeper level, they can be compiled under headings such as 'self-fulfilment at work' or 'culture at work'. And culture is something which the labour movement relegated to leisure time and to the Workers' Educational Association at an early stage instead of demanding that it be introduced at work places. I am convinced that the welcome public debate on a 'popular culture' is foredoomed to remain shallow or confined to leisure time as long as it ignores the manner in which working people find or are refused the right to find meaning, freedom and self-fulfilment in their work and at their work places. Perhaps culture at work is a prerequisite for culture during leisure time?

Many of these values applied without question to the farmers, smallholders and craftsmen who could, once upon a time, only be forced into the towns by sheer need and there formed the first generation of industrial workers together with destitute children and other paupers. That was precisely why they found it so difficult to move. As one of the workers at LM said of his grandparents: 'They were crofters and they could just about make ends meet, but they had freedom in those days. Now they are all sitting at LM and what sort of freedom do they have slaving here?'

Many of these values apply just as unquestionably to the farmers, small businessmen and craftsmen who have none of the benefits which the industrial workers have fought for and won – five-day week, contractual wage agreements, statutory holidays, etc. – but who still refuse to allow themselves to be proletarized until it is absolutely necessary. This is because they, too, know that they have access to work values which the industrial workers can only dream of, at least during working hours. But three quarters of the skilled factory workers in England who were interviewed in *The Affluent Worker* (Goldthorpe et al.) dream of starting something of their own, a workshop or a business, and many of the workers at LM devote a great deal of their leisure time to tinkering with their cars, painting their boats, building houses, sewing clothes, doing joinery work in the cellar or digging in their gardens – because *then* they feel their work has a meaning. Many of these values apply just as unquestionably to the numerous housewives and housemen who devote themselves full-time or part-time to taking care of children and households. I say apply 'unquestionably' because many people do not seem to realize the values involved until they lose them, for example when they are forced to take a job in an industry.

All ye who enter here, abandon hope.

As far as I know no agreement negotiation has yet devoted any attention to freedom, status, meaning and coherence in and at work. It is as though these qualities lay outside the *real* union work, the work which consists of negotiations and disputes (or at least threats of disputes). These values and needs can usually be glimpsed in little-known special agreements between the Employers' Federation and the Confederation of Trade Unions, in cooperation agreements about joint works councils, in the agreement on industrial health services, in the new rationalization agreement, etc. It is as though the design and organization of work consisted of collaboration issues on which agreement can easily be reached between the parties concerned. As though these work issues were not every bit as much issues of interest as wages and working hours ever have been!

These values are also frequently mentioned in anxious, though by no means binding, conversations in joint works councils or are investigated in jargon-packed publications from the council jointly set up by the Employers' Confederation, the Confederation of Trade Unions and the Central Organization of Salaried Employees to deal with collaboration issues. At best, they are made the subjects of state reports in which the labour sector has to make a joint proposal with one of the employer-supported parties (as was the case in Paragraph 32 or the environment report) and after a few years, at best, it is time for legislation in the Riksdag (as was the case in the Security of Employment Act or with regard to language tuition for immigrants).

But all of the work values are, in other words, placed outside the central union work. No dramatic initiatives, no night-time negotiations, no mediation commissions, no strike threats, no television cameras and no blazing headlines surround them.

If the individual industrial worker wants to gain respect and satisfaction in his or her work, in addition to whatever respect and satisfaction can be obtained from wages and piece-rates, he or she will have to try to gain it alone. If a worker goes to his union, he will be told that the union has its hands full with more pressing problems. If he goes to his revolutionary comrades, he will be told that these values cannot be gained within the framework of capitalism, and he will have to wait until the working class has seen to it that the means of production have passed into the right hands.

Without his help?

It must be difficult to convince this industrial worker that he and his workmates must carry out a revolution in order to participate in work values which not only farmers and small businessmen but also nursemaids, assistant nurses, agricultural workers and petrol station attendants often participate in already. Just as he does himself during his leisure time, down in his basement when he is not too tired. Without any revolution whatsoever. Almost as though it were a matter of self-evident rights. Which of course it is. And of course, it has not been possible, so far, to convince very many industrial workers of the necessity of revolution – at least not in this way.

In fact, this line of reasoning may become more defensible if it is turned the other way around: no work values, no independent workers – no revolution.

I am aware of the fact that many of those for whom the wage struggle is sacred – more sacred than working human beings? – regard the designation 'leisure-time demands' as offensive and contemptuous, and perhaps even reactionary. But the viewpoint which Jaakko Stenius indicated to me is so important that I shall have to take that risk. And not even the most faithful of wage strugglers can reasonably deny that the designation 'leisure-time demands' is quite adequate and realistic in essential respects. Higher wages and shorter working hours *are* two demands which are concerned with labour as a market product only; they have very little to do with the work values which the individual worker can experience.

Both of these demands are very much quantity demands, measurable in kronor and hours, and the value of the worker cannot be measured in this way since human values are qualities.

Both demands aim at increasing the yield which the worker gets *from* work and not to increasing the yield which the worker gets *in* his or her work.

Both demands aim at making the worker a more powerful consumer, not making the worker a more powerful producer.

The whole point of wage increases is that leisure time becomes richer, and the whole point of working hour reductions is that leisure time becomes longer so as to provide an opportunity to enjoy the riches which have been earned. Those who receive wage increases can, admittedly, enjoy these during working hours too, since their standing will be raised in the eyes of their supervisors and their comrades. Piece-rate workers in particular can congratulate themselves on not being a burden to anyone since they are paid for exactly what they produce, neither more nor less, and can feel that they do their bit each day. In addition, those who receive more leisure time may also have the satisfaction of knowing that this increases their possibilities of having the energy to deal with their work. But it is, nevertheless, mainly during leisure time – can anyone deny this? – that wages and free hours can be utilized to the full and can be converted into material sources of joy and social satisfaction.

Against this background, it seems almost symbolic that the reform which not only the political but also the union labour movement has fought hardest for during the entire post-war period and usually points to with particular pride as a success has been a reform aimed at securing the longest continuous leisure time in the workers' lives. I am thinking now of the general supplementary pensions scheme (ATP) and not of the excellent National Pension Insurance Funds which could easily be used to finance clear-cut work demands as well.

A strange shadow falls, as I have said earlier, when one regards union work from the point of view of man as a worker, standing at a machine or sitting working on components. And it is precisely there that the strangeness begins. After all, what perspective could lie closer at hand than that of working human beings when the movement leaders study union work and try to determine its functions? It is, after all, for working human beings that the trade union movement has been created. How, then, can it be that so many of the movement leaders do not seem even to have noticed the existence of the shadow? Have they grown used to studying union work from another perspective than that held by the workers? And if so, from which? Don't they see Jaakko Stenius or any of the others before them when they organize the increasingly centralized union work? Don't they see Jaroslav and Desirée the cleaning woman and Kent-Åke the apprentice? If not, who then *do* they see?

Perhaps not human beings at all but only wage-earner groups

and money factors? It is as though they had never sung 'Arbetets söner' ('The Sons of Labour') to the end or had forgotten the two last lines in the first verse:

> We demand the return of human dignity
> The struggle for justice, freedom and bread.

But they have, after all, sung it to the end many times, and they simply have forgotten these two lines. Even those who do not have the song off by heart usually remember these particular lines.

Does this mean that the trade union leaders have interpreted them in a different and more limited way than Henrik Menander must have intended when he wrote them, as though *bread* were the only important word and the rest were rhetorical?

Does this mean that it was only during their leisure time that the sons and daughters of labour were to demand human dignity – in the form of material welfare? Was it only during their leisure time that the sons and daughters of labour were to demand freedom – in the form of free Saturdays and paid holidays? In that case, the union leaders must have believed that human value, justice and freedom *at work* would automatically follow once a reasonably decent leisure-time standard had been achieved.

But nothing follows automatically, least of all if it is concerned with labour. Everything must be worked for. And this means that the most important goal for the trade union movement still remains to be implemented. 'Freedom is won where the struggle is held.' Not during leisure time but at work.

'True, we've given high priority to the basic material issues', I can hear an experienced trade union leader object. 'But this does not mean that we have forgotten all the issues connected with the value and dignity of work and with the worker as a producer. We have quite simply been forced to concentrate on the basic issues and put the others aside because what you call work demands have been out of our reach. That wretched Paragraph 32 has been an obstacle to us there. It's an obstacle to everything! But it's one we shall soon have removed.'

This is a justified and, to a certain extent, hope-inspiring defence. But it is, above all, an inadequate defence. In the first place, it is by no means self-evident that the basic union issues consist of wages, working hours and security alone. This would mean that the dignity and value of work was not a basic issue.

In the second place, the negotiating position and labour legislation would have been completely different today if the trade union movement had not, as Bernt Schiller points out, waited for 60 years before even *putting forward* demands on the right to direct and allocate work. If this had been done, it would be possible to negotiate about work organization, employee policy, machine investments and teamwork today and these would have been issues which could be negotiated just as self-evidently and with just as much backing as wage increment negotiations are. In the third place, the *employers* have not put these work issues 'aside' during the long period when the trade union movements have done so and this fact has, perhaps, been particularly disastrous for the workers.

It has only been possible to put through the long negotiable wage demands, working hour demands and security demands at the expense of a marked impairment of the value and dignity of work and of the worker as a producer. These assets have been reduced bit by bit, they have shrunk, been vandalized and, in many cases, been taken completely from the workers. This is particularly true of the post-war period when Swedish industry and commerce took the step from small-scale to large-scale operations and from national to international competition with all the difficult adjustments this entailed for the employees.

And this makes the problem more serious. I have already described the dehumanizing effects of machinery. But increases in real wages have, as Jaakko indicated, been accompanied by an equal number of evils as far as the value and dignity of work is concerned, e.g. a tremendous increase in the piece-work volume which has only been halted recently; a continuous increase in the work rate and, consequently, in risks to health; an increase in carelessness and injustice and, consequently, a reduction in the quality of the work combined with more carping and envy; a widening of the *local* wage gaps which are always most painful when they occur at close range; a marked increase in the transfer of human beings between various parts of the country, various lines of business, departments and work benches; an inhumanly rapid structural change which has forced many workers to make their way to impersonal large-scale work places with stiffer supervision, increased absence due to sickness, rapid employee turnover and a gaping hole where a sense of belonging had once been.

It is not money but solidarity which is the most sacred of all the issues within the trade union movement, the union leaders usually claim. And they refer to things like the organizational unity and the loyal wage policy. I, too, regard a loyal wage policy as an *essentially* progressive deviation from the struggle for maximum wages – take everything you can get straight across the line! – which enticed so many left-wing organizations to support high-income earner strikes both inside and outside the Confederation of Trade Unions. But if the trade unions led by the social democrats had really valued solidarity more than money they would not have combined this equalization policy with continued approval of the individual wage-setting methods which have contributed directly in so many companies to undermining the solidarity aimed for by the unions. The 'bloody carrot' has been permitted to drive home thousands of wedges between the workers. Above all, the Metalworkers' Union would not have signed the new merit-rating agreement which really does give the employers every possibility to deal individually with the workers from the wage point of view.

But it is not only the increases in real wages which have entailed unpleasant surprises for the workers. The supplements for inconvenient working hours have been accompanied by an increasingly rapid development of shift work, not least of the particularly unpopular shift forms which entail closely spaced changes between day work and night work with all the concomitant dangers to health and social isolation. At the same time, many enterprises have changed over to semi-continuous or continuous operations so as to get the most out of their expensive automatic machines. What a joy it must be to work the night shift during major holidays like Easter Sunday and Easter Monday when one knows that one is free on the very next ordinary working day! The machines have acquired power over working hours too. Holiday pay has been accompanied by (not to say openly bought at the expense of) diabolical qualification rules. A worker in the engineering industry can claim holiday pay if he works all of the preceding and all of the following working day. If he gets an hour off on the day before Christmas Eve or comes ten minutes too late on the day after Boxing Day he cannot claim any compensation for the intermediate holidays. Not even a bullying commanding officer could have designed a more diabolical carrot.

Every increase in over-time compensation has, at the same time, further reinforced the prevailing compulsion to say yes to all over-time work which does not exceed 150 hours per year. Free Saturdays have, as all employees know, been accompanied by an increased work load during the remainder of the working week and the fourth, separate holiday week is usually preceded or followed by extra busy days, as every office worker knows. Will the proposed fifth holiday week be any different?

Note that I have, as a rule, written 'accompanied by' and not 'bought at the expense of' since the causal connections are complicated in many of these cases. It may sometimes happen that a detested machine is installed or that operations are cut back precisely when a new wage agreement has been signed without these two occurrences being in any way connected. It may also sometimes happen that the Confederation of Trade Unions signs a collaboration agreement – such as the health-care agreement of 1967 or the rationalization agreement of 1972 – in which job satisfaction, health and other positive features are linked to efficiency and productivity without making it clear which of these values are to be regarded as superior or subordinate in difficult cases. This is a fatal lack of clarity as long as the employers' sector retains the sole right to lead work and can, thus, decide which factor is to carry the most weight.

What chance does job satisfaction then have against efficiency?

But one cannot make a general claim that the trade union movement, despite its single-minded support of the 'technical development has *consciously* sacrificed the pleasure and satisfaction a worker may get in his or her work in order to push through material demands. The problem does not quite lie on that level.

The Confederation of Trade Unions, the Labour Party (SAP) and the Communist Party (VPK) have always been able to claim that there has been economic room for all of the leisure-time demands they have made. Company profits have, quite simply, been so high that they could easily have financed the improvements – without the workers having to accept impairments in other respects. But everyone knows how inventive employers are when it comes to obtaining compensation once they have signed an agreement, even if their profits have been sky high. If they don't obtain part of the increased wage costs or the shortened working days in the form of increased prices for their products, capital exports or labour lay-off, they obtain it in the form of increased performance demands at work: higher machine speeds, more over-time, reduced piece-work rates, a lower number of workers in the highest wage group, increased shift work or the like. They can also obtain compensation by sabotaging agreement interpretations at local negotiations where the peace obligation and the employers' right to interpret agreements still tie the hands of the shop unions.

The employers always try to obtain compensation wherever they are allowed or wherever they can – and since it is precisely those values which are directly connected with work which are not negotiable, the employers have been particularly free to take out their compensation here and the trade union movement has not been able to prevent them.

That is where the problem lies: the trade union movement has not been able to prevent them. Or rather: the trade union movement has not seen to it that it has acquired the weapons necessary in order to prevent them. 'Wage issues have been more important and will, in all likelihood, continue to be so.'

At every negotiation, the delegations have been able to compromise between wage demands, working-hour demands and security demands and have put most of the weight behind general wage increases or low-income group increments on one occasion so as to be able to concentrate on a reduction of night-shift hours – as though the *length* of the working hours were one of the more important problems facing the shift workers. But it has only been possible to compromise between the negotiable demands and, thus, protect them to a passable degree against attack. I say and mean 'to a passable degree' because price increases have not exactly been brought under control nor have journeys to and from work. But it has not been possible to defend or use the demands concerning the work itself as a compromise argument even passably since most of these demands are covered by the right to direct and allocate work. The unilateral right enjoyed by management to organize, arrange, mechanize, automate, distribute, take apart, check and transfer both work and workers as they please is still in force today – and it is precisely this advantage which the employers have been able to utilize.

They have, so to speak, agreed to improve the conditions of

the workers during leisure time by retaining the right to impair their conditions at work. They have agreed to reinforce the position of the workers as consumers – and very willingly, too, since the workers can then afford to buy industrial products such as telephones – by retaining the right to impair their position as producers.

The work itself has always lacked trade union protection. I'm sorry to be going on like this, but the fact is undeniably remarkable: the work itself has always lacked trade union protection. The work has remained the remotely located, unilluminated merry-go-round which has always run at a loss since all the union investments have been concentrated on the centrally located, neon-lighted and headline-capturing leisure-time swings.

Compare the number of economists and wage experts employed by the trade unions with the number of sociologists, industrial physicians, mechanical engineers, building engineers, architects, and psychologists and compare what the wage negotiations usually cost with what the experiments in industrial democracy have been permitted to cost.

It is easier to see what the difference between negotiable and non-negotiable issues means in reality if one imagines, for a moment, that the *working-hour issues* were granted the same union status as the *work issues*. If they were, we should probably have holiday legislation with as many loopholes and escape clauses as the labour welfare legislation contains today. Just as many 'as far as possible' and 'wherever it may be deemed necessary' qualifications. A state commission would now be at work discussing various methods for abolishing the ten-hour day without impairing the competitiveness of the companies at the same time; a final report would be promised in time for the 1979 election. A collaboration agreement between the Employers' Confederation and the Confederation of Trade Unions would have established the fact that the parties have common interests in all essential respects with regard to the length and organization of working hours, that it should be possible to solve the problem in a spirit of cooperation and that the five-day week should be adopted as a rule, that over-time work should not be arranged during nights and Sundays 'as far as possible' but that efficiency requirements must 'wherever it may be deemed necessary' be given precedence over the rules. How otherwise can

FROM LEISURE-TIME DEMANDS TO JOB DEMANDS   143

exports be kept up and provide the economic room needed for
the reforms of a strong society?

In practice, it would be possible to obtain compensation for
the costs entailed in each wage increase and in each security
reform by means of increases in working hours – just as they
are compensated for today by means of impaired working conditions.

Or just imagine that a battalion of foot soldiers is let loose on
an open plain without support in the form of aircraft, armour,
artillery or even machine-guns. Ordinary privates, recruits with
submachine-guns. The majority is sacrificed and only the strong,
the fast, the daring and the young survive, in other words those
who have always been lucky and managed best in every situation
in almost every type of society. But the trade union movement
was not created once upon a time to protect *that* particular
minority. Wasn't the trade union movement created, instead, so
that the majority – and the *weak* minority – would not be mown
down or wounded out on the disloyal plain? But it is precisely
out there, and precisely in their work, that the workers still lack
the right of decision, the right of veto, the right of strike and the
right to negotiate in most issues, the right to move freely, the
right to agitate, the right to refuse over-time and the right to
refuse to carry out dangerous jobs. They lack all the union and
political fire support which is required in the fight for meaningful
work and for human dignity in work places.

It is only at home in their flats or their houses that they enjoy
all these rights. At home when they have fallen asleep and left
their rights behind them.

A strong and active trade union movement which has fought
successfully for 75 years to improve the conditions of the workers
and has contributed actively to providing them with a material
standard which may be the highest in the world – this is the
bright picture of the Confederation of Trade Unions which one
gets as long as one confine's one's view to the central leisure-time
demands. A weak and passive trade union movement which has
not dared to question the unilateral right of the employers to
direct and allocate work during its first half century of activity
but has, on the contrary, contributed to reinforcing this right and
which has managed to nibble so little at the edges of Paragraph
32, the industrial peace obligation, the piece-work system and the

authoritarian management that the value and dignity of work has been impaired step by step and the worker has been deprived, step by step, of his position as a producer. This is the gloomy counter-picture one gets of the Confederation of Trade Unions if one turns one's gaze towards the central work demands.

It was not until this distortion emerged in all its glaring clarity that I myself completely understood the contradiction which has characterized the reaction of many trade unionists to the critical portrayals of industry which I and others have put forward.

On the one hand, most of them agree that the industrial workers have seen their working conditions deteriorate markedly in many ways, not least since the end of the 1940s when the time-and-motion studies, the supervision and the rejection of workers started seriously and the pace began to become accelerated. On the other hand, they claim forcefully that the union work carried out during the same period has shown considerable success. One reform has followed closely on another and things look very promising indeed for the trade union movement as long as its work can be continued, step by step, without being disturbed by wildcat strikes and the like.

Major successes for the trade union movement and major defeats at the same time for the workers – I found it impossible to get this to add up at the beginning. But the answer is that the trade unionists think only of the trade union contributions made with regard to wages, leisure time and security. When they, at the same time, deprecate the deteriorations which have occurred, they do so honestly but in an odd way as though these deteriorations really did not have very much to do with trade union work. The workers' situation has deteriorated at work but has been improved with regard to union matters.

To define 'union matters' in this way so that the work itself is not covered by the definition is *one way* of contributing to the flight from work. And the question arises of whether the trade union movement must not, paradoxically, be included amongst the organizers of this flight.

A well-nourished population which associates welfare, standard happiness, status, companionship and wealth with a high rate of consumption of industrial products provides the best life insurance for the employers. After all, if they cannot sell their products they will be ruined. The insurance premiums have cost thousands of millions of kronor, not least in the form of advertising financed by the consumers. But the trade union movement has also permitted its members to be weakened as producers and has confined itself to reinforcing them as consumers. Why?

It has always been in the interest of the governing labour movement to ensure that Sweden has an efficient industry and large export revenues so that the major social reform projects can be financed. Consequently, the social democrats have agreed to rationalizations, the piece-work system, the closing down of factories, population transfers, large-scale operations and other phenomena which increase the cash inflow to the State funds. At the same time, the work within the social democratic movement has been allocated in such a way that the party has, for the most part, dealt with the attractive tasks which are connected with the dream of a 'people's home',* the tasks associated with social policy, with full employment, and a considerable proportion of security issues – *inter alia* so as to win the elections – while the trade union movement has been directed, in the main, towards material issues such as wages and working hours. This means that the governing Social Democratic Party has told the Confederation of Trade Unions: agree to all the changes which increase industrial productivity and implement the wage struggle at the same time in such a way that your members will be able to afford to purchase the products manufactured by industry so that we can create a society fit for human beings. Or, in other words: the faster the workers wear themselves out the faster we shall have implemented the people's home here. The governing party says the same thing to the electors, although seldom straight out: the more you eat, drink, smoke and so on, the sooner we shall be able to afford to push through the dental-care reform!

The snag is that neither the employers nor the labour movement have dared put their trust in the productive forces inherent in the value and dignity of work and in the capacity for initiative of working human beings. They have associated efficiency with technical development and with larger production units. They have put their trust more in machines than in human beings. They have not dared believe that a human being, given encouragement and participation, can move mountains, whether he or

* See footnote, page 65. (Trans.)

she be 16 or 75 years of age. The trade union movement has also forced less profitable enterprises to close down in the name of a loyal wage policy – without even considering the fact that a more meaningful mode of work and the right of co-determination could have made many of these enterprises profitable!

Above all, none of the parties on the labour market has dared believe that anything other than material advantages, in the form of money and increased welfare outside of work, might attract and persuade the workers to work better and produce more. Not even the trade union has dared put its trust in this.

Bearing this in mind, it is easy to understand why many people reacted so vehemently and in such a hurt manner when I wrote earlier about prejudices concerning the working class. Far from appearing self-evident, it seems to be deeply disturbing to be reminded that the working class consists of individuals and that all workers are human beings with human needs – when one's every action shows that one does not regard them in this light. The employers have seen the workers as production factors or as one-armed bandits, the trade union movement has seen them as wage groups or wage categories. And they have both acted in accordance with their respective points of view.

Consequently, it is scarcely surprising that the workers' protests remain individual protests. Consequently, it is scarcely surprising that each worker who still persists in believing 'not on bread alone' feels abandoned. He has nowhere to turn. If he approaches management and asks to be allowed to decide over his own work, he will be told that his supervisors and the machines have been entrusted with that task for him, but that he should not let this get him down since he can, by serving a machine, earn more after a week's practice than he could as an independent skilled worker after years of difficult training. If he approaches his trade union and asks for more meaningful work, he will be told that there is no stopping technical development, but that he should not let this get him down since he can soon count on wage increases and on having a fifth holiday week.

And as a result he flees into his leisure time. As a result he, too, becomes an economist or tries to become one or pretends to become one. He concentrates on earning as much as possible, stops going to union meetings, begins to grow careless in his work, transfers all his non-economic hopes to his leisure time, longs ever more intensely for the end of the working week and hurries home to his family with bursting supermarket bags, 'on bread alone', 'on bread alone'.

In order to consolidate his newly acquired materialism, he becomes, perhaps, one of those fast workers, piece-rate stars and drifters who are, according to Jaakko, becoming more and more common in the workshops, by letting the 'bloody carrot' set the tone. 'Why, don't they concentrate the working-hour reductions to Fridays?' he begins to say. 'Why do only the low-income groups get an increase and not us?' he begins to say. 'Why don't they cut the lunch break in half so we can get home earlier?' he begins to say. 'This year we'd better get 15%, otherwise we're going on strike', he begins to say. And most spontaneous strikes have, right enough, been wage strikes.

In the meantime he sits at home and plays 'the accordion to ease the aches in his soul', as Helmer Grundström has put it. Unless, of course, he needs stronger medicine to forget work: complicated football pools systems, nerve pills, intensive participation in the Hammarby supporters club, constant standard improvements at home, pop music, alcohol, dogged and constant tidying up in the garden, holy roller religion or, perhaps, bingo. I do *not* mean glancing through the paper, getting a little tight now and then, sitting half-passively around the telly, all of which are entertainments which can accompany even the most meaningful work. But the more drastic or narcotic attempts at flight – don't they indicate that the leisure-time culture is doomed to a lowly position as long as the work culture has a lowly position? The results are determined by the activities to which one devotes the best of one's strength. But even these attempts at flight can, at the same time, be regarded in a more positive light. They too are protests, sick expressions of a healthy need – and the expressions *could* have been as healthy and as common as the need if the trade union movements and the labour parties had not turned their gaze in a different direction.

'Aching souls' seem, at any rate, to be immune to even the most powerful anaesthetics.

The situation would have been simpler if the parties on the labour market had been the only ones to encourage the workers to turn their backs on work and concentrate on their leisure time. But this leisure-time materialism is so widespread and well-established nowadays that the parties – or at least the trade union movement – have plenty of scapegoats to put the blame on.

If, for example, one raises one's gaze a little, one can see those authorities who decide where different sorts of buildings and institutions are to be located in Sweden today. When LM Ericsson moved out from central Stockholm to Telefonplan 35 years ago, the management ensured that dwellings and day nurseries were provided around the new factory to a reasonable extent and the municipality supplemented these with a post office, a library and a youth centre.

In those days there were, evidently, people who could plan. Work and leisure time were neighbours.

But the housing areas and the social institutions which have been built in the Stockholm region since then have not been built in the vicinity of Telefonplan or similar industrial areas but in the suburbs which *lack* major work places, and the only new buildings which have been constructed around Telefonplan are factories and offices of the same type which lay there before. The same thing again and again instead of planning. Those who work at LM today live somewhere else, they fetch their children from nurseries which lie somewhere else, they take their exercise somewhere else, they take further-education courses somewhere else, they shop somewhere else, they amuse themselves somewhere else – and this seems to be the case in most of the large municipalities all over Sweden.

Work places by themselves and housing areas by themselves, often spaced miles apart. Work by itself and leisure time by itself, because that is what the landlords and planning directors have determined. So even dwelling houses, service facilities and the very trees which grow out of the ground all participate nowadays in the flight from work. Take a look at the factory areas along the road to Södertälje! It is almost as though the industrial environment were infected with a plague – which, of course, it becomes when factories are isolated like this.

But the leisure-time materialism seems to have infected the language we use too, not the least the political language.

I have already mentioned the catchwords 'progress' and 'development' but giving 'priority to human beings' is scarcely better. Because if this catchword is to tally with reality during the last forty years in Sweden, its scope must immediately be reduced by at least 50% – priority has been granted to *half* of each human being and not even the more important half. It has been granted to leisure-time man and not to working man. To man as a consumer and not to man as a producer. Or take the phrase which says that 'things have improved for the vast majority of us in Sweden during the 20th century'. One is expected to agree with this, if one is not to risk being dismissed as grumpy and unreasonable in one's social criticism. And should one dare as much as breathe a word that money and social security are not everything in life, one risks running into an uppercut like this, particularly if one is a poet or a journalist:

> All talk of the futility of wealth, of the minor significance of material advantages, of happiness as being independent of all external things, of the low, earthbound aims of a programme which gives priority to the abolishment of poverty and to a more equal distribution of welfare, all of this preaching from certain groups of the priests and poets, philosophers and journalists of the wealthy and the flourishing is foredoomed due to its own lack of honesty. No one believes this creed to be serious.

These are the words of Ernst Wigforss, PhD (in the *Arbetarrörelsens Årsbok 1971,* * p. 17), and there is no doubt that they contain an important truth. But the question still remains: is it so completely self-evident that 'much better' *must* mean material welfare and social security – and not, for example, freedom, equality and brotherhood? Or human digntiy, culture and power? Wigforss has put the question himself. The headline above the words I have just quoted is 'Not on bread alone'.

Or take an expression like 'immediate requirements' which is constantly used in socialist debate. Why should it be that immediate requirements can only consist of such extremely palpable things as higher wages, shorter shifts and better work environment? Or the right to local strikes, to take a more militant example? There is no reason why this should be, as far as I can see. But it is precisely palpable features of this type which are always said to be immediate requirements while larger or less easily

* The Labour Movement Year Book.

defined requirements are usually postponed, even if their inclusion on today's agenda is just as important or even more important. Are such rights as the right to produce and the right to a form of work which befits man's dignity inadequate as immediate requirements? Is it too early to make such requirements today? Should we wait and not include them on the agenda until computer-controlled fascism has taken over?

Or take such common value-words as 'wealth', 'living standards', 'democracy'.

A Swede who visits a village in Turkey or in some similar agricultural land in the southern hemisphere may well express his surprise, on returning home, at having found so much joy and satisfaction amongst the villagers there. 'I could scarcely believe my eyes, but despite the fact that we were in a poor, developing country with a low standard of living and an anti-democratic régime, we found a surprising amount of hospitality, vitality, humanity and even work satisfaction in these villages.' One can hear such reports in these astonished tones. Astonished and almost anxious because people might think one had adopted the old slavedriver mentality of the Boers about the 'happy savage'. Or that one might have forgotten the political prisoners in the country.

But as soon as these general evaluations are given a different meaning than their material meaning, the visitor may begin to regard the satisfaction and pleasure of the villagers as less paradoxical. It may suddenly occur to him that many of the villagers are happy because they are, in essential respects, rich; because they enjoy, in essential respects, a high standard of living; and, because they have access, in essential respects, to democratic values even if their houses are tumbledown, their food monotonous, their women oppressed and their country lousy with colonels. In the toil and companionship of their work, when they till the earth or cultivate the forest, when they fish or build, they may well enjoy advantages denied many materially well-off Swedes. They are often permitted to carry out a whole job; they are often permitted to work in their own way and at their own pace; they are often permitted to carry out a job together with friends and relatives instead of with foremen and strangers; they are often permitted to regard the work as theirs; and they are almost always permitted to see the final result. Much as crofters and smallholders were permitted to do, in the midst of oppression, in Sweden. Is this poverty, is this underdevelopment? Yes, from the economic and industrial points of view. But from the human point of view? From the human point of view, the technically advanced work carried out at Midsommarkransen seems considerably more impoverished and more underdeveloped.

As far as work is concerned, the developing countries would seem to lie in the northern hemisphere.

There is much talk today about the importance of extending and deepening the concept of 'democracy' just as there is of the importance of orienting the concept 'standard of living' towards 'quality of life'. Excellent. But as soon as a child or a foreigner puts the question, the unhesitating answer is: Sweden is a democracy and the Swedish living standard is high. It is as though the daily dictatorship of work had nothing to do with the democratic status of the country, as though the laborious life spent at work had nothing to do with the standard enjoyed by the citizens. It is only the more or less exhausted leisure-time life which is counted as far as this standard is concerned.

The leisure-time fixation seems to have obtained so deep a grip on the language used in public debates in Sweden that even the most serious of debaters appears to forget the existence and possibilities of work. 'We must reduce working hours considerably so that people will have time and energy for joint and individual decision-making', writes one of these debaters. 'One can't devote all one's life to working, one must have time for living too', writes another. In other words, it is quite out of the question that joint and individual decisions could be made during working hours (and thus provide many workers with more energy for decision-making during their leisure time, too). It is equally clearly out of the question that one might be able to 'live' during working hours.

What deeper shadow could fall over work?

When work and leisure time are relegated to different worlds and when both sides try to get over this divorce by developing their differences only, then working human beings are invited to split themselves in two.

One half, which lives as long as the sun is up, is offered a minimum of freedom, variation, self-fulfilment, right of determination, status and peace, and this half is expected to accomplish a maximum of work. The other half, which is born like the trolls of old when the sun goes down and which dies when the sun comes up, is offered everything it might ask – variation, self-fulfilment, right of determination, status and peace, and this half is not expected to accomplish anything.

If only it were the other way around!

If only it were the free, self-fulfilled, influential, respected and peace-filled half which were expected to accomplish a maximum of work! If, at least, it were the thoroughly rested half which was offered freedom, variation, self-fulfilment, the right of determination, status and peace so that it could enjoy all these riches!

But things are not like that. Nor is it easy to split one's self in two. If a human being lives day after day and year after year in a work environment where the decision-making process is highly centralized, where everyone talks about money, where both management and the union are almost completely male-dominated and where no one who has a say in anything ever asks him for his opinion, for what he thinks and what he knows – then a great deal is going to be required if this human being is to be able to give expression to his suppressed democratic needs during leisure time, to practise equality between the sexes at home, to develop his self-respect without purchasing things to do so and, finally, to use his brain to think and learn things with. Instead, he comes home tired from work and easily falls into an authoritarian manner, into status consumption, traditional sex roles and idle reading.

Obviously not all industrial workers fall into this pattern. But even those who enjoy the benefits of influence, meaning, companionship and variation in their private lives, i.e. during their leisure time, seldom if ever transfer such obvious demands to their working hours.

Personnel department interview

'Department Vt 32 Olovsson, here we have it...Olovsson...'
'Märta.'
'Olovsson, Märta. Exactly. How long have you been working here at Midsommarkransen?'
'For 24 years.'
'Are you married?'
'Yes.'
'And your husband also works within the LM Group?'
'Yes, he's an inspector at Gröndal.'
'And you work on wiring and soldering work here at the main factory?'
'Yes.'
'And where do you live?'
'In Salem.'
'Salem?'
'That's south of Södertälje. At Botkyrka.'
'So you travel by car?'
'Yes, it's a little too far to the train.'
'How many people are included in your household?'
'Five. We have three children.'
'Has the household consisted of the same people all the time?'
'No, to begin with there was only my husband and myself.'
'And you haven't had any turnover in the household since then?'
'Turnover?'
'Yes, turnover of people.'
'Good heavens, no.'

'How old are the children?'

'The girl is eighteen and the boys are thirteen and eleven.'

'And they've lived with you ever since they were born?'

'Of course.'

'They must like living there then?'

'They don't exactly have much of a choice.'

'But surely there are other families in Salem?'

'They can't very well live with them.'

'You mean there aren't any vacancies there?'

'Oh, you mean...No, the boys are too small to work and the girl is still studying.'

'I was thinking of vacant positions for children – parents without children or parents with only one child. After all, you have three. If you get rid of your sons you can reduce your household costs.'

'We're not thinking of farming out any of our children!'

'And no other children have applied to join your household during the years which have passed?'

'What children do you mean?'

'A million people move between various work places in Sweden each year, but the children in Salem seem to be as settled as faithful old servants.'

'Most people have moved in recently. We ourselves lived at Hägerstensåsen when the children were small.'

'Then you had a shorter distance to travel to work?'

'Yes, but our flat was too small.'

'And the children moved with you to Salem?'

'One has to take some responsibility for one's children!'

'Do you rent a flat in Salem too?'

'Yes.'

'How many square metres is it?'

'Ninety, I think.'

'That scarcely leaves room for any partitions?'

'We have four rooms, a bathroom and a kitchen.'

'Five room units in ninety square metres, six including the bathroom...a fair amount of the living area must be occupied by walls and doors then?'

'The flat is fairly sensibly laid out.'

'Do you have separate toilet partitions in the bathroom too?'

'No, we have a separate toilet.'

'In other words, seven rooms. But why do you have all these walls and doors?'

'They were there when we moved in. One can't go around pulling down walls.'

'But if you were allowed to do as you wished?'

'In that case we'd remove a lot of fiddle-faddle that only increases the rent, the bidet and the parquet flooring, the teak boarding...maybe the freezer too. But we certainly wouldn't remove any rooms or doors. We don't want cooking smells all over the flat, and my husband and I want to be able to have our bedroom to ourselves. Our daughter needs a quiet corner when she's studying. And if we couldn't close the door to the boys' room when they're playing pop music on the radio, we'd never have a moment's peace.'

'When your sons play pop music loudly, do you usually have wadding or muffs over your ears?'

'We tell them to turn it down or else we close their door and close our own as well. You can't have too many doors in a flat with teenagers.'

'But a larger open space would surely provide far better possibilities for being together than a rigidly divided set of rooms with a lot of partitions. Have you thought of that?'

'That'd be like living in a gymnasium. Not like a home at all. After all, we moved to Salem to get a four-room flat.'

'But isn't it difficult to keep an eye on the children when you don't have clear visibility throughout the flat?'

'They come out if anything happens.'

'But if an accident should occur?'

'They'll soon make themselves heard. I usually only get worried when they're completely quiet.'

'You seem to have a great deal of trust in your children?'

'Just now it sounded as though all we did was keep them closed in.'

'You misunderstood me. I was advocating a more open way of life with freer spaces, but one must remember the control aspects too.'

'One can't keep an eye on them all the time. And I don't think one needs to either now that they're not small any longer. Sometimes they want to be by themselves, just like my husband and I do.'

'But if your sons damage the fittings and fixtures surely it is you who'll have to pay for it.'

'Yes, the boys don't have any money of their own. But we haven't brought them up to act like hooligans, thank heavens.'

'When you decided to have children, was it the labour requirements in the home, the labour requirements in industry or your own security in old age which formed the basis for your decision?'

'We simply wanted to have children.'

'Wanted to have?'

'Most people who get married want to have children.'

'You had no economic motives at all?'

'No, if we had we wouldn't have had any children. The children's allowance doesn't go far.'

'So your children run at a loss?'

'You could put it that way.'

'Don't you get any returns from them at all?'

'Of course we do.'

'I mean in domestic work?'

'Oh! Well, our daughter helps out quite a lot; she shops, washes, waters the flowers. . .sometimes she fixes spicy salads that my husband is a little suspicious about. But the boys don't go in for household work so much.'

'Then they really are a burden to you?'

'We don't look at it that way.'

'But objectively speaking they are, aren't they?'

'They do the best they can.'

'But not even the girl can repay you in work for what you spend on her in the form of rent, food, clothes, etc.?'

'No, not as long as she's studying.'

'Was it a realization of this fact that made you wait for five years before you had your sons?'

'We needed to save money for a few years so that I'd be able to afford to stay at home while the boys were small.'

'Now I understand you better. After all, marriage is an economic association, too, no matter how much one might wish that emotions alone prevailed. Did your husband have a fixed income at the time of your marriage?'

'Yes, otherwise we probably wouldn't have been able to afford to get married.'

'So it was in order to obtain economic security that you married?'

'No, I had an income of my own then.'

'Did your husband-to-be have a personal fortune?'

'He didn't even have a post office savings book.'

'But why did you marry him then?'

'I liked him.'

'Didn't he have any economic advantages to gain from marrying you either? A dowry for example?'

'I had a secretaire that my grandmother left me. But I don't imagine it was because of the secretaire that he married me.'

'So the two of you had to buy most of your furniture when you began to live together?'

'Yes, bit by bit.'

'Which interior decorator did you employ when setting up your home?'

'We couldn't afford anything like that.'

'But you must have consulted someone when planning your purchases. Otherwise one can easily be cheated.'

'The shop assistants did a lot of talking, of course, but we had a pretty good idea of what we wanted.'

'Perhaps one of you has home furnishing as a hobby?'

'My husband does a little joinery so he knows the difference between proper furniture and rubbish at least. But we bought things we liked ourselves. There isn't really so much to choose from if you only have your wage to go on.'

'But you must have had some help with the furnishing?'

'My mother-in-law had a fair number of suggestions. And my mother helped me to sew the curtains. But we decided most of it ourselves, my husband and I. And this last time we moved, our daughter had a say in it too.'

'So your daughter participated in the decision-making when you last moved?'

'Yes, she had a lot of good suggestions.'

'But she doesn't bring in any money to the household, does she?'

'She has a right to her say anyway, doesn't she?'

'Is it interior decoration she's studying?'

'No, she's going to business school.'

'But the usual procedure, surely, in many sectors where we

ourselves are not specialists is that we allow experts to make the decisions if everything is to function correctly. I assume, for example, that you did not carry out the electrical installation work yourselves in your new flat?'

'No, of course not. That was all done in advance. But furnishing is more a question of taste and opinion.'

'Yes, that's precisely what I mean. An interior decorator has a more highly developed sense of taste than others.'

'I still think that those who live in the flat should be given the final say. Otherwise it'd be like living in an hotel.'

'Did your sons also participate in the decision-making process?'

'All they were interested in was their own room.'

'And were their wishes met there too?'

'Well, I'm certainly not the one who put up all those football teams and fan-club pictures that they've filled the walls with!'

'But you are surely in a position to have these things removed?'

'The boys would just get sour. And if they get sour they go out more often. And if they go out more often they help less.'

'That's interesting. You mean that your children feel a greater responsibility if they are given more of a say?'

'Of course.'

'Very interesting. Do you have curtains in all the rooms?'

'Yes, except in the bathroom.'

'Wouldn't it be more practical with venetian blinds or with completely uncovered window areas? Curtains always block off some of the light.'

'We think it's more cosy with curtains.'

'Cosy?'

'Yes.'

'Did you have to buy new furniture and fittings when you moved to Salem too?'

'No, we inherited some things from my father. My mother doesn't need so much in the pensioners' home, she only has one room there.'

'A cheap alternative for the living-room would, of course, be a long table where the members of the family could sit on Saturdays and work at their various hobbies. One could have space-saving wooden chairs with adjustable back supports along the table. Have you considered this alternative?'

'We may be old-fashioned, but we don't want to sit in a row at home. We like to have the seating a little less rigid, if you know what I mean. So we have a sofa with a couple of armchairs, a large carpet, a few stools my husband has made and a few cushions on the floor.'

'I see.'

'And we have a secretaire, a few plants and a bookcase with knick-knacks and that. The television set is placed there too.'

'Don't you have any books in the bookcase?'

'It's not exactly crowded with them.'

'Don't you have any wooden boxes to sit on?'

'We're not as poor as all that.'

'When you watch television, do you each sit on a separate stool?'

'The boys sit pretty well anywhere when they are not out running about. But my husband and I like to sit a little more comfortably. One needs to relax after work.'

'When your husband feels dizzy or unusually exhausted after work, does he leave the home and take a seat in the nearest doctor's waiting room?'

'That'd only make him worse. He usually stretches out on the bed instead. So do I. That usually helps.'

'So you don't need any qualified doctors?'

'Well, my husband usually visits one because of his back.'

'Do you have any communal activities during your leisure time?'

'If there's anything good on telly, everyone watches it. If it's a nature programme, the neighbours sometimes come in too, they haven't got colour television. On Sundays we usually take a spin in the car or visit relatives. Sometimes we play cards, and everyone joins in then except our daughter.'

'Why doesn't she join in?'

'She thinks card games are silly.'

'And you accept that?'

'We can't very well force her; it wouldn't be much fun playing then. When we eat, we're usually all together. Meal-times together, that's one thing my husband is strict about. Except when he's doing over-time, of course.'

'Do you eat in the kitchen then?'

'Yes, most of the time.'

'Do you have room for two tables there?'

'What would we want that for?'

'So you mean that family members with clean clothes eat at the same table as family members with dirty clothes?'

'We're not so fussy about that. There's only the five of us. Or six, when my mum is there.'

'Didn't you say she lived in a pensioners' home?'

'Yes, but she can't sit there all the time. And sometimes she sleeps at our place over weekends.'

'So you have a guest room too?'

'Our daughter usually stays with her fiancé over the weekends, so her room is often empty.'

'Does your mother pay per night when she sleeps in your home?'

'I can't very well ask my own mother to pay! Besides, she gives a hand, she babysits and that. She's very attached to the younger boy.'

'If I've understood this correctly, you are in charge on the catering side?'

'You might put it that way, perhaps.'

'Has a decision been reached on that?'

'Not that I know of.'

'But how did you arrive at the division of labour you apply?'

'It just turned out that way. My husband is rather lost in the kitchen, and the children prefer to eat what I cook.'

'What sort of domestic training have you received?'

'Nothing special. I have to manage anyway.'

'When you say you have to manage anyway, do you mean that no orders are ever issued?'

'And who'd give the orders, if I may ask?'

'Your husband, for example.'

'He doesn't have any right to give me orders.'

'But he brings in more money to the household than you do?'

'We both work full-time, so he should be grateful as long as I'm willing to cook his food. And he is grateful, too.'

'Grateful?'

'Yes. Just as I'm grateful when he works over-time whenever we need a little extra. He wouldn't have to do that, either, if LM paid me according to my job and not according to my sex.'

'But surely there must be somebody who is in charge in the family?'

'Sometimes my husband puts his foot down and says that he's master of the house, but he usually gets over it pretty quickly. In practice we share the responsibility.'

'The procedure normally adopted in all work organization is that one party directs the work and another carries it out.'

'Sounds crazy. If someone were to stand there and direct my work in the kitchen it would only mean a longer time before the food was ready.'

'But if you are alone in the kitchen, how are the other members of the family to know that you really are cooking the food? Perhaps you're paid a certain sum per meal?'

'If I were, I'd have to pay it myself!'

'But in that case you might easily sit there doing the crossword instead of cooking the food?'

'I don't half feel like it sometimes, I can tell you. Dinner always has to be cooked when you're most tired. But I'm hungry myself too and if the food is late there's a dreadful row, particularly from the boys.'

'Do they pop in and urge you on?'

'Sometimes. But as a rule they're careful not to because I usually tell them to go and lay the table or go out and do some shopping.'

'Do you put the other members of the family to work?'

'Yes, when time is short. Only the girl usually helps voluntarily.'

'Is she paid by the hour then?'

'She helps voluntarily, I said. She's marvellous to have in the kitchen, we never get in each other's way.'

'So you have her as an assistant sometimes?'

'More as a friend. We help each other. If we're having something Italian she takes over.'

'Takes over?'

'Yes, she's bettter at that.'

'Does it sometimes happen that one of your sons takes over from your husband too?'

'That's not so usual. My husband knows best when it comes to the car and that. But when we play cards and there's a squabble about the rules, Nils-Erik usually comes out best. He's the older boy.'

'Does your son decide which rules are to apply?'

'No, but he knows almost all the rules for all the games off by heart. My husband usually has to give in.'

'So you mean that whoever knows best about a particular area is also the one who gets the final say, no matter what his or her position in the family?'

'I don't know if you could say always, but it often turns out like that. If you want something sewn or mended, you have to ask our daughter, if you want to find a photograph you have to ask our younger boy, he has a whole register of all the photos we have.'

'And who knows best what you should eat and which purchases need to be made?'

'We have a freezer now, so my husband and I usually shop on a large scale when we get paid. Otherwise it's my husband or the girl who takes care of the daily purchases, I want to go straight home. The boys have already come home from school then.'

'When you used the word "home" and "at home" are you referring to the family dwelling only or are you also thinking of other premises such as your work place?'

'No, "at home" is at home and that's all.'

'So your husband and your daughter are in charge on the purchasing side, or do you have flexible managerial functions there too?'

'They are different sorts of wishes that have to be taken into account. The boys nag about their favourite dishes, and I usually make a note of things that are needed. My husband usually gets the note when he goes shopping.'

'Well, at least you have a normal allocation of labour in the purchasing sector. You direct the work and your husband or your daughter carries it out?'

'The labour doesn't always get all that allocated! The girl usually thinks of things we need when she's in the shop, I can't keep everything in my head. And my husband sometimes reads my notes more or less as he pleases.'

'As he pleases?'

'Yes, I once wrote fish balls in lobster sauce, and I'll never do it again. He came home with real lobsters.'

'Lobsters?'

'Yes. He wanted to celebrate the fact that his foreman had left, he said.'

'But doesn't that example show that a certain control is, none-theless, necessary?'

'Things work out pretty smoothly for the most part anyway. I mean foremen don't leave all that often.'

'So you *direct* the kitchen work you carry out yourself and you also exercise influence over the purchasing. But there must surely be someone who inspects and approves the work you do?'

'If I burn the food they let me know about it soon enough. The boys don't usually keep their opinions to themselves.'

'So it's the younger children who inspect your kitchen work?'

'We don't have any special inspector. My husband gets an earful when he buys the wrong things, and our daughter gets one when she's careless with the washing. We usually keep an eye on each other; it's as simple as that.'

'But if your daughter is careless with the washing week after week, what do you do then?'

'I tell her to do it better or else I do the washing myself the next time.'

'But you must surely have some form of punishment if the household is to function satisfactorily?'

'No one is made to stand in the corner, if that's what you mean.'

'So some results which are unsatisfactory can continue for several years?'

'We try to make each other listen to reason.'

'And when that is not successful?'

'Then nothing else will be either, I'm afraid. We don't have any domestic help to use instead, and there's not very much we can threaten with either.'

'If you don't want to lay off anybody, you can always threaten to close down.'

'Close down?'

'Yes, the family runs at a loss, doesn't it?'

'Yes, of course. But what would be the point of that? Things would be even more expensive if we were all to live separately. Anyway, no one wants to move. We just have to manage the way we are.'

'But can't you ask the landlord to intervene as an arbitrator when something goes wrong?'

'Just let him dare try!'

'But it's useful to have an impartial body to turn to, isn't it? A priest for example.'

'We want to keep our private lives to ourselves.'

'Do you get any rent allowance?'

'We'd prefer not to have to, but we can't manage without it with the rent we have now.'

'Did you buy your colour television with cash?'

'No, on the instalment system.'

'How do you allocate the remainder of the household work?'

'Everyone does their own beds, and we all give a hand with cleaning up on free days. Otherwise I expect we and the children all do the things we think are least boring.'

'You mean that everyone can carry out the domestic work which they themselves are most interested in?'

'Yes, my husband and our older boy usually deal with any repair work in the flat and take care of the car. Our daughter is good at sewing and mending clothes. Our younger boy is very good at cutting and pasting things, cuttings from newspapers, recipes and all sorts of things although he's only eleven.'

'Cutting and pasting that sounds like therapeutic work of a type common in sheltered homes. Perhaps he could get into a sheltered home?'

'We'll see to it that our own home is sheltered, thank you.'

'But wouldn't things be simpler if you or your husband decided which domestic work each member was to carry out so that unnecessary discussions need never arise?'

'That's exactly when unnecessary discussions *would* arise.'

'I'm afraid I don't understand you.'

'That's when they'd protest. Trouble starts when you begin to use force. Sometimes my husband gets it into his head that he's going to invite the whole family to the cinema and when everyone isn't overjoyed at once or if someone suggests another film, he gets angry and gets out everybody's outdoor clothes and says "no discussion, let's go", but that's when there *is* discussion. Sometimes for hours. And no cinema. It's the same thing with the domestic work.'

'Do you mean that there is a risk of refusal to work if penniless family members are not allowed to participate in the work allocation?'

'Of course. Whatever has to be done will be done more easily if each of us can choose a task which suits us to some extent.'

'So you've gone around and found out what each member of the family wants to do and does not want to do?'

'They're not exactly deaf-mutes, you know.'

'And nobody thinks that most tasks are equally interesting or uninteresting?'

'No.'

'Do you yourself find that certain domestic tasks are more pleasant than others?'

'Of course I do. Cooking food is more pleasant than washing up.'

'But you're not paid for the work you do in the home?'

'Just the same. It's more fun to buy clothes than to wash them.'

'Why is that?'

'It simply is.'

'But there must be quite a few domestic tasks which no one wants to carry out and which must, nevertheless, be dealt with?'

'Then we do it some other way. As I said, the weekly cleaning is done together, by the whole family. On Saturday mornings for the most part. And we usually take turns at washing up and taking care of the rubbish and that. Everyone does it one week at a time.'

'And that usually works out?'

'Not always. Sometimes my husband or our older boy gets it into his head that the car must be attended to just when the cleaning is to start. And the boys' beds are often unmade until after school. But that's not the end of the world. For the most part, it works out.'

'When you implement work rotation on certain of the domestic tasks, isn't there a risk that no one gets a sufficiently fast rate going before he or she is to be replaced?'

'It's not exactly a question of precision work. It has to take the time it takes. It would be far worse if the same person had to wash up year after year.'

'But don't things sometimes get broken when your sons wash up?'

'I usually give a hand when Nils-Erik washes up. And we skip the youngest boy. He puts up names for towels and that in the bathroom and writes out the weekly schedule instead.'

'You mean that an eleven-year-old boy organizes the weekly schedule for the family?'

'We agree on most of it while we're eating, but then he writes it all out and he usually does it so neatly and attractively that we don't have the heart to tell him that we can manage anyway. He loves drawing up tables, our Gunnar. Anyway, it's sometimes handy to have things on paper. If someone tries to get out of doing his or her share.'

'Do you have fixed hours or flexible hours for the domestic tasks?'

'Terribly flexible at times, I'm afraid. When it's my husband's turn to do the washing up, he usually waits until after the television news and sometimes he doesn't wash up until the following morning.'

'Doesn't that seem to indicate that fixed times would be preferable?'

'Our youngest lad wanted to draw up a proper school timetable first so that there'd be plenty of columns to write out. But nobody wanted fixed times. For eating, of course, but not for everything else.'

'Why not?'

'It gets more boring if you have to do something at exactly six o'clock or seven o'clock, or whatever. That's what everyone says. After all, the main thing is that it gets done, sooner or later.'

'Haven't you considered stimulating domestic work by means of a more thoroughly worked-out system of encouragement?'

'We encourage each other all the time. Everyone praises our girl for all the fine things she sews, and no one hesitates to tell Gunnar that he can organize the photos better than any of us. Our older lad finds the going tough in school, but he can always join in and do difficult jobs when my husband is repairing the furniture or the car. My husband says he's very handy.'

'I meant economic encouragement. The domestic tasks could be broken down according to degree of difficulty so that the most advanced work was given a high price and the more routine work was given a lower price. That would spur everyone to learn the more demanding tasks.'

'But it's the interesting tasks that get done first as it is now, without money. We need only give the boys something for cleaning the toilet and other unpleasant work like that.'

'But if your sons only get paid for simpler work, won't they keep on cleaning the toilet all the time?'

'No. They far prefer working on the car or on the photographs in any case. They postpone working on the toilet and taking out the rubbish as long as possible.'

'Why is that?'

'Because they prefer the other work, of course.'

'How odd. All the work studies I know of indicate the opposite.'

'That cleaning the toilet is the most pleasant work?'

'No, but that money is the most effective means of encouragement.'

'Then it must be us that are odd.'

'The fault is probably that the sum used for encouragement is the same no matter how quickly the work is carried out. If you had a supplement for efficiency, many of the routine tasks would become more attractive.'

'If we did, we'd probably have to buy a new set of crockery once a month. And we'd have all sorts of trouble with the time calculations and that. No, we don't want any of that.'

'Perhaps we can leave the duties sector and pass on to the more relaxing domestic tasks. How do you usually pass your free time in the evenings and over weekends?'

'The week-day evenings everyone's usually tired. My husband usually dozes off reading the evening paper, and I find I need only sit comfortably on the sofa and pick up something to read for my eyelids to feel heavy.'

'Do your sons sit and doze too?'

'No, they're always on the move. They're often running about, meeting their friends and that.'

'So they have no obligation to be present in the evenings?

'If they had, we'd never have a moment's peace.'

'But you don't know what they might get up to while they're out?'

'No, that's true. If I worked part-time, I'd be able to devote myself to the boys far more. As things are now, I almost breathe a sigh of relief when they run off, it's awful.'

'What do you do when your sons are out?'

'We mostly look at the telly. We drink our evening coffee and chat a little. I usually have something to knit. If our daughter is at home she usually sews.'

'I thought we'd dealt with sewing and knitting in the duties sector. Or don't you distinguish between domestic work and relaxation?'

'Knitting is fairly relaxing. Sometimes over the weekends my husband spends the whole day working on our country cottage, he enjoys that. We're building an extension out there. When I tell him not to work himself to death, he says that he's not working, he's living. But the result's the same in any case, of course.'

'The result?'

'Yes, the extension to the cottage gets built.'

'Perhaps your husband lacks the ability to relax?'

'That's his way of relaxing, he says. And it seems to be, too. He's never quiet and relaxed like that when he comes home from work.'

'You say that your husband dozes over the evening paper... Wouldn't he wake up if one of your sons stood beside him with a chronometer and counted the number of minutes and seconds it takes him to read each page?'

'That'd only make him angry. He likes to read in peace. You can't get an answer to even the simplest questions when he's reading.'

'Don't you have any timekeeping at all for your relaxation occupations?'

'They wouldn't be relaxing any longer then.'

'But do you never decide in advance how long you're going to spend at a certain thing, for example, eating dinner?'

'We eat until everyone's had enough.'

'And you never decide that you're going to read at such and such a time or that you're going to take a walk at such and such a time?'

'We do things like that when we feel like it.'

'And you don't make any time limits say, for example, that you will play cards for 48 minutes?'

'We usually play until somebody's won.'

'But don't you find it difficult to pass the evenings under conditions like that?'

'There usually isn't any problem.'

'So you don't look at your watches so much during leisure time?'

'Mostly when we have to watch out for a certain television

programme. Or for the communal laundry room. Otherwise I'm
horrified when I look at my watch, at least in the evenings.
Sometimes I've scarcely sat down on the sofa before it's time to
go to bed.'

'But your work is usually finished at four o'clock?'

'The work at home finishes around half past seven, at best.
And the boys are seldom in bed before nine. During the week-
day evenings, my husband and I almost never have a whole hour
to ourselves. And one has to go to bed early when the alarm
clock rings at half past five in the morning.'

'So you would not be interested in any reduction in your
leisure-time hours?'

'No, on the contrary.'

'But it must be easier to find time during the weekends?'

'Yes, and a lucky thing too. There's so much that accumulates
during the week. There's so much one wants to have time to do.
One needs those days to become a human being again.'

'Human being?'

'Yes, a normal human being.'

'But two whole free days must surely be organized and
scheduled a little if the time isn't simply to slip away? Do you all
get up at the same time on Saturdays, for example?'

'No thank you, we want to sleep in then. My husband gets up
and listens to the radio, but he has to shut the door. Anyway,
there are no whole free days in a household.'

'When do you educate and bring up your sons?'

'We don't exactly have any set times, but it's mostly during the
weekends when we're not so rushed. My husband goes out a lot
with the older boy; they get on well together; they go to ice-
hockey matches and everything. The younger lad is more a
mother's boy; he usually attaches himself to me.'

'When you say "get on well" and "attaches himself to" do you
mean that you maintain your parental authority with kid-gloves
or have you given up all demands on obedience?'

'We were brought up to obey, both my husband and I. We
were kept on a fairly tight rein. But we both think that understanding plays a part too. It's not so easy either to get children to
obey nowadays, they're far more cocky than we were. More
obstinate. They say that we're mouldy when we start preaching
things we had to learn once upon a time, my husband and I.'

'What sort of things?'

'That children should be quiet when grown-ups are talking. Or that a couple should be married before sleeping together. They just laugh then.'

'So the children have played an important part in bringing about the forms for consultation, co-responsibility and flexible managerial functions you have described in this interview?'

'Yes, in a way. We don't give them a free hand in everything; we do have certain rules. But being strict simply hasn't worked out; the children have just become obstinate when we've tried. My husband sometimes thinks that we're too easy-going, particularly me of course. And one gets a little lax when one is tired, too. But a more comradely relationship has meant that the children feel more responsible and are more likely to give a hand. They really are. And they are more likely to stay at home too. No drugs and trouble like that.'

'So you don't regret that the strict method has been abandoned?'

'Not when I see the results.'

'But how can you say that you don't want any responsibility for yourself, that you don't believe in consultation, that you think it's a good thing that there are experts to make the decisions, that you want a strict division of labour, that it doesn't matter very much what sort of task you carry out, that money is the only thing that means anything and that people like you shouldn't protest and get involved in things they don't understand?'

'I don't say any of that either!'

'Yes, that's what you said here, in the previous interview we had. It indicates clearly that you have completely different opinions during the daytime than those you have presented now.'

'During the daytime?'

'Yes, during weekdays between 7 o'clock in the morning and 4 o'clock in the afternoon.'

'Oh that! But I'm at work then.'

Suggestions

As soon as I write the word 'suggestions', Jaakko Stenius' words begin to ring in my ears. 'They say at work, some of them say at work, he don't have any answers in that book, that Palm, no suggestions, like...but we're the ones who have to answer, I say. We must answer, not him.'

And yet it must surely be rather disconcerting if, after hundreds of pages of brooding and cackling, I leave it up to the reader to produce the eggs. Besides, most of the suggestions made below do come from discussions with workers and salaried employees at LM. In other words you and your colleagues *have* answered, Jaakko; otherwise it would not have been possible to make the suggestions at all.

The following then is *one* possible procedure which might be adopted for preparing, designing and developing a teamwork system at a work place like LM.

Remove the worst obstacles to...

The labour legislation must be rewritten so that work finally becomes as negotiable as leisure time – work and everything connected with work in the form of management, distribution, transfers, personnel appointments, technical organization and planning, primarily on a departmental level.

The payment-by-results system must be done away with, so that jobs which have been broken down can be put together again, so that splintered groups of workers can be united again and so that the work pace can be determined by the workers themselves, individually and in groups. No individual merit-rating system must be permitted to replace the individual piece-work rate.

The trade union must be decentralized, so that it becomes possible again for individual members to make their voices heard and so that it becomes meaningful again for individual members and groups of members to participate actively in union work, in the first place on a departmental level, in the second place on a shop union level, in the third place on a confederation level.

The workshop rules must be rewritten, so that each employee can move freely within and between the departments at his place of work, and so that he is encouraged to use his own initiative to get to know the production contexts and the company as a whole, including the office sector, etc. (Unfortunately the new workshop rules give no clear indication of how much of this is still prohibited.)

There are other obstacles, too, which must be removed, such as compulsory over-time and union disunity, particularly amongst non-organized labour. Everyone working in the same workshop should belong to the same trade union.

But if no form of teamwork were to be tested before *all* of these obstacles had been removed, one would have to wait for decades. Experimental activities on 'in-depth democracy' at, for example, the Statsföretag factories have been made more difficult but have not been made impossible by Paragraph 32 and the Collective Bargaining Act; if group activities are started at LM, this could be regarded as an experimental contribution to the work being carried out by the commission set up to review Paragraph 32. In my opinion, the individual piece-rates *must* be done away with if the teamwork is not to be threatened by disunity right from the start. Joint piece-rates or group bonuses need not, on the other hand, necessarily be an obstacle to trial activities. The kitty would then be placed at the disposal of each work team and would be distributed as the team considered best. As far as the agreement on individual merit rating, which the Metalworkers' Union idiotically signed, is concerned it should be enough to make use of the paragraph which says that the agreement may not be implemented until a local solution has been agreed on. The shop union should refer to the planned trial activities on teamwork and postpone any such solution or get the employers to accept that the agreement be implemented collectively only so that the work teams and not the team members are merit rated. The workshop rules constitute a minor problem since they have already been toned down and here it is mainly the right to move between the departments and to converse in groups which must be established before the teamwork can be started; the right to agitate, which the top union level seems extremely anxious to retain for itself, need not be won from the beginning and can be demanded when the teamwork has developed to a certain extent. I think much the same can be said of the important decentralization of the trade union. What is needed from the beginning, is a general go-ahead from the union and from the shop union committee saying that they regard the teamwork ideas in a favourable light. It should not be difficult to obtain a go-ahead of this type since the Metalworkers' Union recommended some form of 'production groups' in its report to the congress in 1973. I think that a union decentralization, particularly a distribution of authority from the committee level to the departmental level, will not only become possible but will be made necessary by the development of the teamwork system.

Many of the workers will probably not really regard a number of these obstacles *as* obstacles until they have been provided with an opportunity to see in a concrete manner what the obstacles have prevented them from attaining. It is not until they experience teamwork as something worth developing that they will, I think, have a sufficiently powerful motive for examining and wanting to fight against those paragraphs and decrees which stand in the way of a development of this type. And this factor – that concrete experience usually carries most weight – also indicates that activities can be started more or less immediately, at M and in other quarters to introduce

...teamwork...

One thing is obvious: one need not invite any special expert delegation to take part, one need not refer the issue to any collaboration committee' which will brood over it for years, and one need certainly not empty any particular department and design it specially for democratic purposes or recruit a selection of group-minded elite workers from various parts of the factory. One need not even clean up before teamwork is introduced.

The more or less loosely composed production groups which

already exist in most industries, the work groups which are
served by the same charge-hand or those which carry out
different component tasks within the same production section
can, quite simply, be used as a starting point.

As I mentioned before, each large department in the LM workshop is organized like a company in an army division with the
supervisor as company commander, the foremen as platoon
leaders and the charge-hands as (working) section commanders.
And it is the members of these groups – the number can vary
from five to twenty – which I think can form the most natural
work teams. Without any major arrangements having to be
made.

Unfortunately the tasks which have been located adjacent to
each other are, in some places, so dreadfully alike that there
would be no point in joining them together or so dreadfully unalike
or specialized that they cannot be formed into a meaningful
whole. A certain amount of reorganization will, undoubtedly, be
required in such cases before functional production teams can be
formed or other methods will have to be chosen to give the jobs
meaning and variation.

Methods such as broadening the scope of the work (job enlargement) for example.

But if one starts in the assembly section or in Jaakko Stenius'
department, one will find large numbers of groups which could
easily be developed into work teams. Most of the tasks carried
out in conjunction with handling sheet metal are easy to learn,
and yet they are not so similar that the working week would
become monotonous no matter how one distributed them within
the team. Some of the jobs are more qualified and are based on
drawings, others are extremely simple; some are so heavy that
less robust workers could only manage them for a few hours at a
time, others are light; standing machine jobs with large metal
sheets are blended with sitting work-bench tasks on small com
ponents. This department also has one of the technical pre
requisites for enabling the workers to work together without
difficulty, viz. the machines and components which the worker
need are all close at hand. The usual state of affairs in the en
gineering industry is that all machines of the same type are
located together so as to increase specialization. This means that
the overall context of the production is broken down and i

sometimes impossible to see. All automatic lathes are located together, all eccentric presses are located together, etc. But in Jaakko Stenius' department and, fortunately, in many other departments too, common sense has finally prevailed – eccentric presses, plate shears, edge pressing machines and everything else which is required for the initial stages of the sheet metal and plate work are combined to form machine groups known as centres.

If trial activities are introduced at LM one can, for example, follow the path of the rack frames through the workshop from the pressing and spot welding operations in Department 11 via the surface treatment operations in Department 16 up to the assembly and wiring operations in Department 36 and establish six or seven work teams along this path. This will have the advantage of providing a meaningful production connection between the various groups as well as within them. The long distances can be bridged over by telephone and with the aid of the truck drivers. If the six or seven work teams are served by the same truck drivers, the drivers can deliver messages and complaints between the teams in addition to the goods they transport, particularly when there is a lot to do and the team contact men cannot leave their positions. This would also be a means of making the truck driving job less haphazard and subordinate in general. More meaningful routes would be combined with messenger duties. This is an example of job enlargement.

Another favourable circumstance which already exists in addition to the production groups and the machine centres, is the fact that the charge-hands are not supervisors but workers. Ordinary metalworkers. Consequently, there are no union or legal obstacles to permitting them to be included in the teamwork in a natural way. Nor need they necessarily be appointed as spokesmen for the teams.

In other words, the present groups are called work teams and then go on working as before? No, they do not go on working as before. The very fact that the jobs are taken in turn by the members of the team in the order decided by the team itself is an important change.

I remember what the 'work rotation' was like in Department 36. Suddenly there was a shortage of units and the rack assemblers had to give a hand and solder a stock of units for a week

or two. Suddenly there was a shortage of racks and the unit
solderers had to give a hand and assemble a stock of racks for
a week or two. Six month periods with exactly the same job
interrupted by brief changes for half a week or a week, this was
the only form of work rotation offered. If the tasks I have mentioned here together with the assembly of the copper rails were,
instead, to be combined to form a single work team then more
closely spaced shifts and a more even flow could be achieved.
Nor need any time-consuming problems arise from changing
over or as a result of forgetfulness if only hours or days pass
between each period spent at the stations belonging to the team
instead of weeks and months as is the case now.

If the tasks pass from one member of the team to the other,
the instruction duty should also pass from one member to another
so that the team member who carries out a certain task instructs
the team member who is to take over from him or her. The proper
instructor need not interfere until the team member in question
is unable to make himself understood. In cases where linguistic
problems arise, those who are good at languages can give a hand.
One can easily fall into a comfortable and unenterprising attitude, not only with regard to instructions but also with regard to
simple repair work, if a charge-hand is close at hand. 'That's what
he's there for.' But why should more qualified tasks be restricted
to one person? They too can be passed on from member to
member through the team. And if a spirit of comradeship is
engendered in the teams, the most skilful workers will soon share
their experience and special artifices with the others instead of
keeping them to themselves as they usually do today so as to
increase their own piece-work earnings.

Let us now deal with the more noticeable changes.

The work teams must be able to take over quite a lot of the
tasks and the authority which devolve on others today. Some of
these should be taken over right from the start, others stage by
stage. I am thinking partly of all the duties connected with the
responsibility which the foremen traditionally take care of and
partly of an increasing proportion of the duties connected with
service tasks which are carried out today by workers who work
only on inspection, sorting, packing, waggon transport, cleaning
etc. (Service tasks which require vocational training cannot be
added to the work team in the same way, but not only a specific

truck driver but also a specific repairman should be at the disposal of each work team and should, thus, be loosely linked to the teams.)

Despite the fact that I have given a great deal of thought to the matter, I cannot find a single weighty argument in favour of retaining the post of foreman, that remnant from the days of boss-rule, that daily reminder that management does not trust the rank-and-file. Supervisors are, undoubtedly, needed or at least a department head. The charge-hands, of course, are also required, every group of workers requires someone who can provide instruction and can set out the jobs. But what is the need of platoon leaders when there is no need for platoons? The work teams should reasonably be responsible directly to the supervisor or the shop engineers.

Without any buffers and intermediaries.

Note that I do not say that the foremen themselves should be removed; I only say that the post of foreman should be removed. I do not want anyone to get the sack. And besides, there are many competent former charge-hands and skilled workers amongst the foremen who could suitably return to these tasks. In a labour market situation where graduate engineers act as supervisors and Bachelors of Arts work as semi-skilled workers, the loss of prestige involved should be fairly easy to bear. And many foremen may even find it a relief finally to be released from the ticklish intermediary position they now occupy. Besides, the transition must necessarily be slow. During the first running-in period for the work teams, assistant department heads or at least a couple of roving charge-hands or advisers would be required in addition to the charge-hands linked to each team.

I do not, however, think that it will be enough to let the foremen remain foremen and simply rename them charge-hands or the like. Just as it is not enough to do away with the time-and-motion engineers by renaming them and calling them merit-rating engineers instead.

In other words, the work teams would take over all responsibility for introducing new employees to the work done and for taking out hand tools, cupboard and locker keys and employment books; they would also take over the responsibility for the everyday production planning and stock ordering. Filling in individual job cards will, of course, disappear when piece-work disappears, but the combined daily and weekly production of the team members must be presented. At the same time, the work team will take over all contact with the supervisor and the department offices as well as all contact with the store and the dispatching departments. The charge-hands already deal with some of these tasks in many cases today, particularly on behalf of elderly foremen, and most of the tasks connected with responsibility are sufficiently simple for interested team members to learn them fairly easily. If a charge-hand acts as spokesman for his team during the running-in period, it will also be natural for him to deal with the tasks formerly dealt with by the foremen, particularly all contacts with the department office.

But bearing in mind the experience obtained from work teams on building sites, I think it is important, however, that the power of the charge-hands be limited right from the start. Otherwise it may suddenly turn out that the number of foremen has simply increased since the old foreman system was done away with. One means of preventing a concentration of power is that each team would appoint a second spokesman from the beginning. This spokesman can take over the 'foreman tasks' when the charge-hand is away and can also deal with the team contacts with their union, with the industrial safety officers and with other teams on his own. Another means is to assign the run-through of the production plan and production results to the team meetings in which all members take part, e.g. a brief team meeting each morning and a longer run-through each Friday afternoon or Monday morning. A third means is to distribute, step by step, an increasing number of the various responsibility-tasks to the different team members (and to elect spokesmen each year).

The manner in which the responsibility-tasks are distributed can only be decided within each work team. Individual aspects must be taken into consideration just as they must in the production job. Interests, endurance and the ability to adjust differ from one individual to another (just ask Märta Olovsson, the employee interviewed by the personnel department in the previous chapter). No sensible rotation arrangement gives each member of the team the same schedule. One member may, perhaps, deal with the transport contacts, another may be particularly suitable for acquiring material and other store contacts, a third may be particularly suitable for entering the production results in the books, etc. A work allocation of this type does not exclude rotation. If each team member has one or two *main* tasks, they can rotate the rest of the time. The most important thing, I think, is that no one should need to be restricted to the same job constantly and that each individual production and responsibility task should be mastered by more than one member of the team so that anyone – including one of the spokesmen – can be ill for a week without *any* part of the activities having to be stopped.

Not only am I convinced that a team which functions reasonably well can deal with the old foreman tasks just as competently as the foremen do today; I also believe that some of the tasks will not be *properly* dealt with until they have been transferred to the teams.

Take the induction of new employees, which many foremen deal with superficially today if they have time to deal with it at all. It feels more natural in every way that a workmate should go around and introduce a newcomer to the industrial safety officer, the union contactmen and the neighbouring teams. It is also more practical and time-saving if some member of the team who happens to be going there anyway brings the newcomer along with him to the store, to the packaging department, to the pay office, to the health centre, to the union office and, by no means least, to the various departments where the products manufactured by the team are pre-processed or post-processed. Downtime can also be utilized for this purpose. A preliminary introduction of this type, taking perhaps an hour a day during the newcomer's first week, should be enough to provide a sufficiently good picture of the most immediate production context for the newcomer to be able to get a grasp, during the following week, of the overall production system – which the more official ten-hour introduction is intended to give all new employees.

Next comes the inspection function which lies on the border between responsibility-tasks and service tasks.

Those workers who belong to the inspection function are already dispersed all over the entire workshop today, and the fact that they are solely occupied with inspecting what others produce is not merely a manifestation of the idiotic specialization which still characterizes work organization in industry but also a reminder of the consequences of authoritarian leadership, no matter whether it be adults or 11-year old boys who are to be 'led'. A great deal of time and labour must be devoted to supervising, quality inspection and counting components; otherwise it is difficult to keep production up at the same time as the rank-and-file are kept down. If, instead, we have a system based on teams which apply democratic leadership the team members can be depended on to keep an eye on each other, and the team itself can be entrusted with checking and inspecting its own work. The inspectors, who have usually not received any particular vocational training, can be offered jobs as ordinary producing members in the various teams.

Generally speaking, I envisage the team as a slowly-growing unit.

But why should the teams have to take care of tasks of a purely service nature as well? If most people find it easy to see why the teams should not have foremen and others *over* them, they should find it just as easy to see why the teams should not have anyone *under* them either, e.g. a collection of servants. 'We have only one type of slave here: machines', I'd write on my team notice board if I were to start at LM again. In other words, the team members should be responsible for keeping their own area clean, for running their own errands, for pulling their own waggons, for repairing or replacing their own hand tools, for carrying out a thorough cleaning once a week, and they should learn to find their way around in the store sufficiently well so that they can fetch anything which is missing when orders must be supplemented.

These tasks may not appear particularly attractive and the system adopted by the Olovsson family can be used for those which are most boring, viz. they can be dealt with by several or all of the members of a team on a certain day or each member can deal with them once a week. They may still be boring but the more the work team can deal with its own service tasks, the freer it can work as a team.

The next problem arises in conjunction with packing. This is a task which is more difficult for a team to take over since it is usually carried out quite a distance away from the stations where the components in question are produced or assembled. Well, the packing function can always be moved and assemblers who now carry the racks down to the cellar should easily be able to learn to pack them in crates as well. Under the supervision of a packer.

It goes without saying that employees who deal with large-scale cleaning operations will be needed, just as employees who keep things in order in the stores will be needed. Nor do I nourish any dreams of doing away with all of the service tasks. I just wonder why so many people must devote themselves *full time* to sorting, packing, cleaning, pulling waggons, or inspecting – tasks that anyone can learn and that can even be *pleasant* to have as a change now and then as long as one does not need to do them all the time. If the teams take over more and more of this work, the number of compulsorily specialized service workers can gradually be reduced. After a time, there will be no need for so many employees in the stores, in the packing department, in the transport department, in the cleaning groups and those service workers who want to can then be offered positions in the various teams. I say 'want to' because I do not believe in compulsory membership, whether it be to political parties or to teams. Besides, it is by no means certain that only unskilled service workers long for more variation in their jobs today; even skilled maintenance workers will benefit from being linked to a team. If they retain their main functions, they can still follow an increasing part of the rotation schedule of the team in other respects.

The point about a gradual expansion of the scope of activities of the work team and about internal recruitment is not only that negative specialization can be counteracted and that the gap between production and service can more easily be bridged over, the most important point is that the teamwork can contribute to abolishing the present degrading breakdown of the labour force into 'A' teams, 'B' teams and 'C' teams – a segregation which corrodes solidarity from within.

If teamwork is introduced, I think that it is vitally important that efforts be made from the beginning to avoid having the elite workers and the low-income workers form separate teams. I think this is just as important as ensuring that the service workers who are gradually added to the teams really become full members and are included in the rotation schedule so that, for example, a former cleaning woman will not be confined to cleaning and keeping order. Each team should have as variegated a composition with regard to age, sex, nationality, work capacity and initiative as the various tasks demand and permit.

Or to express this objective in the coarsest of shop-floor language: 'at least one cripple, one idiot and a couple of wogs in each group together with a few women, otherwise there'll be nothing but elite performers all the way'. This is not just demanding that the teams make a social contribution, it is also a means of making a sensible work order possible. If a team consists only of 'elite performers' or only of 'idiots', i.e. only of members who want the same tasks and, consequently, also want to *avoid* the same sort of tasks, then it will be extremely difficult to draw up a rotation schedule which suits everyone. It will also be extremely difficult to get more than a certain number of the many different tasks which are entrusted to the team properly carried out. In other words, the team members should preferably be as variegated as the tasks.

The Olovsson family is a good example here, too. The very fact that the various family members have such different interests means that many different tasks are properly carried out. So even if one were to disregard the social viewpoints involved, it could still be a direct advantage for the team to have a variegated composition.

This does not mean that the entire range of possibilities must be included from the beginning. If one starts with the groups which have been formed around the charge-hands today it may, on the contrary, be justified to *limit* the variety during the transition to teamwork. An example which immediately springs to mind is those production sectors where the administration, in its wisdom, has placed a Turk together with a Finn, a Yugoslav, a southern Swede and a Greek. None of them understands the other. When the teams are formed, everyone should be provided with a chance to move so that fellow countrymen, old friends, relatives, etc. are finally given the opportunity to work together. As long as there are not too many of them. Those who think that the teamwork system is already burdened with sufficient social tasks should remember that I am only talking about internal recruitment here. When the word spreads that teamwork has been introduced at LM, the 'alert youngsters' which top management has so long been asking for will probably begin to make their own way into industry. And external recruitment will no longer consist only of the young, fast workers, careless workers and piecerate stars who are attracted now but also of youngsters who want more meaningful work.

I think that youngsters of this type and former housewives will put a bit of life into many a work team.

'But you still want to burden the teams with several of the social problems which management has created and which management should solve on its own?' Yes, I do. It goes without saying that management *should* solve these problems itself, but I do not believe that management is capable of doing so. If it were, it surely would have solved them by now instead of simply making them worse. Above all, I do not believe that the managers are capable of putting a stop to *internal* rejection and discrimination now that the legislation dealing with employment security has partly deprived them of the right to lay off workers. Since the breakdown into 'A' teams and 'B' teams damages employees most of all, individually *and* collectively, the only way out seems to be for the workers to try to solve the problems themselves. So that the old solidarity can arise once again.

Teamwork is probably the best instrument which can be found for this purpose. The LM plant must become a sheltered workshop.

There are engineering workers today who feel so finished and rejected or who have carried out the same tasks tucked away in a corner for so long that they prefer to continue as they are rather than subject themselves to the strains of teamwork. Others will need precisely that protection which a team can provide, particularly if they are over 60 and have already experienced how those in charge want to transfer them until they request early retirement. If these 60-year-old workers were included in a team and felt that they were permitted to participate, many of them would undoubtedly find their enthusiasm revived and would in no way be a burden to the team as some elite performers may fear. The feeling of belonging with which teamwork would provide members like this, whether they be old or young, is one of the most important measures of the strength and endurance of a team.

However, it is not my purpose to describe an ideal situation but rather to sketch a reasonably realistic model. So I do not mean that the teams should undertake to solve any problems free of charge. Just as they have a right to be paid for their production work, they also have a right to be paid for their rotation arrangements, for their supervisory functions, for their induction of new employees, for the work they devote to integrating labour which is, as the phrase goes, difficult to place. The production work must provide a fixed monthly wage to each member in accordance with the wage class systems in force. But how is the other work to be paid? In money? Some form of group bonus? As soon as the word bonus is mentioned, everyone thinks of money but a group bonus can, fortunately, be paid in currencies which have a more lasting value.

Time and influence, for example.

But once again, as soon as the word time is mentioned everyone thinks of leisure time. But I do not mean leisure time, I do not mean that the employees should go home; I mean the time spent at work which is not devoted to production or service. It is often said, from radical as well as from other quarters, that working hours must be shorter not only for the children's sake but also so that employees will have time for further education and union activities. It is as though it were self-evident that leisure time and the home were the only base for activities of this type. On the contrary, I think that work places should provide the natural base for them. Part of the working hours should be devoted to activities such as educational courses, practical experience in other departments, language tuition, industrial safety, department meetings, shop union meetings, loudspeaker information, reading notice boards, distributing leaflets, going through contracts and agreements, etc. Exercise would also come under this heading. I do not mean five minutes gymnastics during a break but an exercise track around the LM plant, football, tennis, sauna bathing, etc. for at least one hour a week in conjunction with the lunch break. And time spent at activities of the type mentioned here need not be confined to group activities but could also be used individually. To wander around the factory. To go to the dining-room and play the piano for a while. To study the work carried out in the design department. To sit down and read or to stretch out on the sofa in the rest room.

Managers obsessed with performance and results will probably be unable to believe their eyes when they see some of these suggestions. But I think that the production work would be improved if there were a possibility of making a short, sharp break now and then. Of doing something completely different. Just as many people do when they work at home. I think it is vitally

important for trade union work that central meetings, departmental meetings and study circles be regularly arranged during
working hours and that the loudspeakers be used for union and
other messages. And I think it just as important, if everyone is to
be given a feeling that there is a future in his or her work, that
practical experience, training, continued education and study
activities should not remain rarities which management graciously
grants to specially selected employees but should rather be a
right available to all. One member of a team may wish to devote
all the bonus time he can get from the team kitty to attending the
truck driver school, another may want to combine studies and
exercise, a third may want to devote his or her time to industrial
safety service and union activities.

One advantage of taking out one's share of the group bonus in
time instead of in money is that the team can adapt these with-
drawals to suit the production flow. Intensive production periods
with little time over for continued education or individual activities are succeeded by calm periods during which a production
stoppage or a pause while waiting for material provides considerable opportunities for using several of the study hours, meeting
hours, practical experience hours, curiosity hours, exercise hours,
etc. which have been accumulated during the intensive period.
In fact, I believe that management and labour have a common
interest in this type of flexibility. The workers suffer today not
only from being forced to rush when work accumulates but also
from being forced to wait when something goes wrong. And the
managers are faced not only with the problem of persuading the
workers to work over-time or accept shift work when work
mounts up but also of occupying the workers in a meaningful
way during a stoppage. They quite frequently do not know what
to do. A team system which can, from the point of view of time,
be extended and compressed like an accordion would solve these
problems – on condition that the accordion were never completely
pressed together. All time devoted to activities other than production must not be relegated to the quiet working periods.
Just as the planning, control and service of the teams must be
dealt with continuously, the studies, practical training and meetings of the team members must also be granted a certain con-
tinuity. The members must have time to 'live' at work even when
deliveries are in a hurry.

The group bonus which is not taken out in time could, suitably, be taken out in influence so that the teams can gradually expand the scope of their responsibilities. Influence is more difficult to measure than time but no particularly large measurement problems should occur in practice. I mean that a team which management considers to be particularly successful in checking its own production could abstain from taking out bonus time for this and instead ask to be permitted to participate in the more advanced production checking and inspection. Or a team which has dealt with its 'foreman tasks' particularly well might ask that these be expanded to embrace permission to grant leave of absence, to allow members to work part time and the right to a certain amount of flexible working hours within the team (for example so that those who are tired in the morning could come an hour later). But a freer form of negotiation should also be conceivable. When the supervisor comes to a team which has accumulated a large number of bonus points and asks the members to work over-time once a week during a rush period, then the team in question – if it should agree – should have excellent chances of having some of its requests granted. Such requests might be that some of the members be permitted to take portable components home and carry out their work on them there while the other members start late the following day, or that all of the team members be placed in the same wage class, or that the team get a sound-absorbent wall so that they can work in a more undisturbed environment, or that the team be allowed to try a different work organization.

I am presenting things in broad terms here to emphasize the different sorts of possibilities which present themselves once one begins to think in terms of influence and time instead of in money. But certain risks are also associated with a bonus system of this type. The 'benefit gap' between those teams which function best and the others may very quickly become large; other differences may also become so great that discord and dissatisfaction arise. Because of this, it is important that the contactmen for the various teams keep in touch with each other continuously so that the demands pushed through do not differ too widely. It is just as important that a certain fixed proportion of the influence and time due to all of the teams be divided equally amongst them so that each team receives a 'basic quantity' of influence and time whereas the bonus part is only granted to the best teams. If limitations of this type are not introduced, a team which is still seeking the form which suits it best may be deprived of the possibility of finding it.

'So the bloody carrot is still there?' I can hear Jaakko Stenius mutter. Yes, in a way. For my own part, I am only really afraid of the carrot when one can hear the rustle of banknotes in the background and if these banknotes are distributed individually. I am less afraid as soon as the banknotes are put in a common kitty just as the commission is paid to sales assistants in a department store or as the group bonus is paid to sprayers in a toy factory. And if the bonus is taken out only in the form of time and influence then I have very little fear left at all, so little in fact that I can well imagine only part of this bonus being distributed equally within the team, i.e. some of the workers getting a larger share than the others.

It should be borne in mind that the problem here is more of a principle nature than a practical one. In practice, two members of the team – the spokesmen – have more influence than the other members right from the beginning. In practice those teams which function best from various viewpoints will end up first in line when benefits of all sorts are being distributed no matter whether a bonus system is introduced or not. In practice only the teams themselves can decide which type of distribution suits their members best. One can only hope that an individual distribution of time and influence will not be confined to favouring those who are already privileged due to their skill or their positions as leaders but that some consideration also be given to the fact that special encouragement to team members who are in a worse position may frequently be more to the advantage of the team as a whole. But should disagreement arise within the teams, and this is bound to happen, and should it turn out that this disagreement can be reduced if those who are industrious are granted more extra time than those who are careless and if those who are enterprising have more of a say than those who are passive, then this is no catastrophe. On the contrary, perhaps one should be grateful that there is such an innocent – from the viewpoint of comradeship – bonus method available.

After all, it is not amongst civil servants who are used to working on the same salary grade level, no matter whether they are competent or incompetent, that the teamwork system is to be introduced. It is to be introduced amongst people who have been accustomed for decades to seeing that speed and industry in work immediately result in increased earnings. And many of those working in the factories would almost certainly experience it as a direct injustice if 'layabouts and drifters were given the same benefits as those who toil in the sweat of their brows'. And until a certain period of practical implementation has passed it will not be possible to see whether the spirit of community engendered by the teamwork functions sufficiently well for those who toil in the sweat of their brows to feel that it is *worth* making personal sacrifices, e.g. abstaining from bonus time so that it can be transferred to a less prominent teammate who wants to go off and study.

Does this model correspond to the basic work requirements I listed earlier on? Let's see.

Variation, training opportunities, integration, responsibility, companionship, freedom and the right of decision in and at work all seem to be values which the teamwork system can offer in plenty. Freedom and the right of decision will be limited at first but a seed will, in any case, have been sown.

Values such as meaning, personal involvement and respect are a little more uncertain. A meaningful link between the various tasks is scarcely enough as long as many of the individual tasks themselves remain monotonous, and values such as involvement and respect are highly dependent on the spirit and atmosphere which prevails in the individual teams. But I believe that the very first time a team manages to obtain a right on its own, the involvement of its members will be noticeably increased and should the variegated composition of the team make it possible to draw up a rotation schedule which suits most of the members, then I also believe that there is every hope of dealing with one of the worst stumbling blocks in factory life, namely lack of respect for those who deviate.

The teamwork system runs into more difficulty when it comes to offering independence and the right to be undisturbed at work. The fact that the teams are independent and free from foremen does not automatically mean that the individual members will experience any particular independence in their own work. And the right to be undisturbed may be even more difficult to achieve when members constantly work close together. In fact, those workers who have a very pronounced need to work on their own will probably never feel fully at home in any sort of team. Other instruments will be required here. If the workers in question are qualified and skilled then they will already have access to several of the values which only teamwork can offer semi-skilled workers (integration, variation, responsibility, etc.). While the rank and file are building up their team with the aid of the instructors and the union contact men, these 'individualists' should be able to go in the opposite direction, i.e. stop sitting in a line in noisy large-scale departments and instead see to it that compartments and workrooms are partitioned off so that those who have the greatest need can work as undisturbed as I do myself when I write. Or as they themselves may already do during their leisure time, at home at a carpentry bench in the cellar or at a loom in the living-room.

But there will almost certainly also be many amongst the qualified and skilled workers who will find some form of team-work a more attractive solution to their needs, too; perhaps the lone wolves could be loosely linked to these teams.

Finally, we have quality, health, and human dignity, three demands made necessary today by the piece-work system, the poor work environment, the continued rule of company dictator-ship and the domination of machinery. It does not seem possible to cure these illnesses; they can only be forestalled or treated within the framework of each individual team. The fact that each team will check its own quality, favour accuracy and keep an eye on carelessness, take care of its own equipment, carry out its own environmental improvements, limit the dominion of the machines by means of work rotation, keep the rule of management at a distance by making the position of foreman superfluous – all of these comprise important steps in the right direction. But the works managers still remain and they still assess the results pro-duced by the teams. Nor is the individual team a sufficiently large and powerful unit to overthrow the dominion of the machinery, to change the external design of the department or to have a say in the profit distribution.

The teams will have to be coordinated if they are to proceed any further and they will have to attack their remaining problems on a higher level, namely

...in semi-autonomous departments...

Before I say anything about what departments of this type can look like, I shall try to persuade those sceptical readers who are shaking their heads at my reformatory zeal to shake their heads a little less.

Those who took the initiative for the Norwegian experiments with semi-autonomous groups felt that several times during the experiments they ran into a general distrust, on the part of the workers, towards the changes. A number of the participants in these experiments opposed the new ideas despite the fact that the researchers assured them that the changes would be to the advantage of the workers themselves – which turned out to be the situation in many cases. I quote from the Swedish edition of their research report (Thorsrud–Emery: 'Medinflytande och engage mang i arbetet' published 1969):

> We found that the prevailing work arrangements and work specifications, frequently linked to the agreements, formed the basis for complicated defensive action in the face of the new work forms to a greater extent than we had expected. We found that individuals and groups barricaded themselves behind this defensive system – *vis-à-vis* their workmates too – in order to retain the advantages they had acquired. We had, in certain respects, overrated the workers' inclination to regard their own work situation critically and to want to improve it. We had – in certain respects – underrated the distrust they showed *vis-à-vis* the company when changes in their work situation were discussed...nor did we fully realize the way in which existing wage systems – in this case individual piece-rate – tied the workers to traditional solutions...

But why did the workers resist? Why do workers frequently resist when proposed changes are presented to them?

Is it so, despite all, that conservatism has a particularly firm grip on the workers – or is it, perhaps, so that the workers are particularly accustomed to the fact that changes which come from above or from without usually mean deteriorations of some type?

Is it because of a primitive distrust towards scientific experi ments that many workers throw a spanner into the works when well-meaning researchers appear – or is it because they know that the researchers are backed by the management when they carry out their experiments?

Is it purely as a result of red-tape pedantry and uncomradely egoism that many workers obstinately defend their contractually or individually acquired privileges – or is it also because they have had to struggle to acquire the few privileges they have and they know through bitter experience how easily they can lose them?

Is it mainly or even partly as a result of a general inability to collaborate that many workers who are paid by results quarrel and wrangle – or is perhaps because the piece-work system invites quarrels and makes collaboration difficult?

Is it, finally, due to contentment or a lack of clearsightedness that many workers abstain from criticizing their own work situation when talking to researchers – or is it, perhaps, because they say 'no thanks' to sympathy from outsiders whose aims they are not quite sure about?

If the researchers approached management with their measuring instruments and, with the best of intentions, suggested to the managers that they deepen industrial democracy by removing the walls between them and placing all individual benefits in a common managers' kitty they might find that the 'distrust towards changes' is fairly widespread even on a managerial level. Besides, Thorsrud and Emery did not have to approach the managers to discover that management, when it came down to brass tacks, was more inclined to combat the group experiments than were the workers or the salaried employers. The managers, who were polite and helpful at the beginning, were just as negative when it turned out that the idea of semi-autonomous groups stimulated employees to question wage systems and managerial rights. The employees grew enthusiastic about the group idea when they fully realized that it was to their advantage – and then the managers brought in time-and-motion engineers, UMS and MTM instead.

The Industrial Democracy Delegation* in Sweden had exactly

* The Swedish Labour Party's policy of socialization within the general framework of a 'mixed economy' is to nationalize individual companies within different industrial sectors. These companies are grouped to form

the same experience, both at the Uddevalla shipyard and at the State tobacco factory in Arvika.

At the beginning it was the managers who smiled while the remainder of the employees glared, but after a time their positions were reversed. The managers approved of 'deepened industrial democracy' as long as the 'deepening' effect was limited to a few pits with railings round about and as long as a consultation group with the local manager as chairman was given control. But when other departments wanted to try the new ideas and when the workers realized that the prerequisites for a successful team were a monthly salary and increased authority to manage their own work – then the smiles of the managers froze. What might not this lead to? The top management of the state-owned Statsföretag AB in Stockholm glared most of all, so the Industrial Democracy Delegation was disbanded in 1974.

There is certainly plenty of conservatism, passiveness and un-comradely egoism on most shop floors, just as there is on most other floors where human beings work, are suppressed, have to compete with and eliminate each other. But before one turns about completely and begins to propose the daring thesis that the workers in particular are *specially* egoistic or conservative, one should ask oneself if the workers, just like most other people, are not mainly opposed to those changes which they know or believe will be to their disadvantage?

Take the well-known opposition to in-company transfers. Is this due to general conservatism or is it possibly due to the fact that many workers have learned to their detriment that transfers often entail lower incomes, worse jobs, a return to the beginner's stage, being ordered about without being asked first, losing their old comrades and being deprived of an environment where they may have begun to feel at home? A certain conservatism would seem sensible in cases like this. If the workers were *thoroughly* conservative they would never ask to be transferred. But they do so frequently, at any case at LM. They do so because they hope they will get a better job, a more pleasant environment, a higher income or more acceptable working conditions (and then it sud-

---

one major corporation – Statsföretag AB. The Department of Industry set up the Industrial Democracy Delegation to participate in and document the experiences gained from experiments involving new forms of worker participation in the state-owned companies. (Trans.)

lenly seems as though the *managers* were the ones who disliked transfers).

If the workers appear *particularly* inimical to changes they are so, I think, because of the fact that they have particularly poor experience with changes, and if the workers appear *particularly* distrustful of even positive proposals they are so, I think, because the workers are particularly accustomed to the fact that no one makes any notice of their own proposals. Anyone who puts forward an idea without getting any response easily grows distrustful when the opposite party puts forward a totally different idea later on.

And I wonder if exactly the same position does not arise in conjunction with the much discussed unwillingness of the workers to take responsibility, i.e. that this is a myth which the employers have created so as to be able to retain the responsibility for themselves.

If my publisher should step into my study with an extremely expensive electric typewriter which I have not asked him for and tell me that it is high time to increase my productivity, if he should remove my own beloved typewriter and offer me use of a new one, without cost, on condition that I take full responsibility for it and treat it as an infant in arms since the publishing house may otherwise suffer the most dreadful losses – if all this were to happen I am not at all sure I should want the 'responsibility'. What is wrong with my old Torpedo? If my publisher should, despite all, get his own way and then give me a telling off every time the supposedly foolproof machine breaks down, even when the fault is not mine, and also has a habit of referring to the *machine* when the typescripts are well-written and only refers to me when the typescripts are poorly written – then I most certainly do not want the 'responsibility'.

But this is exactly the type of pseudo-responsibility which is constantly 'offered' to the workers at LM. They are offered the responsibility for expensive machines which simply stand there one morning when they arrive at work. The responsibility for errors which the machines or the foreman permit. The responsibility for complicated automatic machines to which they have received only the most fleeting of introductions. The responsibility for following safety regulations even when safety arrangements are lacking or are deficient. To say nothing of the camouflaged piecework which is called 'economic responsibility' and which means that the hourly earnings of, for example, the transport workers are reduced when the goods are delayed, even when the delay is not their fault.

In other words, it is fairly understandable that Märta Olovsson should say 'no thank you' to 'responsibility' at work. But things are different at home in Salem. There she has just as much responsibility as the managers do at LM, and she has no more desire to avoid it than they do. This is because the responsibility she has at home in Salem is not a pseudo-responsibility but a real responsibility. In fact, she seems to appreciate the life-value called responsibility so much that she is prepared to share it with her children – and not in the way commanding officers do when they want subordinates to put the blame on at the same time as they retain all the power for themselves. She shares the burden of responsibility, but she also shares its bright and attractive aspect – authority, trust, freedom. If Märta and many like her say 'no' to responsibility at work, they do not appear to be doing so due to any unwillingness to take responsibility in any form but only due to a thoroughly justified unwillingness to accept the twisted forms of responsibility which are normally offered to them at work.

Responsibility without control. Responsibility without influence.

The study material which Paul Blumberg has compiled (*Industrial Democracy: The Sociology of Participation*, Constable) seems to permit an unequivocal conclusion on this particular point. Satisfaction at work constantly increases the more influence and, consequently, the more responsibility the workers get. When a change is to be introduced, Blumberg concludes, the worst effect is usually achieved if management carries out the change on its own without even informing employees in advance. A somewhat better effect is achieved if management first informs the employees and then decides on the change. A still better effect is achieved if management opens a discussion with the employees on the planned change before any decision is finally made. But by far the best effect is achieved if the employees are permitted to discuss the proposal and then to reach a joint decision on the change. It is first then – when joint responsibility is greatest – that all of the visible signs of a general job satisfaction can be noted a pleasant atmosphere in the departments, few disputes, notice-able pleasure in work, low employee turnover, low absenteeism, even production flow and, as a rule, high production.

If workers as a whole had been unwilling to take responsibility, almost none of the many studies on which Blumberg bases his con-clusions would have given the results they have given.

Are you still shaking your head? If so, perhaps you doubt the teamwork idea for a completely different reason. If so, you may be afraid that the assumption of responsibility which teamwork entails, not least in conjunction with the assumption of the fore-man tasks, can lead to the workers becoming involved with management and being made jointly responsible for unpopular decisions which management reaches? If you do, then I find it easier to understand your doubt. I myself also believe that there is a risk in this type of involvement when responsibility is distri-buted, particularly on the higher levels in the company hierarchy and particularly when the responsibility is distributed from above and not from below.

That is one of the reasons why I consider that the social demo-crats got hold of the wrong end of the stick when they introduced the 'social renewal of working life' by pushing through a law on board representation for employees. It is particularly easy to get involved up *there*. It can be easy enough to get involved on a joint works council level – particularly as long as no responsibility has been acquired on a departmental level. But how great is the risk of becoming involved on a departmentel level? The workers themselves obviously deem the risk worth taking since they have reacted so positively to the assumption of responsibility which group experiments have offered them, not only in the US but also in West Germany, England, Yugoslavia, Norway and Sweden. They seem prepared to take responsibility on the level on which they themselves work, in their own departments, with all the risks that this may entail.

Those who do not see this willingness in a positive light and con-tinue to shake their heads, continue to warn the workers for every type of joint responsibility and collaboration, and continue to exort them to satisfy themselves with demands – in themselves excellent – like the right to veto and the right to strike, have completely mis-understood the whole teamwork idea. The idea is not that the workers should collaborate with management more internally so that solidarity can be reinstated. Nor is the idea that the teams should take over the foremen's positions but rather that they should make them superfluous. In any case, one may well wonder how those who produce could ever take over the means of production if they are reluctant to take responsibility over their own work benches. But, of course, they are not reluctant. The workers do not fight shy of more responsibility if it entails influence and participation. It is only the nervous and frightened cell-forming branch of the left which fights shy.

Are you still shaking your heads?

If so, you may be afraid that teamwork would be so successful that the workers might settle down and fence in their teams with cosy walls at the same time as the managers walk about smiling contentedly at the willingness to work and the low rate of absence of the workers? In that case I can only say that I hold a different opinion. I do not for one moment believe that the workers – or any other employees – will settle down with a teamwork system which is functioning reasonably well if they can see that the idea can be developed to their advantage. I think that their appetite will grow to match the opportunities available. If those who have long been forced to eat from a single bowl at work – the money bowl – are given a taste of responsibility, meaningfulness and freedom then they will ask that these bowls too be refilled. Particularly if the teamwork has brought about improvements which even management can appreciate – increased presence, better agreement, a more even production flow, etc. – because then the work teams can negotiate from a strong position.

Refilling the money bowl will only become a thing of the past.

No department can become autonomous overnight. The change must be carried out in stages. To begin with, the first work teams must find the form and composition which suits them best, both as individual teams and in cooperation with other pioneering teams along the same production line. But even during this trial period, the groups which work together in a more disorganized manner could study activities and prepare new work teams. Both Norwegian and Swedish experiments show that it is easier to develop group activities than to start them – each team can learn from the mistakes of the trial groups.

The first step towards semi-autonomous departments is taken as soon as several different teams evolve in the same department, on condition that these teams do not isolate themselves from each other. Nor will they isolate themselves from each other if they can see that they have more to gain from collaboration. One means of demonstrating this is for the union group council to push through demands on behalf of several teams, demands which the various teams have tried unsuccessfully to push through individually. The right, for example, to obtain team over-time in the form of compensatory free time (which can be accumulated to whole days) or the right to say 'yes or no' to new tools, production methods or conveyor belts after a trial period.

Another step towards semi-autonomous departments is taken when all of the work teams are represented on the production committees which already exist in the shop departments, at least at LM. These committees function today more or less as minor consultation groups with limited authority and few meetings and are clearly dominated from above. But when the foremen have been replaced by the team spokesmen at the same time as the union contact men are retained, the atmosphere should change and the production committees can gradually extend their authority. Weekly and monthly plans for the production in the department could be ratified in these committees. Dissatisfied or harassed team members could put their complaints to these committees and could arrange for transfer. Work teams and department supervisors could discuss important questions in these teams; in order to avoid double loyalty these discussions would, in difficult cases, be passed on to the union department council for regular negotiation.

The extent to which the workers will be able to hold their own in these discussions will depend to a considerable extent on how successful the teamwork is, even when measured in the manner traditionally used by management. If productivity is reasonable, quality is high, absence is low and the production flow is even then the prospects should be excellent for the subsequent stages listed below:

the right of veto and the right of proposal, for the teams as a whole, in conjunction with rebuilding projects, machinery replacements and the appointment of supervisors within the department;
special rewards for independence and organizational

ability as well as for technical imagination and social
solicitude when calculating the group bonus (in time
and influence) for each team;
the right for the trade union council in each department (i.e. elected members and industrial safety
officers) to negotiate on wages directly with management and to reserve a department kitty out of company profits, in time *and* in money, for individual
distribution and for special purposes.

In my opinion, these special purposes should not only cover
wage increases for those at the bottom of the scale and special
benefits for parents of small children but also initiatives of a
type which can counteract the considerable disunity which prevails today between various groups of workers. As things are at
present, it is almost assumed that management alone should take
the initiative for measures such as rest and study rooms in the
departments   which is why the measures remain, as a rule, on
paper. But if the worker's representatives in the joint industrial
council were to ensure that money, from the environmental fund
which is now to be established in each company, was allocated
to cover the basic costs, then the workers in the respective departments could cover the remainder through voluntary time with-
drawals from both the department kitty and the team bonus
kitty. In other words, the workers themselves would acquire the
necessary furniture and select the colours, would paint or at least
select pictures and other embellishments, would make contact
with the municipal library to obtain a bookcase, would employ
a psychologist for personal advice once a week, would acquire
physical training appliances and study material, would set up
notice boards, make or paint tables and chairs. With or without
the aid of personal contacts in the workshop. If all of the teams
were engaged on various parts of this furnishing work then I feel
sure that the solidarity and the feeling of belonging enjoyed by
the members would be considerably reinforced. The finished rest
and study rooms would be regarded as the workers' *own* rooms
in a completely different way than they would if management
had arranged everything 'for the good of the workers'.

Later on, a project for rebuilding the entire department could
be carried out along the same lines. When this is done, machine

entres, departments and even whole workshops may well take a hape which is very different from any which older metalworkers and managers) can imagine today. Everything would be clearly haracterized by the opinions and tastes of those who work in he various production sectors. If the employers' right to direct nd allocate work has been abolished by then and if the union ctivities have been decentralized so that the union department ouncils have a right to negotiate in all labour questions, the vorkers can put force behind their demands in critical situations y the use of go-slow actions, spot strikes and other forms of what he metalworkers in Italy call 'escalated negotiations'. But even hen, one should remember that the most powerful weapon in the ands of the workers is not the right to stop work but rather the roduction of good results. The higher the demands the workers nake and the more eagerly they threaten to strike, the more in-lined management will be to adopt repressive measures. This is omething workers know today. Only if they can point to excel-lent results all the time, results which are not confined to the number and quality of the products but also to planning, organ-ization, service, presence, agreement, and continued education, will management find it extremely difficult to say no to the demands put by the labour sector.

This is because they will have to say no against all common sense, i.e. against the growth interests of the company – and if they do that then there is every reason to escalate the negotia-tions.

But what I have in mind is, on the whole, a highly peaceful transition to autonomous departments. If the extreme radicals and other madcaps manage to persuade workers to follow a more militant line – constant small strikes, for example, or a rapid abolition of the post of supervisors – then I think the result will be a setback. If, instead, the teams take over increasingly quali-fied tasks step by step and if the team representatives on the production committee take over an increasing proportion of the old lower management functions (not formally but in practice), the position of supervisor will soon prove to be superfluous. The supervisor will suddenly find that he has nothing to do. The teams will then be directly responsible to a worker-controlled produc-tion committee. And the production committee, which will then lead and distribute the work of the department in collaboration

with the teams, will be directly responsible to the works engineer
The works engineer will place an order with the production
committee for a quantity of those products which the department
can produce and which LM has received an order for – in much
the same way as LM orders products from subcontractors in
other localities today.

Without involving itself in how these products are manufactured.

Then one can really begin to talk about semi-autonomous
departments. The teams in these departments will devote an
average of six hours a day to production work, one hour to
administration and service, and one hour to study, practical training in other ·departments, meetings, etc. The key to the official
noticeboard will be held by the production committee. Both
management and work teams will have to ask permission of this
committee before putting up their messages. The loudspeakers
would be used to broadcast messages from the trade union and
music chosen by the workers as often as it is used by management
today to broadcast muzak. The workers would edit their own
house magazines together with the workers in other departments.
The information resources would be equalized, at least on the
basic level.

When all the employees in the department are loosely or
permanently linked to various teams, no individual worker need
stand up alone any more against management. The team then
becomes the smallest unit which management can negotiate with,
a security factor of no little importance for all those workers who
feel none too secure today for various reasons. A prerequisite for
this, however, is that the various teams take the responsibility
for and protect those members who may be burdensome in
certain respects – instead of squeezing them out by means of
constant complaints. But which body is management to negotiate
with and which body are harassed workers to seek support from
when not only the teams and the trade union department council
but also the production committee is elected and controlled by
the workers?

How is one to avoid worker being pitted against worker?

In this situation, too, I believe that the union as manifested by
the department council (and, in more difficult cases, by the shop
union and the federation) must deal with all decisive negotiations

with management and at the same time deal with complaints from dissatisfied workers. Otherwise there is a danger that the production committees will have too much say in what is going on. It is sometimes said in Eastern Europe that the workers in worker-controlled enterprises have no need to strike, but history contains too many examples of workers in leading positions who have abused their powers for us to abstain from a conscious dispersion of those powers. I believe that even in semi-autonomous departments there are powerful arguments for defending the independence of the teams and at the same time separating the powers of the production committee and the department council.

The manner in which the power should be distributed in detail lies outside the scope of this book. There is a great deal (both positive and negative) to be learned concerning the distribution of power and election procedures from the workers' council system which has now been in operation for a quarter of a century in Yugoslavia.

I have spoken here of semi-autonomous departments instead of semi-autonomous groups because a unit which is as small as a group or a team can never be semi-autonomous in the proper meaning of the term.

This is probably why the various work teams have been isolated from each other at the new Volvo factory at Kalmar (with their own entrance, their own rest rooms, etc.) – so that the team idea does not 'infect' higher levels. But how far can a *department* become autonomous and how high up in the hierarchy can this autonomy be spread as long as the company as a whole still retains its authoritarian structure and is included in a private capitalistic community with innumerable ramifications, both nationally and internationally?

Not all of the way, but a fair bit.

It must be borne in mind that each team, right from the start, will keep continuous contact with other teams along the same production line, even those in different departments. The very fact that all the workers in a department are permanently or loosely linked to various teams means, in practice, that the contact network between the departments is so thoroughly developed that all of the production lines are covered. If each individual team, with the aid of telephones, truck drivers and personal visits keeps continuously in contact with about five teams elsewhere, then this in itself is an important step towards something far more comprehensive than semi-autonomous departments, namely autonomous workshops.

And by then there should also be far better possibilities than there are today for having things accomplished in the higher level consultation and decision-making bodies which have already been introduced or have been proposed in industry: employee committees, health councils, wage-earner funds, environment funds, extended works councils, company boards with trade union representatives, etc. As things are today, it is the durable shop union members who sit on all these committees and groups, and the majority of the workers have not got a clue about what is going on. But if there is a thoroughly developed network of work teams, independent production committees and department councils which are entitled to negotiate, if all of these are spread over the entire workshop, then the ordinary workers will be able to participate and propose representatives, press them on in various issues and even continuously check what they accomplish in a far different way than is possible today. If the workers manage to develop the production committee on a departmental level so that it becomes an effective instrument for their own interests, then they should be able to develop the wage-earner fund, for example, at a later stage in the same way.

But central measures of a different sort will also be required, in all likelihood, in order to safeguard the department-level control and to clear the way for a worker-dominated management throughout the workshop.

In addition to the economic 'employee consultants' for which legislation has now been passed, the teams and production committees will also need mechanical engineering consultants who can help them to sketch alternative production forms and machines more suited to human beings as well as building consultants who can help with drawings and estimates when machine centres or whole departments must be rebuilt. Consultants will also be required at Group level when whole factories are to be rebuilt or new factories constructed. If the labour sector cannot present economically and technically realistic alternatives in good time to the proposals put forward by the company architects, then the factories will be located and constructed more or less as management decides. And, on a Group level, the workers will also need

leeper contact with production committees and shop unions in
LM's subsidiaries and subcontractors all over the country – as
they will later on with LM employees abroad.

Contacts of this type are difficult to make for geographic
reasons, but if they are not made at all then there is a danger that
the autonomy will be limited to the plant at Midsommarkransen
and will, consequently, die out due to lack of nourishment.

But what is required above all is a totally different collaboration between workers and salaried employees, between the workshop and the office, than that which exists today. Collaboration
from a production point of view and from a union point of view.
'I find it very difficult to imagine that were the employees to take
over the running of the factory, they would make a worse job of,
for example, the work distribution, wage setting, personnel welfare and decision-making than top management does at present',
I wrote earlier on in the first part of this book (published in
Swedish in 1972). And my opinion has not changed since then.
Many of the salaried employees and directors who read the first
part of the book then thought, however, that my idea was that the
workers alone should take over the entire operation of the plant.
But by 'the employees' I meant all types of employees – workers
and salaried employees at all levels. Competent technicians,
salesmen and administrators will, of course, be required in an
LM Group controlled and owned by the employees, just as they
are required today. Should it turn out that the employees want
the present Managing Director to remain, then they will ask him
to stay on. The only condition, of course, is that the present
Managing Director be willing to work as devotedly on behalf of
the employees as he works today on behalf of the major share-
holders.

The fact that the objectives sketched out here still seem a
long way off is, of course, not only a result of the terror which the
central political measures required for ensuring a coordinated
autonomy within industry still seems to strike in the hearts of all
the major political parties; I think it is also a result of the fact
that workers and salaried employees at all levels still live and act
so dreadfully separated from each other that they have seldom as
much as sensed what they have to gain from collaboration,
particularly with regard to trade union matters.

I heard a radio programme recently about 'the ardour which

died out'. A few of the old workers were asking themselves where the ardour and enthusiasm from the beginning of the labour movement had gone. There was solidarity and a spirit of sacrifice in the old days, they said, but where is it now? They did not feel they could find any satisfactory explanation, no matter whether they were temperance veterans or trade union veterans, social democrats or communists.

But ardour, enthusiasm and solidarity evolved once because the struggle against naked destitution and the struggle for the vote demanded a broad and intensive suport. It was not enough that a few struggled on behalf of many. Fortunately, the issues at stake were also large and vital enough to fire the imaginations of many. The struggle for higher wages and shorter working hours is of a different type, particularly today, when a reasonable livelihood and a five-day week have already been gained. This is not the sort of struggle to fire imaginations, but nor does it need to. No popular movement is required to arrange the routine wage increments and working-hour reductions, only an apparatus.

But the struggle for the value and dignity of work and for a meaningful life even during those hours when the sun is up would, on the other hand, seem to require as broad and intensive a support as the struggle against naked destitution ever did. It is not enough here that a few fight on behalf of many; those who belong to that many must also join in. It still remains to be seen if these issues will be regarded as large and vital enough to fire the imaginations of the majority. For my own part, I am inclined to think that the struggle for the value and dignity of work and for a meaningful working life may fire so much ardour and enthusiasm that the old veterans of the popular movement will scarcely believe their eyes.

When ordinary workers and salaried employees begin to realize that a real influence over their daily work is actually within reach and *can be achieved*, then it will be possible to revive the old solidarity in a stronger form than ever before and the 'immense power of the wage earners', so frequently spoken of, will no longer be just a pretty phrase.

. . .and soon the employees can take over.